KW-481-556

CONTENTS

page

List of abbreviations 7

**Introduction – Minority rights, human rights: a review
of basic concepts, entitlements and implementation procedures
under international law** 9

Gaetano Pentassuglia

What do we mean by the concept of international minority rights? 9

What is the content and legal status of international minority rights? 12

How can international minority rights be enforced? 20

**Chapter 1 – The United Nations treaty monitoring
bodies and minority rights, with particular emphasis
on the Human Rights Committee** 29

Alexander H. E. Morawa

Introduction 29

The implementation mechanisms under the International Covenant
on Civil and Political Rights 30

Rights of relevance to minorities 39

The treaty monitoring bodies and minority rights activism 45

**Chapter 2 – The role of the United Nations
Working Group on Minorities** 55

Asbjørn Eide

Introduction 55

Major issues identified by the WGM 60

Conclusions and prospects for the future 68

Chapter 3 – The International Court of Justice 71

Frank Selbmann

Introduction 71

Jurisdiction of the International Court of Justice 71

The proceedings before the ICJ 75

Relevance for NGOs in the field of minority protection 77

3

**Chapter 4 – Using the European Court of Human
Rights to protect the rights of minorities** 83

Fernand de Varennes

Introduction 83
The European Court of Human Rights mechanism.............................84
The rights of minorities and the ECHR mechanism.........................87
Some practical guidance 103
Conclusions..104

**Chapter 5 – The Framework Convention for the Protection of National
Minorities** 109

Alan Phillips

Introduction 109
Description of the FCNM 109
Achievements of the FCNM..114
Practitioners and the FCNM 121
Conclusions..126

**Chapter 6 – The European Charter for Regional
or Minority Languages** 131

Stefan Oeter

Introduction 131
The construction of the mechanism..132
The main results of the monitoring scheme..140
What are the possibilities under the ECRML
for minority rights practitioners?..148
Concluding remarks 154

**Chapter 7 – Implementing minority rights in the framework
of the CSCE/OSCE**..159

Claus Neukirch, Katrin Simhandl, and Wolfgang Zellner

Introduction 159
The CSCE/OSCE mechanism regarding minorities............................159
Main results in the field of minority rights 167
Recommendations for minority rights practitioners 179

**Chapter 8 – European Union standards and mechanisms for
the protection of minorities and the prevention of discrimination**..........183

Kyriaki Topidi

Introduction: from market integration to human rights
and non-discrimination 183
Description of the mechanisms: the EU contribution
to the development of standards and mechanisms for the protection
of minorities..184
Main results: legal and political apparatus of the EU
on non-discrimination and minority rights..188

Critique and evaluation of the practice: a mixed record 196
Conclusions 199

Chapter 9 – Bilateral agreements and their implementation 203

Emma Lantschner

Introduction 203
Description of the mechanism 204
Discussion of the main results in the field of minority rights 210
Guidance for minority rights practitioners 217
Concluding remarks 220

Useful websites 225

Selected bibliography 229

Appendices

Appendix 1 – Extracts from the European Charter
     for Regional or Minority Languages 239

Appendix 2 – Extracts from the Statute of the International
     Court of Justice 241

Appendix 3 – Extracts from the Convention on the Prevention and
     Punishment of the Crime of Genocide 243

Appendix 4 – Extracts from the European Convention for the Peaceful
     Settlement of Disputes 245

LIST OF ABBREVIATIONS

ACFC	Advisory Committee on the Framework Convention for the Protection of National Minorities
CERD	Committee on the Elimination of Racial Discrimination
CFSP	Common Foreign and Security Policy
CoE	Council of Europe
CoM	Committee of Ministers (Council of Europe)
CSCE	Conference on Security and Co-operation in Europe
EBLUL	European Bureau for Lesser Used Languages
EC	European Community
ECHR	European Convention on Human Rights
ECJ	European Court of Justice
EcommHR	European Commission of Human Rights
ECOSOC	Economic and Social Council
ECPSD	European Convention for the Peaceful Settlement of Disputes
ECRI	European Commission against Racism and Intolerance
ECRML	European Charter for Regional or Minority Languages
ECtHR	European Court of Human Rights
EU	European Union
FCNM	Framework Convention for the Protection of National Minorities
FRY	Federal Republic of Yugoslavia
HCNM	High Commissioner on National Minorities
HRC	Human Rights Committee
ICC	International Criminal Court
ICCPR	International Covenant on Civil and Political Rights
ICERD	International Convention on the Elimination of All Forms of Racial Discrimination
ICESCR	International Covenant on Economic, Social and Cultural Rights
ICJ	International Court of Justice
ICTY	International Criminal Tribunal for the former Yugoslavia
ICTR	International Criminal Tribunal for Rwanda
NGO(s)	Non-governmental organisation(s)
OJ	Official Journal
ODIHR	Office for Democratic Institutions and Human Rights
OSCE	Organisation for Security and Co-operation in Europe
PCIJ	Permanent Court of International Justice
RMDSZ	Democratic Alliance of Hungarians in Romania
TEU	Treaty on European Union
UDHR	Universal Declaration of Human Rights
UN	United Nations
UNDM	United Nations Declaration on the Rights of Persons Belonging to National or Ethnic, Religious and Linguistic Minorities
UNTS	United Nations Treaty Series

MINORITY RIGHTS, HUMAN RIGHTS: A REVIEW OF BASIC CONCEPTS, ENTITLEMENTS AND IMPLEMENTATION PROCEDURES UNDER INTERNATIONAL LAW

Gaetano Pentassuglia*

What do we mean by the concept of international minority rights?

Generally speaking, international minority rights designate a special set of norms regarding numerically inferior and non-dominant groups possessing particular characteristics, most notably a distinctive ethnic, linguistic and/or religious identity which makes them different from the rest of the population of the state where they live.[1]

The first system of minority rights protection was set up by the League of Nations in the aftermath of the First World War. It was designed to accommodate nationals who belonged to racial, religious or linguistic minorities living within the newly emerged or enlarged states that resulted from the redrawing of boundaries caused by the disintegration of three multinational empires, that is, Austria-Hungary, Prussia and the Ottoman Empire. The system consisted of special treaty- and declaration-based obligations undertaken by the affected states, whose external "guarantee" was vested in the League of Nations. The Council of the League was indeed made competent to address cases of actual or potential infractions of minority obligations brought to its attention by council members, while the Permanent Court of International Justice (PCIJ) was empowered to deliver impartial decisions over differences of opinion on questions of law or fact arising out of the relevant regimes. Although they did produce a measure of protection, the League of Nations norms came under attack as they were not intended to be for general application nor did they give the minorities concerned *locus standi* vis-à-vis the League Council or the right to appear before it or other competent bodies for oral hearings. The exploitation of the "minority card" by Nazi Germany for the purpose of revising the 1919 Versailles settlement further contributed to the eventual demise of the League of Nations' experiment along with the League of Nations itself.

The gradual disenchantment with the League system progressively generated the belief that there should be no special guarantees for minorities but only protection of basic human rights for all. Although the League of Nations norms, by referring not only to minorities but also to all inhabitants or citizens in relation to the enjoyment of general freedoms without discrimination, did contain to a large extent the human rights seeds which were to flourish after 1945, their overall rejection paved the way for minority provisions being excluded from major post-Second World War documents, such as the Charter of the United Nations (UN Charter) and the Universal Declaration of Human Rights (UDHR). A study of the UN Secretariat of 1950[2] concluded that the post-1919 minorities treaties had generally ceased to exist. At the same time, the issue of minorities was not removed from the post-1945 international agenda. Resolution 217C (III), adopted by the UN General Assembly in 1948, emphasised that the UN could not "remain indifferent" to the fate of minorities and referred the matter to the Economic and Social Council (ECOSOC) with a view to producing a "thorough study" about the problems of minority groups. The mandate of the Commission on Human Rights allowed it to follow up minority issues by submitting proposals, recommendations and reports, while its sub-commission was established with a specific remit to address the protection of minorities, together with the prevention of discrimination.

As a result, the minority rights discourse continued to develop, though at a slow pace. Important progress was made many years after UN General Assembly Resolution 217C (III), culminating in the inclusion of a minority provision in Article 27 of the proposed International Covenant on Civil and Political Rights (ICCPR), finally adopted in 1966. In contrast with the post-1945 hesitation or even neglect, minority issues regularly come up in present-day activities within multilateral forums. The upsurge of ethnic tensions following the break-up of the former Soviet Union and Yugoslavia and in states of other continents, largely fuelled a considerable process of reconsidering the protection of minorities at universal, regional and sub-regional level, which is still under way.

One important theme arising from the continuing presence of the minority question on the agenda of the international institutions which are fundamentally concerned with the protection of human rights in general, is the seemingly problematic relation between the concept of minority rights and that of human rights. Although the basic framework of human rights protection rests on rights held by individuals as such, some group rights, namely rights directly ascribed to collectivities, have unquestionably entered the realm of international law, for instance the right to self-determination and the right to be protected against genocide. Are minority rights individual or collective? Or both? Are minority rights human rights? There is no doubt that minority rights form an integral part of the international protection of human rights. For instance, Article 27 of the ICCPR situates the protection of minorities within a general context of human rights entitlements. The Framework Convention for the Protection of National Minorities (FCNM), opened for signature by the Council of Europe (CoE) in 1995, confirms this by explicitly recognising minority rights as a human rights issue (Article 1). The same notion is reflected in the preamble to the UN Declaration on the Rights of Persons Belonging to National or Ethnic, Religious and Linguistic Minorities (UNDM), adopted by the General Assembly in 1992, and paragraph 30 of the Document of the Copenhagen Meeting of the Conference on the Human Dimension, adopted in 1990 by the Conference on Security and Co-operation in Europe (CSCE) (renamed in 1994 the Organisation for Security and Co-operation in Europe – OSCE).

This assumption, though, also reveals that minority rights and human rights are not identical notions. The general concept of human rights is something qualitatively different in that the rights of all individuals are placed under international protection. In terms of rights supervision, the League system somewhat reflected this approach when distinguishing between internal (constitutional) protection for all inhabitants or citizens of the minority states and international guarantee for members of minorities only.[3] Human rights means equal enjoyment of basic rights for everybody, whereas minority rights can be described as special rights recognised to the exclusive benefit of minority groups. Thus, basic rights for all combine with special rights for minorities: these rights are complementary and mutually reinforcing.

But, as has been mentioned, minority rights pose the issue of their individual or collective nature in international law. The international instruments on minority rights invariably refer to persons belonging to minorities, not minorities as collectivities. Therefore, minority rights as such are not construed as group rights. Article 27 of the ICCPR epitomises the hybrid approach to minority rights under human rights law. While referring to "persons belonging to minorities", Article 27 is clearly designed to protect a collective interest, since minority members have to exercise the rights "in community with the other members of their group". As recognised by former UN Special Rapporteur Capotorti,[4] "[it] is the individual as member of a minority group, and not just any individual, who is destined to benefit from the protection granted by Article 27". In sum, Article 27 recognises individual rights premised on the existence of a distinctive community. The interaction between individual rights and group protection aspects is clearly reflected in the relevant case-law of the Human Rights Committee (HRC) pursuant to the first optional protocol to the ICCPR (see *infra*), and confirmed by the 1992 UNDM, inspired by Article 27, which recognises rights of persons belonging to minorities, while at the same time providing for a state duty to protect the existence and identity of a minority as a whole (see *infra*, Article 1).

While special in nature and scope within the canon of international human rights, minority rights are not privileges. As early as 1935, the PCIJ held in its advisory opinion concerning the Minority Schools in Albania[5] case that minority rights represented some of the implications of the concept of substantive equality, as opposed to formal equality (equality in fact as distinct from equality in law). They are indeed intended to remedy the structural imbalance between minorities and majorities in areas critical to the preservation of cultural integrity. In that case, the PCIJ insisted on the notion of equality in fact and held that the closing of the minority schools in question by the Albanian government was incompatible with equality of treatment between a majority and a minority. In fact, general or specific anti-discrimination clauses, as contained in a variety of international human rights instruments, may pave the way, to a greater or lesser extent, for this goal to be achieved, by not only outlawing unreasonable distinctions against minorities but also producing, under proper conditions, differential treatment benefiting them. Indeed, it is now established in international human rights law that the principles of equality and non-discrimination do not require identical treatment in every instance but may well justify (and sometimes may even mandate) difference in treatment which is reasonable and objective as well as proportionate to the aim sought to be realised. This approach might therefore allow the favouring of a distinctive minority group over rights of others, as confirmed by minority rights instruments themselves. In other words, distinctions may well be upheld when they are designed to advance the specific position of a minority and thus to ensure full equality. And yet, as stated by the PCIJ in the Minority Schools in Albania case, the protection of minorities falls beyond purely anti-discrimination objectives generated by the purpose of "achieving perfect equality with the other nationals of the State";[6] it specifically aims at preserving the characteristics which distinguish the minority from the majority, satisfying the ensuing special needs.

Hence, whereas the prevention of discrimination in general demands equality, including special, temporary measures designed to remove not only legal but also social and/or economic obstacles to the enjoyment of rights and freedoms, the core of the protection of minorities lies in special, essentially permanent measures which are intended to safeguard the identity of certain groups, and must themselves conform to the principles of equality and non-discrimination.[7] From the angle of the prevention of discrimination, minorities come into play, along with other groups, in terms of the achievement of their full integration into all sectors of society. Integration so understood is, for instance, the objective of the International Convention on the Elimination of All Forms of Racial Discrimination (ICERD), adopted in 1965. In the field of the protection of minorities, the focus is on what makes minority groups non-assimilated into, and thus different from, the rest of the population, though clearly rejecting a policy of apartheid.

One general implication of the qualitative distinction between the anti-discrimination approach and minority rights is that the issue of respect for minority rights is *au fond* independent of whether minority members are treated in a non-discriminatory way. Indeed, even if they are, these persons are still entitled to special rights regarding their identity. To put it differently: anti-discrimination standards are not "minority rights" but rather set out indispensable starting points to enable their protection.[8]

What is the content and legal status of international minority rights?

At the universal level, Article 27 of the ICCPR and the 1992 UNDM represent the most important instruments embodying minority rights, of a conventional and extra-conventional nature, respectively. Article 27 provides that where ethnic, religious or linguistic minorities exist within the territory of a state party, their members shall not be denied the right, in community with the other members of their group, to enjoy their own culture, to profess and practise their own religion, or to use their own language.

The opening phrase, which was intended to meet the concern of Latin American countries that immigrants to these countries might form separate communities claiming minority rights, may in fact prove a tool in the hands of states for denying that they have minorities on their territory. France has indeed entered a declaration in which it is stated that "in the light of Article 2 of the Constitution of the French Republic, Article 27 is not applicable so far as the Republic is concerned".[9] Although the HRC has considered such a declaration as being a reservation which releases France from the duties established by Article 27,[10] it has unambiguously dismissed the notion that the existence of minorities is somehow premised on an admission of discrimination, as implied by the French view that no minority rights can be recognised by a state as long as that state complies with anti-discrimination norms by affording human rights to all individuals under its jurisdiction. The HRC has insisted on the factual nature of existence criteria, not requiring any prior decision by a state party.[11]

The basic aim of Article 27 is to protect the ethnic, religious and/or linguistic identity of minorities, as indicated in the HRC General Comment No. 23 (50) regarding this provision. The collective dimension to Article 27 rights is reflected in a marked interaction between individual rights and group protection aspects as resulting from the jurisprudence which is being developed by the HRC in the context of the individual communications procedure. The leading cases brought before the HRC reveal such an interaction in terms, for instance, of the: i. identification of minority membership based primarily on "objective ethnic criteria" and exercise of the rights in the place where the community exists; ii. free choice made by the persons concerned as to whether to invoke such rights to be enjoyed in a specific community context; iii. restrictions on individual rights justified by the legitimate aim of minority group survival and well-being, pursued through proportionate means; and iv. protection of the group through the protection of its members.[12]

As shown by Sandra Lovelace v. Canada[13] and Ivan Kitok v. Sweden,[14] the area of conflicting interests of a minority and its members raise particularly sensitive issues. In the Apirana Mahuika et al. v. New Zealand case,[15] the HRC found the measures impugned, designed to protect the group to which the complainants belonged, to be compatible with Article 27, while at the same time emphasising that, since Article 27 continues to bind the state party in relation to the authors' rights to enjoy their own culture, those measures must be carried out in a way that such rights are respected.

The repercussions of the protection of Article 27 rights on the position of the entire group is indicated, to a greater or lesser extent, by the HRC views in Bernard Ominayak, Chief of the Lubicon Lake Band v. Canada,[16] I. Länsman v. Finland,[17] J. Länsman v. Finland,[18] Apirana Mahuika, and J.G.A. Diergaardt et al. v. Namibia.[19] Interestingly, the HRC has also developed the notion that the right to self-determination in Article 1 may be relevant to the interpretation of Article 27. However, on a procedural level, the HRC has firmly rejected the standing of communities or legal entities to lodge an individual communication under the first optional protocol, although, in the Lubicon Lake Band case, it made the interesting procedural point (recalled in later cases) that there was no objection to communications submitted by a group of individuals claiming to be similarly affected by alleged breaches of the ICCPR.

Non-forced assimilation, enjoyment of the traditional way of life or aspects of it, including protection against erosion of the sustainability of traditional economic activities as part of minority "culture" as well as consultation with minority members on decisions affecting them, feature among the major themes of HRC case-law at this juncture (some such themes are also mentioned in the HRC general comment on Article 27). Further develop-ments will, of course, depend on the number and quality of Article 27 cases which will be taken to the HRC.[20]

According to the language of Article 27, minority members "shall not be denied" certain rights concerning their ethno-cultural identity. Therefore, states appear to undertake the mere negative duty of not interfering in the enjoyment of those rights, rather than an obligation to take positive action to protect them. And yet, active state duties have been construed both in terms of the protection against infringements by "other persons within the State party"[21] (so-called "horizontal" protection) and in terms of the effective preservation and development of minority identity. In the latter respect, though, a dividing line can be drawn between the interpretation that focuses on direct positive duties under Article 27 and the one that, more cautiously, establishes indirect duties to adopt positive measures as a major constraint on proactive domestic policies affecting minority identity in accordance with the anti-discrimination clauses contained in the ICCPR.[22] The HRC has become increasingly assertive with regard to positive measures, notably to address the situation of minority indigenous groups, while it has appeared unclear as to the relation of such measures to typical minority issues such as language use. Although its approach seems primarily to be grounded on indirect anti-discrimination assumptions, that is, on the notion that positive action can be justified as long as it is compatible with the principles of equal-ity and non-discrimination, the HRC view should be considered as part of an evolving incremental understanding of Article 27 rights, whose ramifications are in fact a function of the support from states parties. At this stage, the notion of direct positive duties seems to be favoured by a growing number of states concerned.

The UNDM was adopted by consensus by the General Assembly in Resolution 47/135 of 18 December 1992. As indicated earlier, it is inspired by, not "based on", Article 27. Therefore, while non-legally binding, this text is essentially intended to further expand the substance of minority rights within the UN system. Indeed, the UNDM uses a more constructive language than Article 27 does. For instance, pursuant to Article 1, paragraph 1, states "shall protect" the existence and identity of minorities and "shall encourage" conditions for the promotion of such an identity. Article 2, paragraph 1, replaces "shall not be denied the right" in Article 27 with the positive "have the right". Paragraphs 2, 3 and 4 of Article 2 importantly introduce the con-cept of participation rights, including a specific right to participate effectively in local decisions affecting the minorities concerned, "in a manner not incompatible with national legislation". The last paragraph of Article 2 impor-tantly elaborates upon contact rights, including transfrontier contacts with "kin-members". Article 4, paragraph 2, provides that states "shall create favourable conditions" for the expression and development of minority cul-tures, "except when specific practices are in violation of national law and contrary to international standards". The next two paragraphs deal with, respectively, "adequate opportunities" to learn the minority language and to receive instruction in that language and minority participation in economic progress. Articles 5, 6 and 7 invite states to ensure that minority interests and rights are duly taken into account in national planning and international co-operation. The remaining clauses embrace assumptions which are typically reflected in other minority rights instruments, namely that the entitlements in question may not prejudice existing obligations and commitments undertaken by states, that minority rights may not undermine the human rights and fundamental freedoms of others although they are prima facie compatible with the anti-discrimination precept, and that the instrument may not be used to ground claims jeopardising the territorial integrity of states.

Flexible wordings or clawback clauses such as "whenever possible" or "where appropriate" expose the respective provisions to a negative reading. Still, the text appears, in general, to be an important contribution to international minority law making. In UN practice, a declaration is indeed a formal and solemn instrument which imparts a strong expectation that members of the international community will abide by the principles it contains.

At the regional level, the OSCE has enshrined minority standards in a variety of instruments, the most significant of which remains the Document of the Copenhagen Meeting of the Conference on the Human Dimension of 1990. While lacking legally binding status (like all OSCE standards), such a document has proved so far the most influential elaboration of international minority rights provisions. Indeed, both the UNDM and the FCNM have benefited from the Copenhagen text as one of their main sources of inspiration. Moreover, the instrument has been incorporated as a legal obligation in recent bilateral treaties, such as the 1995 basic treaty between Hungary and Slovakia (*infra*). In terms of substantive entitlements, particular emphasis is laid on the implications of the right of minority members to identity, free of any attempts at assimilation against their will, such as the use of mother tongue in private and in public, association rights, transfrontier rights, mother tongue education, etc. Interestingly, paragraph 35 refers to autonomy arrangements as one possible means of realising the right of persons belonging to national minorities to effective participation in public affairs, in connection with the protection of the identity of such minorities. A report produced by an expert meeting convened in Geneva by OSCE participating states in 1991, further elaborates upon such issues by offering, *inter alia*, a shopping-list of advisable domestic policies.

The CoE has never ceased to be interested in the minority question, though the idea of elaborating specific legal standards in this field regained momentum only following developments in eastern Europe throughout the early 1990s. The European Convention on Human Rights (ECHR) and its recent Protocol No. 12 (not yet in force at the time of writing) do not address minority rights. However, as increasingly suggested by the Strasbourg jurisprudence in such areas as political and religious pluralism, education as well as way of life (the latter aspect, interestingly reflected in the case of Chapman v. United Kingdom),[23] such texts and further protocols might generate some form of protection for minorities and their members in relation to their general needs and interests as a result of the functioning of pertinent substantive provisions (most notably Articles 8 to 11 of the ECHR and Articles 2 and

3 of Protocol No. 1) and/or their respective anti-discrimination clauses (notably Article 14 of the ECHR, and Article 1 of Protocol No. 12, once it has entered into force).[24] Various proposals have been put forward by either political or specialised bodies or individual countries. The Parliamentary Assembly has long been most active in attempting to develop minority rights standards. In 1993, it adopted Recommendation 1201 on an additional protocol on the rights of national minorities to the European Convention on Human Rights. The text further develops previous Assembly proposals, particularly by focusing on individual rights, and complementing the rights framework with a definition of "national minority" (Article 1), a clause regarding restrictions on the rights recognised (Article 14), as well as a far-reaching right to autonomy regimes (Article 11). Its provisions on language and education rights are also noteworthy (Articles 7 and 8).

In the same year of its adoption, this Assembly proposal failed to be endorsed by the CoE member states. Nevertheless, the instrument has since triggered important legal consequences, both as part of "commitments" undertaken by new member states of the Organisation upon admission (in connection with the human rights requirements set forth by the Statute), and through its incorporation by reference in important bilateral treaties. Moreover, the Assembly has recently reaffirmed the need for an additional protocol to the ECHR based on the principles contained in Recommendation 1201 (1993) (Recommendation 1492 on the rights of national minorities, adopted in 2001). However, in its reply of 13 June 2002, the Committee of Ministers considered it "premature" to reopen the debate on this project.[25]

Apart from possible new standard-setting achievements, the FCNM and the European Charter for Regional or Minority Languages (ECRML) set out norms which are either focused on minorities or impinge upon their situation. Indeed, while the former contains minority rights provisions, the latter is not per se concerned with linguistic minorities, nor does it establish individual or collective rights for the speakers of the languages protected. Rather, the ECRML provides guarantees for the benefit of the historical regional or minority languages of Europe, with a view to promoting and protecting multilingualism in the fields of education, judicial authorities, administrative authorities and public services, the media, cultural activities and facilities, economic and social life and transfrontier exchanges. The ECRML also differs from the FCNM in that, with the exception of a set of fundamental principles and objectives on state policies and practices applicable to all regional or minority languages spoken within the territory of the contracting state (Part II), it allows each party to select a minimum of 35 paragraphs or subparagraphs covering the areas addressed in the operative provisions of its Part III, in respect of each language specified upon adherence to the ECRML (Article 2, paragraph 2, and Article 3, paragraph 1). There is reason to believe that the wide range of options offered to states by such operative provisions, while positively allowing for accommodation of specific circumstances, in practice precludes a great deal of *ipso facto* protection. As yet, this treaty, adopted in 1992 and entered into force on 1 March 1998, has attracted fewer ratifications than one might expect of an eleven-year-old instrument. It should be noted, however, that the ratifications have doubled over the past few years, and that, in general, time may be needed to assess the legal and political implications of ratifying the ECRML.

The FCNM resulted from the CoE Vienna Summit of 1993, as an alternative to the adoption of a protocol to the ECHR as suggested by the Assembly. Unlike the stringent rights and duties embraced by Recommendation 1201 (1993), the treaty contains programme-type provisions setting out objectives which the parties undertake to pursue. As a result, the provisions are not directly applicable, leaving the parties a measure of discretion in the implementation of the instrument, in view of particular local factors. The FCNM builds upon previous texts. As indicated earlier, the CSCE Copenhagen Document inspired it to a large extent. In fact, the treaty was generated by an attempt to translate the political commitments endorsed by that document into legal obligations. The FCNM came into force on 1 March 1998. So far, it has been ratified by many, though not all, European countries.

In addition to providing a link between minority rights and some rights and freedoms already established under the ECHR, special provisions are meant to directly address the particular needs of minorities. States parties are under a duty to promote the conditions necessary to maintain and develop minority culture, and to preserve the essential elements (that is, religion, language, traditions which are not in violation of national law or international standards, and cultural heritage) of minority identity, as well as to abstain from any attempt to assimilate minority members against their will (Article 5). Articles 10 to 14 are concerned with language and education rights. They well illustrate the flexibility of the treaty mentioned above. They cover such matters as use of minority languages before administrative authorities, use and official recognition of minority names and surnames, display of minority signs and information of a private nature, traditional local names, street names and other topographical indications, access to education, etc. Article 13 provides for the right to set up and manage private educational establishments (paragraph 1), with no financial obligation for the parties (paragraph 2). The right to learn one's own minority language, pursuant to Article 14, paragraph 1, does not imply a positive duty on the parties, notably of a financial nature, while "adequate opportunities" for mother tongue education in areas inhabited by persons belonging to national minorities traditionally or in substantial numbers, are recognised only in a very hesitant way (paragraph 2).

Article 15 aims to ensure the effective participation of minority members in the life of the state, along the lines of Article 2 of the UNDM, although without an explicit right to participation in decisions concerning the minority. However, the explanatory memorandum on the FCNM importantly provides a range of advisable modalities of participation to be considered for adoption within the framework of the parties' constitutional systems, ranging from consultation to decentralisation of power, which are not spelled out in Article 2 of the UNDM. Other provisions encompass important aspects of protection, such as access to the media (Article 9), the prohibition of gerrymandering practices (Article 16), cross-border contacts (Article 17, paragraph 1) and participation in the activities of national and international non-governmental organisations (Article 17, paragraph 2).[26]

The European Union (EU) has not developed an instrument on minority rights. At the internal level, the emphasis is on equality and non-discrimination rather than minority rights. Article 13 (ex Article 6a) of the Treaty establishing the European Community (EC Treaty), introduced by the Treaty of Amsterdam, enables the European Council, under certain conditions, to take appropriate action to combat discrimination on, *inter alia*, racial or ethnic and religious grounds. Although it does not amount to a directly effective prohibition of discrimination binding member states and Community institutions, a so-called anti-discrimination package has been adopted on the basis of this enabling clause, including the Council directive of 29 June 2000 implementing the principle of equal treatment between persons irrespective of racial or ethnic origin,[27] and the Council decision of 27 November 2000 establishing a Community action programme to combat discrimination.[28]

Further indication is provided by the Charter of Fundamental Rights of the European Union, adopted at the Nice European Council of December 2000. Despite the fact that proposals had been submitted for including a minority rights provision in the charter,[29] the final text, couched in any event in a non-legally binding form,[30] limits itself to expanding the anti-discrimination approach (notably through a general clause prohibiting discrimination in Article 21, paragraph 1) endorsed by the Treaty of Amsterdam, and mentioning respect by the Union for cultural diversity – including religious and linguistic diversity pursuant to Article 22 – in accordance with earlier developments (notably under Article 151, ex Article 128, of the EC Treaty). The impact of general human rights provisions enshrined in the Treaty on European Union (TEU) (for example in Article 6) on the protection of minorities within the EU area remains to be seen, as does the role of the European Court of Justice (ECJ) in tackling internal minority issues within the context of its human rights jurisprudence.[31] Importantly, though, the ECJ recognised in the Bickel/Franz case that domestic norms designed to protect minority rights may be "legitimate", and thus compatible with Community law based on a test of proportionality.[32]

At the external level, the core of minority rights activities lies in a range of mechanisms designed to facilitate and/or consolidate transition towards democracy by eastern European countries.[33] They are linked to the admission procedure or to more general policies which pursue the rapprochement of these countries into EC/EU structures. Generally speaking, they are designed to promote the implementation of CoE and OSCE standards rather than establish new norms in the field.

Interestingly, the Stability Pact for Europe of 1995, resulting from a Common Foreign and Security Policy (CFSP) Joint Action approved by the EU Council in 1993, incorporated or spurred on major bilateral treaties between countries from eastern Europe, dealing wholly or partially with minority issues, such as the cited basic treaty between Hungary and Slovakia and the later treaty between Hungary and Romania.[34] They importantly incorporate soft law instruments on minority rights (typically, the Copenhagen Document,

Recommendation 1201 and the UNDM), thereby turning them into legally bind-ing regimes. Nevertheless, they normally do not elaborate upon the content of the instruments and their relation to one another (for instance, the minority language and education rights contained in Recommendation 1201 are far more strongly worded than those embodied in the UNDM).

A new wave of bilateral arrangements is being prepared under the umbrella of the Stability Pact for South Eastern Europe, launched by the EU, within the CFSP, in 1999. The Western pressure for such ad hoc regimes somewhat reflects the present difficulties in achieving more stringent and wider sys-tems of protection at the European level. At the same time, co-operation on the promotion and protection of minority rights has increased not only through bilateral treaties but also through sub-regional multilateral instru-ments. Of particular importance are the Central European Initiative Instrument for the Protection of Minority Rights, and the Framework Convention for the Protection of National Minorities – this latter adopted within the Commonwealth of Independent States – both finalised in 1994. Specific regional minority standards beyond Europe are still virtually lacking, although some minority aspects are creeping into the indigenous rights dis-course within the inter-American human rights protection system and attempts have been made recently to advance minority issues within the African human rights protection system as well.[35]

In terms of the legal status of contemporary minority rights norms, Article 27 of the ICCPR, as the only international global treaty standard on the pro-tection of minorities, seems to be gaining currency as the expression of a norm of international customary law binding all states. In fact, while specific contours of Article 27 rights require further clarification and areas of dis-agreement persist, at least the right to the equal enjoyment of one's identity, and, in particular, to assert and preserve it free of any attempt at assimilation against one's will, nowadays enjoys wide support from the international com-munity, in view of broadly formulated notions of cultural pluralism and repeatedly stated concerns for stability. It might arguably be viewed as a strong candidate for customary law through state practice and *opinio iuris*.[36] The same considerations may partly apply to the UNDM, some provisions of which may indeed be interpreted as either reaffirming customary law (for example Article 1, paragraph 1, in relation to aspects affecting the physical existence of minorities)[37] or probably reflecting customary law *in statu nascendi* (for example Article 2, paragraph 1). Overall, the maturing of the declaration into customary law basically depends on whether, and to what extent, states will respond to the above-mentioned expectation of compli-ance which the adoption of this type of instrument normally carries with it, bridging a recurrent gap between proclaimed principles and their actualisa-tion within domestic systems.

A major source of international minority rights law, and international human rights law in general, is international treaties. In addition to Article 27 of the ICCPR, the treaty approach is in fact gradually recovering from the general disfavour into which it fell (with a few exceptions) following the disenchant-ment with the treaty-based League system in the 1930s. The FCNM and the above-mentioned bilateral treaties provide evidence of such a renewal in conventional regimes.[38] Unlike customary norms, treaty norms of course apply only to those states which have consented to be bound by them. As revealed by the above brief overview of standards, several instruments on minority rights are of a non-legally binding nature, although this is not to say that they are legally irrelevant. In addition to their important moral and/or political force, they indeed help shape the content of international law standards, as is vividly illustrated, *inter alia,* by the incorporation as legal obligation of major soft law texts in the recent bilateral regimes indicated earlier. In general, they can be used by a variety of state and non-state actors, including national courts and NGOs, as a useful tool for advancing the minority rights discourse in conjunction with norms deriving from traditional sources of international law (as far as they are applicable to a given country), and persuading governments to comply with the relevant standards through appropriate domestic laws and practices.

How can international minority rights be enforced?

Given the well-known absence of a centralised power of enforcement at the international level, the implementation of the relevant international standards must be secured through each country's own legal system. Most domestic systems require that international human rights norms be incorporated into specific national laws in order for them to become applicable within this context. At the same time, international human rights norms, including those regarding minorities, either set out, or imply a duty to do so or, where they are not binding, at least generate expectations that states will take internal action in conformity with them. Effective "domestication" of international norms demands an effective system of remedies for violations of those norms as well; as long as this system is put in place by a country, then international supervisory procedures will normally remain unavailable until internal remedies are exhausted.

Experience shows that if implementation of international norms is entirely left to domestic mechanisms, effective human rights protection is less likely to follow. This explains the widely shared notion that enforcement can also occur, or be facilitated, through international action. In theory, under international law states may call each other to account in relation to their human rights violations. In practice, this rarely happens. In fact, the scene of inter-state enforceability of human rights, far from indicating an excessive human rights "vigilantism", has in most cases shown a remarkable lack of willingness on the part of a state to pick up on human rights violations committed by another state. As a result, international enforcement is mostly pursued through a variety of procedures and mechanisms made available within major international institutions,[39] a number of which are discussed at length in this book. The aim of the following is thus not to analyse them in any detail but rather to offer a cursory indication of some major implementation approaches and the purposes they are supposed to serve.

One way of viewing enforcement in relation to minorities is in terms of the various techniques of supervision concerned with the protection of human rights in general, at universal, regional or sub-regional level. For instance, the UN Commission on Human Rights and its Sub-Commission on the Promotion and Protection of Human Rights, essentially employ the so-called "ECOSOC 1503 complaints procedure", set up to identify situations amounting to consistent patterns of gross human rights violations, as well as procedures based on the appointment of special rapporteurs or working groups with country-oriented mandates (that is, authorising to investigate certain human rights violations within a particular state) or thematic mandates (that is, authorising to investigate in general certain human rights matters, such as, for example, religious intolerance). Both special rapporteurs and working groups report annually to the Commission on Human Rights, and their reports are made public. Minorities are frequently victims of a vast range of human rights violations, beyond the specific area of minority rights, whose investigation comes under the scope of many of those procedures. Consequently, pertinent issues, which by and large affect the physical integrity of minority groups and/or the enjoyment by their members of basic human rights on an equal footing with other individuals, have been, or may be brought up by making use of the monitoring opportunities provided by the above procedures, ranging from investigative and/or fact-finding activities to public debate with NGOs. In principle, they might even generate background input leading to a claim under a particular human rights treaty.[40]

Similar examples of human rights global or regional procedures offering avenues to advance the general interests of a minority group, notably in relation to the non-discriminatory exercise of rights and freedoms, include the reporting and complaints procedures before the Committee on the Elimination of Racial Discrimination (CERD) established pursuant to the ICERD, the judicial-like enforcement machinery before the European Court of Human Rights pursuant to the ECHR and its protocols, and the control processes within the inter-American human rights system.[41] It should be noted that the enforcement of human rights may also result from action taken by bodies which have been established with no specific human rights mandate. For instance, such UN bodies as the General Assembly and the Security Council may consider general human rights matters, including those involving minorities, without any formal complaint mechanism, and the latter may authorise enforcement action under Chapter VII of the Charter of the United Nations, encompassing the use of armed force in case of abuses amounting to threats to, or breaches of, international peace and security.

However important these mechanisms may be with regard to minorities, the fundamental way of looking at enforcement benefiting these groups is of course through the supervisory methods that are directly attached to the implementation of minority rights standards. Some such methods are briefly indicated below. As hinted at earlier, the HRC is increasingly effective in securing protection under the ICCPR, especially by providing specific redress for minority rights violations and improving the understanding of Article 27 rights in the context of the complaints procedure set out by the first optional protocol to the ICCPR. The UN Working Group on Minorities, established within the (then) Sub-Commission on Prevention of Discrimination and

Protection of Minorities pursuant to ECOSOC Resolution 1995/31, and partially the High Commissioner for Human Rights, review the implementation of the 1992 UNDM, and consider several related questions affecting the maintenance of peace. The UN working group held eight annual sessions, between 1995 and 2002, in which a wide range of relevant subjects were reviewed. Although this body has been established more as a framework for discussion than as a strict control mechanism, it nevertheless performs de facto an important supervisory work by regularly inviting not only independent experts but also governments, international agencies and minority representatives to offer their perspectives on minority issues. Where NGOs or minority associations make an oral statement or otherwise submit information about the situation of minorities in a specific country, this country is given an opportunity to respond or provide additional information.

At the European level, the Committee of Ministers is entrusted with the task of monitoring the implementation of the 1995 FCNM (Article 24, paragraph 1). To this end, it is assisted by an Advisory Committee on the Framework Convention for the Protection of National Minorities (ACFC), whose members have recognised expertise in the field of the protection of national minorities (Article 26, paragraph 1). On 17 September 1997, the Committee of Ministers adopted a resolution concerning the rules on the monitoring arrangements under Articles 24 to 26 of the FCNM (Resolution (97) 10). Consistent with Article 26, it determines the role of the ACFC, which is established as a body of experts who are elected by the Committee of Ministers but serve in their individual capacity, and therefore its relation with the latter. The FCNM provides neither an inter-state nor individual complaints procedure. Rather, the supervision is based (primarily) on periodic state reporting (after initial transmission of full information under Article 25, paragraph 1), in order to evaluate "the adequacy of the measures taken" (Article 26, paragraph 1); it is basically aimed at encouraging states parties to implement the FCNM properly, rather than at "sanctioning" those states which breach it. In late 1998, the Committee of Ministers adopted an outline for reports to be submitted pursuant to Article 25, paragraph 1, of the convention, regarding their legal, policy and factual components (the outline will be reviewed in the light of the results generated by the first monitoring cycle).

The ACFC has already adopted several opinions on the implementation of the FCNM, while the Committee of Ministers, to which all of the ACFC's opinions have to be submitted for final deliberations, had adopted its own resolutions containing conclusions and recommendations.[42] No binding decision can be adopted by the monitoring body. The non-judicial character of the procedure confirms the little stringency of the treaty as a whole, and clearly reflects states' reluctance to secure supervision based on adjudication and redress. So far, the ACFC has appeared remarkably active with regard to meetings with not only representatives of states parties but also representatives of non-state actors, such as national institutions, NGOs and minority organisations, whose background input has also been sought through shadow reports.[43]

In strictly institutional terms, an important development was the establishment of the OSCE High Commissioner on National Minorities (HCNM) at the Helsinki follow-up meeting of 1992. The HCNM has worked since 1993 as an instrument of conflict prevention, by providing – according to the respective mandate – "early warning" and, where appropriate, "early action", so as to prevent tension from escalating into violence and spreading across national borders. He may collect and receive information from any source (save information from people or organisations involved in terrorism or violence), conduct fact-finding missions in the form of visits subject to the consent of the state concerned, and suggest solutions with a view to fostering dialogue between governments and national minorities. Despite his security rather than humanitarian functions, the high commissioner is also guided by the relevant OSCE and other human rights instruments as a framework of analysis. In fact, he has occasionally reviewed pertinent standards, as, for instance, in the 1999 "Report on the Linguistic Rights of Persons Belonging to National Minorities in the OSCE Area", or facilitated the drafting of special texts, such as the so-called Hague, Oslo and Lund recommendations on, respectively, the education, linguistic and participation rights of persons belonging to national minorities, adopted between 1996 and 1999 by independent experts in support of his efforts, under the auspices of the Foundation on Inter-Ethnic Relations based in The Hague. His essentially mediation strategy, though, remains one characterised by pragmatism and "quiet diplomacy", designed to reach tailor-made compromises rather than secure a progressive, general implementation of existing standards.

The complex of supervisory techniques, particularly their role in the implementation practice, raises a whole host of questions which will be explored in the following chapters. For the purpose of the present introduction, a few general aspects may be worth briefly mentioning. In terms of the nature of supervision regarding minority rights, judicial review is virtually non-existent, while quasi-judicial review is largely confined to the individual complaints procedure established by the first optional protocol to the ICCPR. Whereas judicial-like approaches are generally still resisted by states, most recent responses rest on the recognition of a linkage between rights protection and preservation of peace and the resulting need for more flexible (non-judicial) models which envisage minority issues and minority rights compliance from a predominantly pragmatic context-specific perspective. The FCNM, the recent eastern bilateral treaties, the OSCE HCNM work, as well as a range of further related measures, all provide examples of policy-driven patterns, namely attempts to inspire domestic policies which are responsive to political circumstances.[44] For instance, the flexibility of the OSCE HCNM's mandate, coupled with a number of operational tools he has developed over time, are at the basis of a constructive way of tackling situations of potential inter-state conflict involving minorities, as illustrated by the case of the Hungarian minorities in Romania and Slovakia.[45] On the other hand, non-judicial responses to enforcement are reaching beyond the typical mediation, "non-hierarchical"[46] processes reflected in the patterns described above. The CoE and the EU are stepping up the level of minority rights monitoring in connection with their own human rights admission requirements and/or within the context of a coherent strategy based on the principle of conditionality. Depending on the initiative pursued, a number of sanctions (operating, by contrast, as disincentives) are provided for as a last resort against non-compliant states, ranging from suspension or termination of the relevant trade agreement (under a so-called human rights clause) to other appropriate steps, including suspension of financial assistance and/or trade preferences, to denial of membership. The EU deploys strong political and economic leverage to induce compliance with human rights/minority rights, in line with overall international tendencies to use the financial lever for this aim, which is brought to bear, to a greater or lesser extent, on the prevention of ethnic conflicts.[47] Generally speaking, the monitoring of the implementation of, *inter alia*, minority rights standards, is being carried out on the basis of internal reporting supplemented by available sources from other international organisations or bodies.

Experience shows that there are certainly advantages in adopting such flexible approaches. First, they are unencumbered by those stringent procedural requirements typically set out by formal complaints mechanisms – they may indeed result in loosely undertaken action on the initiative of the relevant body (for instance, the OSCE HCNM, the CoE Parliamentary Assembly or the EU Commission or Council) and/or in an open dialogue meant to favour constructive solutions (for instance, in the context of the FCNM or the recent eastern bilateral treaties). Second, although the impact of the various models may vary depending on a range of factors, it is safe to say that they generally allow for a degree of representation of the group's interests, particularly by enabling minority organisations or third-party NGOs to provide relevant information and make a case for ameliorating protection by the state concerned. Third, policy-driven responses to minority rights implementation tend to address compliance issues in a comprehensive manner, thereby promoting the sort of policy change which is necessary to tackle those systemic problems that group accommodation may raise (namely, long-standing group disputes linked to social and political factors). As effective in facilitating compliance with minority rights standards as they may appear, theoretically or in practice, they also present downsides which should be properly considered. Indeed, as non-judicial or political processes, they normally do not carry with them enforcement possibilities for victims and their representatives, are often exposed to double standard or realpolitik considerations, and/or the issue of minority rights compliance may not surface unless it is visibly linked to a potential or actual danger of conflict. Even more importantly, their contribution to a legal interpretation of standards is limited or difficult to measure, due to either precisely the diplomatic – rather than juridical – characterisation of the work carried out by the supervisory actors (for instance, the OSCE HCNM) or the low-key legal nature of the monitoring process as a whole (for instance, that of the FCNM). In this regard, the Article 27 jurisprudence of the HRC as well as the ECHR jurisprudence are clearly indicative of the far greater role judicial-like bodies play in expounding the norms, applying them consistently, and providing remedies for limited grievances.

At the same time, judicial-like models are focused on individual cases, which may be brought up only by those (be they individuals, groups of individuals or NGOs) who believe to have been victims of a rights violation. To be sure, the victim requirement is not always a sine qua non for petitioning: for instance, the petition procedure before the Inter-American Commission on Human Rights (IACHR) allows for petitions to be filed with the IACHR by a third party on behalf of individual victims, with or without the latter's knowledge or consent; that has occurred so far mostly on behalf of indigenous communities. In the specific context of minority rights supervision, the HRC, though deeming inadmissible complaints submitted by collective entities on their behalf or by third parties on behalf of individual victims, as well as complaints in the form of an *actio popularis*, does allow, as indicated earlier in this chapter, communications from a group of allegedly "similarly affected"[48] individuals such as minority members. As long as minority rights norms are, and remain of an individual nature, judicial-like approaches, in their most progressive versions, might go as far as to confer a procedural faculty of independent action upon minority associations and third-party NGOs, and therefore permit a higher measure of collective representation. Even so, they could not transcend limitations attached to the nature and reach of adjudicatory or quasi-adjudicatory methods.

A plausible contention seems to be that both judicial-like and policy-driven means of enforcement can usefully address certain minority situations, but not all of them. The former approaches arguably reflect the vision of implementing minority rights as "normal", or universal or generally applicable, human rights law, particularly in the sense of resolving questions relating to the content of the relevant provisions and the way they should be applied in practice, as well as seeking consistency of the respective regime of rights and duties. As hinted at earlier, the latter approaches are prompted by considerations of security and are part of wider efforts at preventing, managing and/or solving ethnic disputes or conflicts. It would thus be advisable to better appreciate the advantages and disadvantages of judicial-like and policy-driven international responses in a way that both of them can appropriately serve the fundamental aim of generating effective minority rights protection at the domestic level. Although no dramatic developments on the judicial-like side can be reasonably expected over the short and medium term in international law,[49] discussion as to the complementarity – rather than mutual exclusion – of such approaches can and should go on, while at the same time upholding independent and effective supervision as their veritable mantra.

* Dottore in Giurisprudenza (Bari); Ph.D. (Rome); Lecturer in International Law, University of Munich; Visiting Fellow, Max Planck Institute for Comparative Public Law and International Law, Heidelberg, Germany.

1. On the complex debate about the definition of minority, see Gaetano Pentassuglia, *Minorities in International Law: an Introductory Study*, (Strasbourg, 2002), pp. 55-75 (including extensive references to further literature).

2. UN Secretariat, *Study of the Legal Validity of the Undertakings Concerning Minorities*, UN Doc. E/CN.4/367 (1950).

3. Ibid., 27-28.

4. Francesco Capotorti, *Study on the Rights of Persons belonging to Ethnic, Religious and Linguistic Minorities*, UN Doc. E/CN.4/Sub.2/384/Rev. I (1979), paragraphs 206-210.

5. 1935 PCIJ Series A/B, No. 64, 17.

6. Ibid., 17.

7. For jurisprudential examples of this latter aspect, see Gaetano Pentassuglia, op.cit., p. 92.

8. It is quite revealing in this regard that whereas protection against discrimination, together with protection against genocide, as well as other specific protective contours surrounding these areas, are believed to generate primordial non-derogable rights benefiting minority groups, i.e. rights which, as a logical *prius* to any meaningful protection of such groups, must be respected even during a state of public emergency which threatens the life of the nation (see e.g. HRC General Comment No. 29 (72) on derogation from provisions of the covenant during a state of emergency, adopted on 24 July 2001, *Official Records of the General Assembly, Fifth-sixth Session*, Supplement No. 40, A/56/40, Vol. I, Annex VI, paragraph 13.c to 13.e, this is generally said not to be the case when it comes to the elements of protection regarding the identity of minorities, save perhaps in particular cases and aside from the matter of limitations allowed in normal times (see, for example, Gaetano Pentassuglia, op.cit., pp. 108-109).

9. For comments on this statement submitted by France upon its ratification of the ICCPR, see Sarah Joseph, Jenny Schultz and Melissa Castan, *The International Covenant on Civil and Political Rights: Cases, Materials, and Commentary* (Oxford, 2000), pp. 601-602.

10. Interestingly, in Hopu and Bessert v. France (Communication No. 549/1993, UN Doc. CCPR/C/60/D/1993), the HRC maintained this stand, but five dissenting members considered the French declaration as inapplicable to overseas territories under French sovereignty.

11. HRC General Comment No. 23 (50) on Article 27 of the International Covenant on Civil and Political Rights, adopted on 6 April 1994, CCPR/C/21/Rev. 1/Add.5, paragraph 5.2.

12. For a comprehensive overview, see Gaetano Pentassuglia, op.cit., pp. 100-102.

13. Communication No. 24/1977, views of 30 July 1981, (1981) Annual Report, 166; (1983) Annual Report, 248.

14. Communication No. 197/1985, views of 27 July 1988, (1988) Annual Report, 221.

15. Communication No. 547/1993, views of 27 October 2000, CCPR/C/70/D/541/1993.

16. Communication No. 167/1984, views of 26 March 1990, (1990) Annual Report II, 1.

17. Communication No. 511/1992, views of 26 October 1994, (1995) Annual Report II, 66.

18. Communication No. 671/1995, views of 30 October 1996, (1997) Annual Report II, 191.

19. Communication No. 760/1997, views of 25 July 2000, CCPR/C/69/D/760/1996.

20. A case is currently pending before the HRC, raising issues under Article 27 in connection with the recognition of one's minority name (Tadeusz Kleczkowski (Tadeuš Klečkowski) v. Lithuania, Communication No. 1032/2001, submitted on 3 October, 2001).

21. HRC op.cit., paragraph 6.1.

22. Gaetano Pentassuglia, op.cit., pp. 104-108.

23. Gaetano Pentassuglia, op.cit., pp. 120-127; Benoît-Rohmer, "La Cour de Strasbourg

et la protection de l'intérêt minoritaire: une advancée sur le plan des principes?", 12 *Revue trimestrielle des droits de l'homme* (2001), pp. 999-1015; *idem*, "La Cour européenne des droits de l'homme et la défense des droits des minorités nationales", 13 *Revue trimestrielle des droits de l'homme* (2002), pp. 563-586; Gilbert, "The Bourgeoning Minority Rights Jurisprudence of the European Court of Human Rights", 24 *Human Rights Quarterly* (2002), pp. 736-780.

24. Unlike Article 14 of the ECHR, which proscribes discrimination only in so far as it relates to the enjoyment of any of the Convention rights, Protocol No. 12 contains a freestanding, general prohibition of discrimination. While broader in scope *ratione materiae*, the legal effects of Article 1 of this protocol would appear prima facie to reproduce on a larger scale, rather than qualitatively exceed, those of Article 14 of the ECHR, especially in the light of the most recent Strasbourg jurisprudence (see Thlimmenos v. Greece, Application 34369/97, ECtHR., Judgment of 6 April 2000).

25. Reply adopted on 13 June 2002 by the Committee of Ministers of the Council of Europe to Parliamentary Assembly Recommendation 1492 (2001), REC_1492 (2001), GR-H (2002) CB8.

26. For an overview of substantive aspects brought up in the context of the initial activities concerning the monitoring of the implementation of the FCNM, see Rainer Hofmann, "Review of the Monitoring Process of the Council of Europe Framework Convention for the Protection of National Minorities", *European Yearbook of Minority Issues 1* (2001/2), pp. 435-460, at pp. 447-458.

27. 2000/43/EC, OJ 2000 L 180/22.

28. 2000/750/EC, OJ 2000 L 303/23.

29. Guido Schwellnus, "Much Ado about Nothing? Minority Protection and the EU Charter of Fundamental Rights", *Constitutionalism Web-Papers* (2001), at http://les1.man.ac.uk/conweb

30. However, the Laeken European Council in December 2001, which established a "convention" charged with considering the future of the EU prior to the Intergovernmental Conference in 2004, adopted a declaration setting out the issues that the convention is expected to consider, including whether the charter should be included in the basic treaty. At the time of writing, the discussion on this matter is still under way.

31. Minority issues were addressed by the ECJ in the cases of Bickel/Franz (Case C-274/96, Criminal Proceedings against Bickel, (1998) ECR I-7637) and Angonese v. Cassa di Risparmio di Bolzano SpA, (2000) All ER (EC) 577). See generally Gaetano Pentassuglia, op.cit., pp. 144-146.

32. See in more detail, Rainer Hofmann, "National Minorities and European Community Law", *Baltic Yearbook of International Law* 2 (2002), pp. 159-174.

33. Gaetano Pentassuglia, "The EU and the Protection of Minorities: The Case of Eastern Europe", 12 *EJIL* (2001), pp. 3-38.

34. Arie Bloed and Pieter van Dijk (eds), *Protection of Minority Rights Through Bilateral Treaties: The Case of Central and Eastern Europe* (The Hague, 1999).

35. Thio, L. "Battling Balkanisation: Regional Approaches Toward Minority Protection Beyond Europe", 43 *HILJ* (2002), pp. 403-468.

36. The HRC has implicitly recognised the customary law status of Article 27 in paragraph 8 of its General Comment No. 24 (52) on issues relating to reservations made upon ratification or accession to the covenant or the optional protocols thereto, or in relation to declarations under Article 41 of the covenant, adopted on 2 November 1994, UN Doc. A/50/40.

37. For the physical integrity of minority groups in international customary law, see Gaetano Pentassuglia, *Minorities in International Law*, op.cit., pp. 79-84.

38. For a survey and bibliographic references, ibid., pp. 181-196.

39. Ibid., pp. 199-227.

40. For instance, a case of alleged genocide consistently made within this context

might be then taken up by a state party to the 1948 Convention on the Prevention and Punishment of the Crime of Genocide before the International Court of Justice (Article 9).

41. Thio, L. op.cit., pp. 434-444.

42. The Advisory Committee's opinions and the Committee of Ministers' conclusions can be consulted at http://local.coe.int

43. For a comprehensive overview of the initial monitoring practice of the Advisory Committee, see generally Rainer Hofmann, "Review of the Monitoring Process of the Council of Europe Framework Convention for the Protection of National Minorities", op.cit. See also the Third Activity Report delivered by the Advisory Committee covering the period from 1 November 2000 to 31 May 2002, ACFC/INF(2002)001, at http://www.humanrights.coe.int/minorities

44. See generally Gaetano Pentassuglia, "On the Models of Minority Rights Supervision in Europe and How They Affect a Changing Concept of Sovereignty", *European Yearbook of Minority Issues* 1 (2001/2), pp. 29-64.

45. Steven R. Ratner, "Does International Law Matter in Preventing Ethnic Conflict?", 32 *New York University Journal of International Law and Politics* (2000), pp. 591-698.

46. Antonia Handler Chayes and Abram Chayes, "Mobilizing International and Regional Organizations for Managing Ethnic Conflict", in David Wippman (ed.), *International Law and Ethnic Conflict* (Ithaca, London, 1998), pp. 178-210.

47. Gaetano Pentassuglia, "The EU and the Protection of Minorities: The Case of Eastern Europe ", op.cit., *passim.*

48. Bernard Ominayak, Chief of the Lubicon Lake Band v. Canada, Communication No. 167/1984, views of 26 March 1990, (1990) Annual Report II, 1, paragraph 32.1.

49. At the European level, see, for example, the reply adopted on 13 June 2002 by the Committee of Ministers of the Council of Europe to Parliamentary Assembly Recommendation 1492 (2001), REC_1492 (2001), GR-H (2002) CB8.

THE UNITED NATIONS TREATY MONITORING BODIES AND MINORITY RIGHTS, WITH PARTICULAR EMPHASIS ON THE HUMAN RIGHTS COMMITTEE

Alexander H. E. Morawa*

Introduction

The United Nations treaty regime

This chapter intends to show how the human rights treaty regime set up by the United Nations (UN), and in particular the International Covenant on Civil and Political Rights (ICCPR)[1] and the International Convention on the Elimination of All Forms of Racial Discrimination (ICERD),[2] may be relevant for those who want to give effect to and improve the rights of minorities and why its implementation bodies, such as the Human Rights Committee (HRC) and the Committee on the Elimination of Racial Discrimination (CERD), if used wisely, can be an appropriate forum for testing the scope of minority rights by means of international human rights implementation and litigation.

Apart from the two above mentioned bodies, four more exist: the Committee on Economic, Social and Cultural Rights,[3] which monitors compliance with a whole range of rights within the framework of its mandate, the Committee against Torture (CAT),[4] the Committee on the Elimination of Discrimination against Women (CEDAW),[5] and the Committee on the Rights of the Child (CRC)[6], which are more "specialised".[7] Reference to the practice of these bodies will be made in so far as it is relevant in the minority rights context.[8]

The International Covenant on Civil and Political Rights

Drafted by the Commission on Human Rights between 1948 and 1966, the International Covenant on Civil and Political Rights is part of what is called the "International Bill of Human Rights",[9] which consists of the Universal Declaration of Human Rights, the two covenants – the second being the International Covenant on Economic, Social, and Cultural Rights (ICESCR)[10] – and the optional protocols (OPs) thereto.

The ICCPR entered into force in 1976. By December 2002, a total of 149 states had ratified it.[11] Of these, 104 have also accepted the competence of the HRC to receive individual communications alleging breaches of the rights guaranteed.

The International Convention on the Elimination of All Forms of Racial Discrimination

States parties to ICERD "undertake to pursue by all appropriate means and without delay a policy of eliminating racial discrimination in all its forms and promoting understanding among all races".[12] Since the CERD's working methods correspond by and large to the ones of the Human Rights Committee, it will not be discussed separately, but wherever necessary its particular features and practice will be noted.

The implementation mechanisms under the International Covenant on Civil and Political Rights

The Human Rights Committee is a "treaty-monitoring body".[13] It consists of 18 members who are elected by secret ballot by the states parties to the ICCPR and serve in their personal capacity. While there are less formal guarantees for their independence than, for instance, for the judges of the European Court of Human Rights, nominees have usually been of a very high quality. "The Committee convenes three times a year for sessions of three weeks' duration, normally in March at United Nations headquarters in New York and in July and November at the United Nations office in Geneva."[14]

The HRC employs various means when monitoring state compliance with the ICCPR, including a state reporting system, general comments and an inter-state complaint mechanism, accompanied by the system of individual complaints under the optional protocol (OP).

The state reporting procedure

The state reporting approach is in many ways the less effective approach to human rights implementation compared to judicial proceedings. Most UN treaties provide for a reporting mechanism accompanied, in several cases, by an individual complaints procedure. It is probably fair to say generally that the "stronger" treaties allow individual petitions, while the "weaker" ones do not, at least not initially or automatically. That is true for Europe as well: the FCNM and the European Charter for Regional or Minority Languages (ECRML), for instance, are "reporting treaties."[15] The European Social Charter (and revised Charter of 1996)[16] was a "reporting only" treaty for decades, but has recently morphed into a limited "petitions treaty", allowing collective, but not individual complaints. Thus, there is always the possibility to make treaties "stronger". The ICCPR utilises both systems, with a mandatory system of state reports, but the individual communications procedure being optional.

The ICCPR and the HRC's practice provide for different forms or stages of reporting: states have to provide an initial report, due within one year after the entry into force of the covenant; supplementary reports may be requested by the committee if a state report contains insufficient information; finally, periodic reports on the domestic implementation of the covenant are due every five years.[17]

There are crucial questions to be asked when assessing the efficiency of a reporting procedure: What are states obligated to report about? Can the supervisory body engage in an open dialogue with the states parties? What is the outcome of the whole procedure? Is the public aware of the process?

The HRC has set forth fairly precise rules for state reports which are now available as "consolidated guidelines",[18] published in February 2001. They distinguish between the *initial* reports, which have to be comprehensive and written on an article-by-article basis, and targeted periodic reports, geared primarily to the committee's specific concerns. "In their *periodic* reports states parties need not report on every article, but only on those articles identified by the HRC in its concluding observations and those articles concerning which there have been important developments since the submission of the previous report."[19] Thus, it has been said that there is an "evolution as far as the effectiveness of the study of reports is concerned".[20] As regards the contents of the reports, the guidelines furthermore stipulate that "legal norms should be described, but that is not sufficient: the factual situation and the practical availability, effect and implementation of remedies for violation of Covenant rights should be explained and exemplified".[21] States should thus also describe "the practices and decisions of courts and other organs of the state party as well as further relevant facts which are likely to show the degree of the actual implementation ... [of] the Covenant, the progress achieved and factors and difficulties in implementing the obligations ...".[22]

With respect to the right not to be discriminated against, which is particularly relevant in the given context, the HRC reiterated that it "wishes to know if there remain any problems of discrimination in fact, which may be practised either by public authorities, by the community, or by private persons or bodies. The HRC wishes to be informed about legal provisions and administrative measures directed at diminishing or eliminating such discrimination".[23]

These guidelines notwithstanding, state reports received by the committee continue to "lack ... information on the implementation of the Covenant in practice".[24] That has prompted the HRC to strategically develop further mechanisms within the state reporting scheme to increase its effectiveness, in particular so-called "lists of issues". Once an initial report has been dealt with, the committee's reaction will guide many states and facilitate the preparation of their next periodic report. To emphasise even further what information is needed, the HRC now also uses lists of issues outlining the areas of concern with respect to particular states. These are "adopted at the session prior to the examination of a report, thereby allowing a period of at least two months for states parties to prepare for the discussion with the Committee".[25] The lists of issues are particularly useful when it comes to the more ambiguous provisions of the ICCPR, such as Article 27 safeguarding minority rights.[26]

Central to the consideration of reports is the oral hearing, where a state's delegation has an opportunity to answer specific questions from members of the committee. Thus, the HRC encourages states to use the list of issues in order to better prepare for a constructive discussion, but does not expect written answers at that stage.[27] The oral hearings themselves should not be confused with court hearings. They reflect the overall purpose of the state reporting procedure to assist states in their efforts to implement the ICCPR, but not to formally hold a state in breach of its obligations.

The various inquiries and discussions on the basis of state reports lead to the committee's concluding observations, which it has been adopting since 1992.[28] The observations are by no means general in nature, but tend to reflect the concerns the HRC and its members have in light of the explanations, or lack thereof, given by the state delegations in the course of the discussion of their national reports.[29] With respect to newly independent states the committee has shown a degree of lenience and has emphasised the "efforts" by the governments to remedy a situation of widespread human rights violations they inherited from their predecessors[30] and the "clear progress in securing civil and political rights".[31] Finally, the HRC does not hesitate to draw and publicise positive conclusions if mandated.[32]

As regards follow-up in the state reporting process, the HRC routinely demands from states that their "... next periodic report[s] ... contain material which responds to all the present concluding observations ...".[33] Finally, especially in light of the end of the Cold War and the emergence of numerous new states facing far-reaching human rights problems inherited from their predecessors, the committee adopted a "current events" approach: whenever events come to its attention that indicate that the enjoyment of ICCPR rights is in jeopardy, the HRC requests accelerated "emergency reports" from states parties.[34] When examining Croatia's report in April 2001, for instance, the committee "... asked [the state party] ... to forward information within 12 months on the implementation of the Committee's recommendations regarding ... the discrimination faced by minorities, in particular the Serb ethnic minority ...".[35]

Publicity plays a vital role in the implementation process. "The Committee [usually] requests that [the] concluding observations and the next periodic report be widely disseminated in [the country concerned]."[36] States parties are urged to publish them "in appropriate languages"[37] and to make them accessible, in particular, to "civil society and non-governmental organisations operating ..."[38] in the country. Occasionally the committee even requires states to implement "a programme of dissemination of human rights texts and ... systematic training ...".[39] There is, furthermore, significant interaction between the HRC, as well as the other treaty monitoring bodies, such as the CERD,[40] and non-governmental organisations. NGOs are providing country information and critical reports on the human rights situation in certain countries, information which the committee may take into consideration and use as a starting point for asking questions.[41] NGOs also participate in the meetings of the chairpersons of the human rights treaty bodies.

General comments

General comments "spell out the meaning of various provisions of the Covenant".[42] The HRC, building upon its practice in the state reporting and individual communications procedures, summarises its interpretation of individual rights and develops general guidelines on how they are supposed to be implemented domestically.[43] While this sounds harmless, the HRC has occasionally utilised general comments as a tool to evolve the interpretation of the ICCPR.[44]

Inter-state complaints

The optional inter-state complaints procedure provided for in Articles 41 and 42 of the ICCPR should also be mentioned briefly. It would allow states parties who have recognised the HRC's competence to do so, and on the basis of reciprocity, to submit claims that another state party is not fulfilling its obligations under the ICCPR, thereby initiating a process of mediation and conciliation[45] of little practical value. That procedure was never utilised and scholars have rightly qualified it as "meaningless".[46]

Individual communications under the OP

a. Introduction

The individual complaints procedure[47] is optional, and thus not contained in the ICCPR itself, but in a so-called optional protocol. By ratifying it, a state party "recognises the competence of the Committee to receive and consider communications from individuals subject to its jurisdiction who claim to be victims of a violation by that State party of any of the rights set forth in the Covenant".[48] The complaints procedure was intended as an additional, but equally important mechanism to implement rights complementing the reporting procedure outlined above[49] and has, apart from establishing breaches of the law, a "preventive dimension", just like the reporting processes.[50] The HRC itself has emphasised that the complaints procedure "aims at helping victims rather than condemning States parties for violations of the Covenant. The Committee therefore welcomes the early co-operation by States parties in finding solutions to human rights problems."[51] The role of the HRC in deciding individual cases differs, nevertheless, quite significantly from its primary role as an adviser and consensus-builder in the course of the evaluation of state reports. The committee here acts as a tribunal, not a mediator, and its working methods resemble in many ways those of international courts, such as the European Court of Human Rights. That is reflected, for instance, in the increasing number of cases decided by majority vote rather than by consensus, and the habit of committee members to append dissenting or concurring opinions to views and even admissibility decisions.[52] By the same token, the committee places individuals who complain and the states which are alleged to have violated their rights on an equal footing throughout its proceedings. Each has an opportunity to comment on the other's arguments.[53] The HRC's final views in cases, moreover, display "a structure closely akin to that of a true judicial pronouncement".[54]

Between 1977 and July 2002 a total of 1 107 individual communications concerning 71 states were registered. Of those, 310 were declared inadmissible, 143 were discontinued or withdrawn, in 404 cases the HRC proceeded to a consideration of the merits and found breaches of the ICCPR in 313 of them.[55] In mid-2002, the HRC had 250 individual communications pending before it, most of them in the pre-admissibility stage.[56] The following table gives an overview of the status of cases from 1997 to 2001.

Table 1.1. Communications dealt with from 1997-2001[57]

Year	New registered	Cases concluded[58]	Pending cases (total admissible and pre-admissible cases) at 31 December	Admissible cases at 31 December	Pre-admissible cases at 31 December
2001	81	41	222	25	197
2000	58	43	182	27	155
1999	59	55	167	36	131
1998	53	51	163	42	121
1997	60	56	157	44	113

b. The handling of cases by the HRC

Incoming communications are reviewed by members of the UN High Commissioner for Human Rights' "petitions team" under the direction of a Special Rapporteur on New Communications, whose competences include the transmission of communications to states parties and the indication of interim measures of protection.[59] Cases are subsequently dealt with by individual members who act as case rapporteur, by the Working Group on Communications and finally by the plenary committee.[60]

It is particularly relevant for petitioners that since 1997 the HRC, except under exceptional circumstances, joins the consideration of admissibility and merits of communications in all cases. "[W]hen a new communication has been received the State party will be requested to submit written explanations or statements relating to both admissibility and merits of the communication. Only in exceptional circumstances will the Committee request a State party to address admissibility only. A State party which has received a request for information on admissibility and merits may within two months apply for the communication to be rejected as inadmissible. Such a request, however, will not absolve the State party from the requirement to submit information on the merits within the set time limit ...".[61]

The treaty monitoring bodies have always – much like the entire UN system – suffered from understaffing and limited financial resources. That has led to the near collapse of the procedure in recent years, prompting the HRC itself to demand improvements and to emphasise "the urgency of finding a solution to this continuing failure in the system".[62] However, it is noteworthy that the working methods of the committee's legal staff have changed dramatically since then, and, especially with the introduction of a specialised petitions team at the High Commissioner's office in Geneva, the efficiency of the procedure has increased. New communications are routinely registered and communicated to the states parties within a few months after they have been received, occasionally even within two months or less. If one considers that the European Court of Human Right's registry hardly ever communicates regular applications – that is, applications that do not require urgent action to prevent irreparable harm to individual interests – less than two years after they are registered, that means that the HRC's procedure is much faster and may thus offer advantages to certain groups of petitioners.

c. Admissibility

In international human rights litigation admissibility means a set of preconditions that have to be fulfilled before a tribunal may proceed to a consideration of the merits of a complaint. These are listed in the OP itself and comprise the following elements:

— communications must not be anonymous, and must come from a person or persons subject to the jurisdiction of a state which is a party to the OP. Routinely communications will be sent in by the individual who claims that his or her rights have been violated, or his/her representative, but when it appears that the alleged victim is prevented from submitting the communication, the HRC may consider a communication from someone who is acting on behalf of the alleged victim. However, someone with no apparent links with the person(s) whose rights have allegedly been violated cannot submit a communication;[63]

— inadmissibility *ratione temporis* (Article 1 of the OP), which means that the alleged violations of the covenant must have occurred after the entry into force of the ICCPR and OP for the state concerned, unless continuing effects exist which in themselves are alleged to violate rights;

— incompatibility of the claims with the provisions of the ICCPR (Article 3 of the OP): "[c]ommunications must raise an issue concerning the application of the Covenant. [T]he Committee cannot function under the OP as an appellate body where the issue is one of domestic law, [but] some communications continue to be based on such a misapprehension; such cases, as well as those where the facts presented do not raise issues under the articles of the Covenant invoked by the author, are declared inadmissible. ... Claims based on alleged rights that are not protected in the Covenant are declared inadmissible *ratione materiae*";[64]

— non-substantiation of claims (Article 2 of the OP): "[a]lthough an author does not need to prove the alleged violation at the admissibility stage, he or she must submit sufficient materials substantiating his/her allegation for purposes of admissibility. A 'claim' is, therefore, not just an allegation, but an allegation supported by a certain amount of substantiating materials";[65]

— non-exhaustion of domestic remedies (Article 5, paragraph 2(b) of the OP): the HRC must ascertain that an author has exhausted all available domestic remedies. However, that "applies only to the extent that those remedies are effective and available. The State party is required to give 'details of the remedies which it submitted had been available to the author in the circumstances of his case, together with evidence that there would be a reasonable prospect that such remedies would be effective.' ... The rule also provides that the Committee is not precluded from examining a communication if it is established that application of the remedies in question is unreasonably prolonged";[66]

- inadmissibility because of submission of the "same matter" to another procedure of international investigation or settlement (Article 5, paragraph 2(a) of the OP);[67]

- abuse of the right of submission: "Article 3 of the OP provides that a communication may be declared inadmissible on grounds of abuse. [So far] the Committee has not determined ... what exactly would constitute an abuse of the right of submission. This jurisprudence remains to be developed."[68] However, one may conclude from a comparative analysis of the practice of other tribunals that "'abuse' may occur if a fundamental procedural rule is knowingly and repeatedly – and despite previous warnings by the [tribunal] – violated with the malicious intent to unduly interfere with the normal course of proceedings, thus undermining the authority of the [tribunal]".[69] It is also possible that an unreasonable and unexplained delay in submitting a case to the HRC may lead to it being dismissed as an abuse of the right to petition.[70]

d. Duties of states in the course of the examination of individual complaints and the "effect" of decisions and views

We have previously discussed the obligation of states to provide the HRC with adequate information about the domestic implementation of the ICCPR in their state reports so as to enable it to exercise its functions properly. In the course of the examination of individual communications a similar "duty to co-operate" exists. In Bleier v. Uruguay the HRC was confronted with the disappearance of a man whom witnesses had seen in a military detention camp and a government unwilling to provide any explanations with regard to these allegations. The committee held that:

> [W]ith regard to the burden of proof, this cannot rest alone on the author of the communication, especially considering that the author and the states party do not always have equal access to the evidence and that frequently the states party alone has access to relevant information. ... [T]he states party has the duty to investigate in good faith all allegations of violation of the Covenant made against it and its authorities, especially when such allegations are corroborated by evidence submitted by the author of the communication, and to furnish to the Committee the information available to it. In cases where ... further clarification of the case depends on information exclusively in the hands of the states party, the Committee may consider such allegations as substantiated in the absence of satisfactory evidence and explanations to the contrary submitted by the states party.[71]

This procedural tool – called "default jurisprudence"[72] by commentators and by the HRC itself[73] – has been utilised by the committee in subsequent cases.[74] One must admit that such prima facie assumptions of violations will only occur in cases of very severe breaches of human rights and when the situation in a given country is such as to support far-reaching inferences: thus, the committee's knowledge of country conditions stemming from the reporting process plays a role in the individual complaints procedure. However, a version of the "default jurisprudence" is being applied as a general rule and also with respect to procedural issues, such as the "exhaustion of domestic remedies" requirement,[75] and has been summarised by the HRC as follows:

> [I]f a states party does not provide an answer to an author's allegations, the Committee will give due weight to an author's uncontested allegations as long as they are substantiated.[76]

The consideration of communications under the OP by the HRC is confidential and takes place in closed meetings.[77] Since a change in the rules of procedure in 1996,[78] however, the author of a communication and the states party concerned may make public any submissions or information bearing on the proceedings, unless the HRC has requested the parties to respect confidentiality. Also, the committee's final decisions – that is, views, decisions declaring a communication inadmissible, and decisions to discontinue a communication – are made public.[79] The duty to actively disseminate information about the ICCPR and its implementation also extends to the HRC's views and the measures adopted to give them effect at the domestic level.

The HRC concludes its views in individual complaints cases with the following general statement:

> Bearing in mind that, by becoming a party to the Optional Protocol, the states party has recognised the competence of the Committee to determine whether there has been a violation of the Covenant or not and that ... the states party has undertaken to ensure to all individuals within its territory and subject to its jurisdiction the rights recognised in the Covenant and to provide an effective remedy in the case a violation has been established, the Committee wishes to receive from the states party, within 90 days, information about the measures taken to give effect to the Committee's Views.[80]

From a legal point of view, the HRC's "views" are not the same as "judgments". Scholars have called them "not legally binding"[81] or "*unverbindlich*"[82] and cautioned that there is a total "lack of sanctions"[83] hampering their enforcement. States have gone even further, particularly when they found themselves as defendants before the committee. The following exchange of views took place during the consideration of the Austrian state report in 1998. A member of the Austrian delegation argued that his government "regard[s] the Committee's views on communications from individuals as non-binding opinions, and [does] not think its obligations under the Covenant extended to acting in accordance with those views. It [does], however, believe that such views should be taken duly into account".[84] Committee member Mr Klein countered by saying "that, while the Committee's views might not have the same status as judgments of the European Court of Human Rights, they were not entirely devoid of legal consequences",[85] a view strongly supported by Mr Buergenthal.[86]

The Committee's long-standing approach is, as it expressed, *inter alia*, in the case of Bradshaw v. Barbados, that "... it is an obligation for the State party to adopt appropriate measures to give legal effect to the views of the Committee as to the interpretation and application of the Covenant in particular cases ...".[87] In recent years it has become even more outspoken by developing this new approach:

A specific *mechanism* should be established to ensure that the Views expressed by the Committee on individual communications under the OP to the Covenant are *systematically* implemented.[88]

The HRC, unlike for instance the European Court of Human Rights, has a mandate to recommend specific measures a state should adopt to remedy a wrong. That includes steps like "the reopening of proceedings that led to a violation of the Covenant".[89] In certain cases the HRC goes beyond recommending actions aimed at remedying the grievances of the individual petitioner. It then usually urges states to amend their domestic laws to be able to implement the HRC's views or, at the very least, not to apply laws in a way that would contravene the ICCPR.[90] In its 2001 views in Blazek et al. v. the Czech Republic, a case concerning reparations for expropriations under the communist regime, the HRC proceeded to:

...[encourage] the states party to review its relevant legislation and administrative practices to ensure that neither the law nor its application entails discrimination in contravention of Article 26 of the Covenant.[91]

Occasionally the HRC has found that the effective remedy should entail compensation, if the circumstances of the case so warrant.[92] Unlike the regional human rights courts the committee does not have the formal authority to award "just satisfaction" or "fair compensation"[93] for breaches of human rights. Irrespective of that, the committee has said that it "may also fix a sum for compensation"[94] and has indeed begun to do that in individual cases.[95]

Finally, a "Special Rapporteur for the Follow-up on Views" was established in 1990 who solicits and receives reports from states parties on particular measures taken to comply with the views in individual cases.[96] So far, in 198 of the cases that ended with a finding of a breach of the ICCPR, the respondent states have submitted such reports. The HRC qualifies the reactions of states as either "satisfactory", if and when they "respond in substance to the Committee's recommendation or represent substantial compliance", or "unsatisfactory", whenever replies do not respond to the recommendations, fail to address the issue of compensation to the victim or constitute "less than substantial compliance".[97] Some 30% of the 198 follow-up responses by governments received up to 2001 were considered "satisfactory in that they display the State party's willingness to implement the Committee's Views or to offer the applicant an appropriate remedy".[98] In some cases, states either "explicitly challenge the Committee's findings, on either factual or legal grounds, constitute much-belated submissions on the merits of the case, promise an investigation of the matter considered by the Committee or indicate that the State party will not, for one reason or another, give effect to the Committee's recommendations".[99] Apart from formal follow-up procedures, the most efficient way to give effect to the HRC's views is publicity, which is used by the committee itself[100] and is also available to petitioners and advocates in the field.

Rights of relevance to minorities

The norms

Core provision and an example for the expansion of the catalogue of rights safeguarded compared to the Universal Declaration of Human Rights,[101] on the one hand, and the beginning of a practice of formulating binding provisions protecting the rights of minorities rather vaguely,[102] is Article 27 of the International Covenant on Civil and Political Rights, which reads as follows:

> In those states in which ethnic, religious or linguistic minorities exist, persons belonging to such minorities shall not be denied the right, in community with the other members of their group, to enjoy their own culture, to profess and practise their own religion, or to use their own language.

Rights of relevance to minorities are contained, for instance, in Article 1, which stipulates that "[a]ll peoples have the right of self-determination. By virtue of that right they freely determine their political status and freely pursue their economic, social and cultural development." The HRC has not admitted complaints from groups claiming a right to self-determination in, for instance, the 1990 case of the Lubicon Lake Band v. Canada,[103] but has treated such claims as possible violations of Article 27. It has also concluded, in its recent views in Diergaardt et al. v. Namibia[104] and Gillot v. France[105] that "Article 1 may be relevant in the interpretation of other rights protected by the Covenant, in particular Articles 25, 26 and 27".

Article 26 corresponds to the general non-discrimination rule in Article 2, paragraph 1, but provides for an independent right to material equality:

> All persons are equal before the law and are entitled without any discrimination to the equal protection of the law. In this respect, the law shall prohibit any discrimination and guarantee to all persons equal and effective protection against discrimination on any ground such as race, colour, sex, language, religion, political or other opinion, national or social origin, property, birth or other status.

Finally, Article 25 reads as follows:

> Every citizen shall have the right and the opportunity, without any of the distinctions mentioned in Article 2 and without unreasonable restrictions:
>
> (a) To take part in the conduct of public affairs, directly or through freely chosen representatives;
>
> ... (c) To have access, on general terms of equality, to public service in his country.

The ICERD's purpose is to prohibit "any distinction, exclusion, restriction or preference based on race, colour, descent, or national or ethnic origin which has the purpose or effect of nullifying or impairing the recognition, enjoyment or exercise, on an equal footing, of human rights and fundamental freedoms in the political, economic, social, cultural or any other field of public life".[106] Amongst the measures states are required to adopt are positive ones, which are then considered not discriminatory themselves:[107] they "shall, when the circumstances so warrant, take, in the social, economic, cultural and other fields, special and concrete measures to ensure the adequate development and protection of certain racial groups or individuals belonging to them ...".[108]

An obligation to provide effective remedies for individuals who become the victims of racial discrimination complements the substantive provisions of the convention.[109]

The Human Rights Committee's general comment on Article 27 of the ICCPR

In 1994, the HRC adopted a general comment[110] on the ICCPR's core minority rights provision, Article 27. Despite criticism that it is not much less ambiguous and framework-like than the norm itself,[111] the general comment is instructive in many respects.

While emphasising that Article 27 provides for a right "which is distinct from, and additional to, all the other rights"[112] under the ICCPR, the committee stressed that it must not be "confused with the right of peoples to self-determination"[113] or the general and specific non-discrimination provisions contained therein.[114] The HRC was critical, in this context, of states "who claim that they do not discriminate on grounds of ethnicity, language or religion" and "wrongly contend, on that basis alone, that they have no minorities".[115]

The "sovereignty and territorial integrity" of states parties notwithstanding, "one or other aspect of the rights of individuals protected under that article – for example, to enjoy a particular culture – may consist in a way of life which is closely associated with territory and use of its resources",[116] as the HRC had said in, for instance, its views in Kitok v. Sweden.[117] This also relates to "the use of land resources, especially in the case of indigenous peoples. That right may include such traditional activities as fishing or hunting and the right to live in reserves protected by law".[118]

Those protected by Article 27 "are those who belong to a group and who share in common a culture, a religion and/or a language. Those terms also indicate that the individuals designed to be protected need not be citizens of the State party".[119] The HRC adds:

> Article 27 confers rights on persons belonging to minorities which "exist" in a states party. Given the nature and scope of the rights envisaged under that article, it is not relevant to determine the degree of permanence that the term "exist" connotes. Those rights simply are that individuals belonging to those minorities should not be denied the right, in community with members of their group, to enjoy their own culture, to practise their religion and speak their language. Just as they need not be nationals or citizens, they need not be permanent residents. Thus, migrant workers or even visitors in a states party constituting such minorities are entitled not to be denied the exercise of those rights. As any other individual in the territory of the states party, they would, also for this purpose, have the general rights, for example, to freedom of association, of assembly, and of expression. The existence of an ethnic, religious or linguistic minority in a given states party does not depend upon a decision by that states party but requires to be established by objective criteria.[120]

That approach has led to disagreement between the HRC and states parties, of which the following exchange is illustrative: Germany, in its 1996 state report referring to the drafting history of the ICCPR, voiced its opinion that "[t]he application of Article 27 must ... be restricted to certain ethnic groups:

'it was agreed that the article should cover only separate or distinct groups, well-defined and long-established on the territory of a State'".[121] The HRC countered by expressing its concern, in its concluding observations, "that the definition of minorities as 'ethnic or linguistic groups who have a traditional area of settlement in particular regions'" was "much too restrictive in terms of Article 27 of the Covenant. The Committee is of the view that Article 27 applies to all persons belonging to minorities whether linguistic, religious, ethnic or otherwise including those who are not concentrated or settled in a particular area or a particular region or who are immigrants or who have been given asylum in Germany."[122] The HRC concludes its general comment by stating that states are "under an obligation to ensure that the existence and the exercise of this right are protected against their denial or violation. Positive measures of protection are, therefore, required not only against the acts of the State party itself, ... but also against the acts of other persons within the State party".[123] With respect to positive measures, the general comment emphasises that they "may also be necessary to protect the identity of a minority and the rights of its members to enjoy and develop their culture and language and to practise their religion, in community with the other members of the group"[124] whereas they have to be undertaken in the context of non-discrimination "both as regards the treatment between different minorities and the treatment between the persons belonging to them and the remaining part of the population. However, as long as those measures are aimed at correcting conditions which prevent or impair the enjoyment of the rights guaranteed under Article 27, they may constitute a legitimate differentiation under the Covenant, provided that they are based on reasonable and objective criteria".[125]

The HRC finally reiterates that "[t]he protection of these rights is directed towards ensuring the survival and continued development of the cultural, religious and social identity of the minorities concerned, thus enriching the fabric of society as a whole".[126]

Examples of the committees' practice and case-law[127]

As stated previously, the committees advance the interpretation of the treaties by monitoring state compliance through the consideration of reports and the adoption of decisions and views on individual communications, whenever a state has ratified the OP. The following section presents merely a few illustrative samples of that practice, primarily of the Human Rights Committee, with particular regard to individual petitions. Recent cases build on a series of cases, beginning with Lovelace v. Canada, where the loss of "Indian status" of a Canadian woman on account of her marriage to a non-Indian was at issue; the marriage later broke up and she wished to return to the reserve where she had been brought up. The committee here held that "[p]ersons who are born and brought up on a reserve, who have kept ties with their community and wish to maintain these ties must normally be considered as belonging to that minority within the meaning of the Covenant"[128] irrespective of their status under domestic legislation. That the committee will take an independent look at the existence of a "minority" within the meaning of Article 27 is also evident in its state reporting practice, where it has repeatedly expressed its concern, as in the case of Ukraine, about "the vague and undefined concept of 'national minorities', which is the dominant factor in the State party's legislation on national minorities but does not cover the entire scope of Article 27 of the Covenant".[129] In the Lovelace case the HRC said that even though the right to reside in a particular place is not safeguarded by Article 27, residence restrictions must have "both a reasonable and objective justification";[130] in Ms Lovelace's case, no such justification could be made, nor was the measure "necessary to preserve the identity of the tribe".[131] That was reiterated in the Kitok case: "[a] restriction upon the right of an individual member of a minority must be shown to have a reasonable and objective justification and to be necessary for the continued viability and welfare of the minority as a whole".[132]

A case already mentioned, Diergaardt et al. v. Namibia[133] involves but does not resolve the question of what minorities are for the purposes of Article 27. The complainants were members of the Rehoboth Baster Community whose communal land had allegedly been "nationalised" by the Government of Namibia at the time it became an independent state in 1989 and after a long period of semi-autonomy. The Baster Community are descendents of indigenous people and Afrikaans settlers. They occupy a limited area in the vicinity of Windhoek where they "developed their own society, culture, language and economy, with which they largely sustained their own institutions, such as schools and community centres".[134]

The first issue was the "nationalisation" of the communal land: the Baster Community "claimed a violation of Article 27 in that a part of the lands traditionally used by members of the Rehoboth community for the grazing of cattle no longer is in the de facto exclusive use of the members of the community".[135] In a decision that is highly ambiguous and prompted numerous members to file dissenting or concurring opinions the committee was:

> ... unable to find that the authors can rely on Article 27 to support their claim for exclusive use of the pastoral lands in question. This conclusion is based on the Committee's assessment of the relationship between the authors' way of life and the lands covered by their claims. Although the link of the ... community to the lands in question dates back some 125 years, it is not the result of a relationship that would have given rise to a distinctive culture. Furthermore, although the ... community bears distinctive properties as to the historical forms of self-government, the authors have failed to demonstrate how these factors would be based on their way of raising cattle. The Committee therefore finds that there has been no violation of Article 27 of the Covenant in the present case.[136]

There was another issue, however, and here the complainants won. The Constitution of Namibia declares English to be the only official language. The Baster Community speaks Afrikaans. In 1992 the government sent a circular to all its civil servants with the following directives: "[a]ll employees of the Government are thus advised to, in future, refrain from using Afrikaans when responding to phone calls and their correspondence".[137] The committee approached this problem from the point of view of discrimination under Article 26 of the ICCPR. It held:

> These instructions barring the use of Afrikaans do not relate merely to the issuing of public documents but even to telephone conversations. In the absence of any

response from the states party the Committee must give due weight to the allegation of the authors that the circular in question is intentionally targeted against the possibility to use Afrikaans when dealing with public authorities. Consequently, the Committee finds that the authors, as Afrikaans speakers, are victims of a violation of Article 26 of the Covenant.[138]

In Communication No. 671/1995, Jouni Länsman et al. v. Finland, decided in 1996, the HRC was requested to assess whether logging in an area which the authors, reindeer breeders of Sami ethnic origin, used for reindeer husbandry violated their rights under Article 27. They challenged "the plans of the Finnish Central Forestry Board to approve logging and the construction of roads in an area covering about 3 000 hectares ... The members of the ... Herdsmen's Committee occupy areas in the North of Finland, covering a total of 255 000 hectares, of which one fifth is suitable for winter herding. The 3 000 hectares are situated within these winter herding lands".[139]

In the states party's opinion, the authors' complaint concerned the question of what types of measures in the areas concerned "trigger the 'threshold' beyond which measures must be regarded as a 'denial', within the meaning of Article 27, of the Samis' right to enjoy their own culture".[140] Finland argued that "if the concept of 'denial' within the meaning of Article 27 is interpreted as widely as by the authors, this would in fact give the Sami reindeer herders the right to reject all such activities which are likely to interfere with reindeer husbandry even to a small extent ...".[141] It referred to the co-existence of interests of forestry management and reindeer husbandry[142] and added that "[w]hile the logging and tracks in the ground will temporarily have limited adverse effects on the winter pastures used by the reindeer, it has not been shown ... that the consequences would create considerable and long-lasting harm, which would prevent the authors from continuing reindeer husbandry in the area under discussion on its present scale".[143]

The authors argued "... that because the economic benefit from reindeer herding is low, many reindeer herdsmen have had to look for additional sources of income. This development has been accelerated as most herding committees have been forced to cut the number of their herds. The necessity to reduce the herds has been caused by the scarcity of herding lands and the poor condition of existing, overused herding lands. In such a situation, suitable winter herding areas are a truly critical resource, which determine the scale of reductions in the number of reindeer belonging to each herdsmen's committee. The authors themselves developed other economic activities besides reindeer herding in order to survive. They work as butchers for other herdsmen's committees, work for private local landowners or conduct small-scale logging within their own private forests. All, however, would prefer to work solely in reindeer herding".[144]

The HRC emphasised that economic activities may come within the ambit of Article 27, if they are an essential element of the culture of a minority. It identified the crucial question to be determined in the present case to be "... whether the logging that has already taken place ... as well as such logging as has been approved for the future and which will be spread over a number of years, is of such proportions as to deny the authors the right to enjoy their culture in that area".[145] The HRC recalled that measures which have a certain limited impact on the way of life and livelihood of persons belonging to a minority do not necessarily amount to a denial of the rights under Article 27. On the basis of all the evidence before it, the committee concluded that the impact of the logging in the instant case would not be such as to amount to a denial of the authors' rights under Article 27. As regards future logging plans, the HRC pointed out that:

> ... the State party must bear in mind, when taking steps affecting the rights under Article 27, that although different activities in themselves may not constitute a violation of this article, such activities, taken together, may erode the rights of Sami people to enjoy their own culture.[146]

That case, and the subsequent case of Äärelä v. Finland,[147] in which the logging of some 92 hectares in a reindeer husbandry area was at issue, demonstrate that the threshold of "denial" of minority rights in Article 27 of the ICCPR is quite high. It raises difficult questions, including the permissibility or even necessity of economic affirmative action in favour of members of minority groups. None of these questions have, as of yet, been answered by the HRC. In particular, the issue of where "erosion", as the committee calls it, of minority rights by virtue of an accumulation of measures affecting them adversely might begin, remains to be seen.

In Mahuika et al. v. New Zealand,[148] the authors belonged to the Maori people of New Zealand and complained about the Fisheries Claims Settlement Act 1992 which was based on a settlement which had been negotiated between the Government and Maori representatives and was intended to settle all Maori claims, current and future, to commercial fishing rights. Pursuant to the act, the Maori were given a 50% stake in a major New Zealand fishing company, as well as 20% of quota issued under the quota management system. The authors stated that they did not agree with the settlement, that fishing was one of the main elements of their traditional culture and that they desired to manifest their culture through fishing to the fullest extent of their traditional territories. The HRC ruled, *inter alia*, on the question of a state's duties to hear a minority's views and take them into consideration in the course of settling matters that affect it:

> In the consultation process, special attention was paid to the cultural and religious significance of fishing for the Maori, *inter alia*, to securing the possibility of Maori individuals and communities to engage themselves in non-commercial fishing activities. While it is a matter of concern that the settlement and its process have contributed to divisions amongst Maori, nevertheless, the Committee concludes that the states party has, by engaging itself in the process of broad consultation before proceeding to legislate, and by paying specific attention to the sustainability of Maori fishing activities, taken the necessary steps to ensure that the ... settlement and its enactment through legislation ... are compatible with Article 27.[149]

The case of Ignatane v. Latvia[150] concerned the right to take part in the conduct of public affairs and to participate in elections pursuant to Article 25 of the ICCPR. The author, a Latvian teacher of Russian origin, claimed that she had been arbitrarily disqualified from running in local elections by means of the Latvian language aptitude test. In 1993 she had passed the test and obtained the highest possible grade of proficiency, yet in 1997, after she had announced her intention to be a candidate, it appears that she had managed to forget most of her Latvian, since a language inspector certified that she lacked the necessary proficiency and she was subsequently removed from the list of candidates. The HRC said:

> The decision of a single inspector, taken a few days before the elections and contradicting a language aptitude certificate issued some years earlier by a board of Latvian language specialists, was enough for the Election Commission to decide to strike the author off the list of candidates for the municipal elections. The Committee notes that the states party does not contest the validity of the certificate as it relates to the author's professional position, but argues on the basis of the results of the inspector's review in the matter of the author's eligibility. The Committee also notes that ... Latvian law does not provide for separate levels of proficiency in the official language in order to stand for election, but applies the standards and certification used in other instances. ... The Committee notes that the first examination, in 1993, was conducted in accordance with formal requirements and was assessed by five experts, whereas the 1997 review was conducted in an ad hoc manner and assessed by a single individual.[151] The annulment of the author's candidacy pursuant to a review that was not based on objective criteria and which the states party has not demonstrated to be procedurally correct is not compatible with the states party's obligations under Article 25 of the Covenant. The Committee concludes that Mrs Ignatane has suffered specific injury in being prevented from standing for the local elections in the city of Riga in 1997, because of having been struck off the list of candidates on the basis of insufficient proficiency in the official language. The Human Rights Committee considers that the author is a victim of a violation of Article 25, in conjunction with Article 2 of the Covenant.[152]

The treaty monitoring bodies and minority rights activism

Minority rights activists and advocates may consider using the treaty monitoring bodies for various reasons and in various ways.

The case-law and, to a lesser degree the monitoring practice, have brought about a body of law that is indicative for a common, and indeed universal standard of minority rights in a certain, limited area. These standards may legitimately be called more advanced than those of, for instance, the European Court of Human Rights, also because that Court has no explicit mandate to address minority issues. Thus, advocates will likely find more guidance in the Human Rights Committee's practice when it comes to assessing compliance of a certain national law or measure with international human rights standards. If used wisely, litigation may assist with advancing these standards and others, since the treaty monitoring bodies' pronouncements add to the emerging universal corpus of norms and, besides that, may influence the interpretation of regional instruments, be they specialised minority rights treaties or regional human rights instruments.

The procedures before the treaty monitoring bodies are simpler and, at least in principle, they are more accessible than the regional human rights courts and similar tribunals with their more formal procedures. Although the committees' views or opinions in individual cases lack the formal legal effect of judgments, they can hardly be ignored altogether. In particular, higher domestic courts can be lobbied to accept the practice as "precious sources of information" – or informal tools to facilitate interpretation – if not formal sources of law, when dealing with similar issues. NGOs and activists can contribute to establishing a "culture" of compliance by not only developing a strategy for bringing test cases before the bodies, but also fostering an environment of compliance by contributing to a higher degree of visibility of their practice and by building public awareness of the role they are playing.

In the reporting procedure, NGOs have always played an important role as the producers of shadow reports and the providers of factual information that allows the monitoring bodies and their individual members to ask governmental delegations those questions that are most relevant. Here, too, publicity is a major tool in fostering efficiency.

In sum, it would seem that the treaty monitoring bodies have not been used to the fullest extent possible by those who seek to advance minority rights standards. These do not evolve in a vacuum, but at different levels and in different fora in parallel; thus, the "cross-fertilisation" factor should not be discounted. Implementation organs, be they universal or regional, general or specialised, and also national bodies look for guidance elsewhere when it comes to resolving questions put to them. The UN treaty monitoring bodies are not only amongst the most likely to look beyond their own confines, but are also quite capable of influencing other practice. Litigation and implementation strategies by NGOs and activists should bear that "parallelism" in mind and make adequate use of the healthy competition amongst human rights bodies.

Mag.iur. (University of Salzburg, Austria), LL.M., S.J.D. (George Washington University), International Legal Counsel and Visiting Professor of International Law, Arcadia University, Philadelphia, PA.

1. Adopted on 16 December 1966, entered into force on 23 March 1976, 999 UNTS 171.

2. Adopted on 7 March 1966, entered into force on 4 January 1969, 660 UNTS 195.

3. Established to monitor compliance with the International Covenant on Economic, Social, and Cultural Rights, adopted on 16 December 1966, entered into force on 3 January 1976, 999 UNTS 3.

4. Articles 17 and 22 of the Convention against Torture and Other Cruel, Inhuman or Degrading Treatment or Punishment, adopted on 10 December 1984, entered into force on 26 June 1987, G.A. Res. 39/46.

5. Article 17 of the Convention on the Elimination of All Forms of Discrimination against Women, adopted on 18 December 1979, entered into force on 3 September 1981, 1249 UNTS 13.

6. Article 43 of the Convention on the Rights of the Child, adopted on 20 November 1989, entered into force on 2 September 1990, G.A. Res. 44/25.

7. For a critical review of the mechanisms see: "Effective Functioning of Bodies Established Pursuant to United Nations Human Rights Instruments, Final Report on Enhancing the Long-term Effectiveness of the United Nations Human Rights Treaty System", note by the Secretary-General, 27 March 1997, E/CN.4/1997/74.

8. A useful online resource dealing with the various complaints mechanisms is: http://www.bayefsky.com/tree.php/area/complain

9. Louis Henkin, "The International Bill of Rights: The Universal Declaration and the Covenants", in: Rudolf Bernhardt and J. A. Jolowicz (eds), *International Enforcement of Human Rights* (Berlin, Heidelberg, 1987), 1.

10. Adopted on 16 December 1966, entered into force on 3 January 1976, 999 UNTS 3.

11. Table available at: http://www.unhchr.ch/pdf/report.pdf

12. Article 2, paragraph 1, ICERD.

13. Manfred Nowak, "The International Covenant on Civil and Political Rights", in: Raija Hanski & Markku Suksi (eds), *An Introduction to the International Protection of Human Rights* (Turku/Åbo, 2nd ed., 1999), pp. 79-100, at p. 91.

14. See http://www.unhchr.ch/html/menu2/6/a/introhrc.htm

15. See Johannes Niewerth, *Der kollektive und der positive Schutz von Minderheiten und ihre Durchsetzung im Völkerrecht* (Berlin, 1996), p. 194.

16. See http://www.humanrights.coe.int/cseweb/GB/GB1/GB1.htm

17. See Manfred Nowak, *U.N. Covenant of Civil and Political Rights. CCPR Commentary* (Kehl am Rhein, 1993), p. 548 et seq., MN 6-8.

18. HRC, "Consolidated Guidelines for State Reports under the International Covenant on Civil and Political Rights", CCPR/C/66/GUI/Rev.2, dated 26 February 2001.

19. HRC, "1999 Annual Report to the General Assembly", A/54/40 (Vol. I), 18, paragraph 40 (hereinafter "1999 Annual Report I", emphasis added).

20. Fausto Pocar, "Current Developments and Approaches in the Practice of the Human Rights Committee in Consideration of State Reports", in: Asbjørn Eide and Jan Helgesen (eds), *The Future of Human Rights Protection in a Changing World* (Oslo, 1991), pp. 51-58, at p. 53.

21. HRC, "Consolidated Guidelines for State Reports under the International Covenant on Civil and Political Rights", op.cit., at D.2.1.

22. HRC, General Comment No. 2, Reporting Guidelines, dated 31 July 1981, at paragraph 3.

23. HRC, General Comment No. 18, Non-discrimination, dated 10 November 1989, paragraph 9.

24. See, amongst many, the Concluding Observations: Ukraine, CCPR/CO/73/UKR, dated 4 November 2001, paragraph 2.

25. HRC, "2000 Annual Report to the General Assembly", A/55/40 (Vol. I), 16, paragraph 48 (hereinafter "2000 Annual Report I").

26. The questions concerning non-discrimination and rights of persons belonging to minorities addressed to the Government of Hungary during the consideration of their fourth periodic report in July 2001 may serve as an example:

"4. Please provide further information regarding measures to prevent and combat discrimination, in practice as well as in law, in relation to access to housing and public places, as well as to employment, particularly with respect to the Roma/Gypsies minority. Please comment on allegations of discriminatory treatment of the Roma/Gypsies minority by the police and the judiciary.

5. What concrete steps have been taken, and with what results, to overcome problems with regard to the placement of Roma/Gypsies children in 'special schools', as well as alleged discrimination in State education facilities ...?

6. Please comment on the extent of allegedly racially motivated violence and harassment vis-à-vis foreigners, including asylum-seekers and the Roma/Gypsies minority, and on allegations about the failure, on the part of the police and judicial authorities, to investigate and prosecute hate crimes. What measures have been adopted by the State party to combat such crimes and to prosecute perpetrators?

... 8. Please provide updated information on the number and proportion of persons belonging to minorities involved in political and public affairs, including the public service, and in economic life."

HRC, List of issues to be taken up in connection with the consideration of the Fourth Periodic Report of Hungary, CCPR/C/HUN/2000/4, dated 25 July 2001, paragraphs 4-8.

27. See ibid.

28. 2000 Annual Report I, 16, paragraph 50.

29. The 1999 observations concerning Norway may serve as an example:

"The Committee remains concerned that while legislative reform work in the field of Sami land and resource rights is in progress, traditional Sami means of livelihood, falling under article 27 of the Covenant, do not appear to enjoy full protection in relation to various forms of competing public and private uses of land. Lawsuits by private landowners leading to judicial prohibition of reindeer herding and high legal costs for the Sami are a particular concern in the absence of satisfactory legal aid."

Concluding Observations: Norway, CCPR/C/79/Add.112, dated 5 November 1999, paragraph 16.

30. See, for instance, the Concluding Observations: Slovenia, CCPR/C/79/Add.40 [A/49/40, paragraphs 334-353], dated 21 September 1994.

31. Concluding Observations: Belarus, CCPR/C/79/Add.5, dated 25 September 1992, paragraph 4.

32. For instance the remarks in ibid., paragraph 4.

33. Amongst many, Concluding Observations of the HRC: Lithuania, CCPR/C/79/Add.87, dated 19 November 1997, paragraph 22.

34. See Sarah Joseph, "New Procedures Concerning the HRC's Examination of State Reports", 13 *NQHR* (1995) pp.13-23.

35. Concluding Observations: Croatia, CCPR/CO/71/HRV, dated 26 April 2001, paragraph 25.

36. Concluding Observations: Norway, CCPR/C/79/Add.112, dated 5 November 1999, paragraph 18.

37. Concluding Observations: Ukraine, CCPR/CO/73/UKR, paragraph 24.

38. Concluding Observations: Kyrgyzstan, CCPR/CO/69/KGZ, dated 24 July 2000, paragraph 24, and Ukraine, CCPR/CO/73/UKR, paragraph 24.

39. Concluding Observations: Kyrgyzstan, CCPR/CO/69/KGZ, paragraph 6.

40. See CERD Committee, 2001 Annual Report to the General Assembly, A/56/18, paragraph 479, where the "Committee by consensus reaffirmed the importance of maintaining members' access as independent experts to all relevant sources of information."

41. See the Report of the Chairpersons of the Human Rights Treaty Bodies on their Thirteenth Meeting, A/57/56, dated 5 February 2002, paragraph 52.

42. Buergenthal, *International Human Rights*, at p. 46.

43. See, for a description of the process of drafting and the legal significance of General Comments, Torkel Opsahl, "The General Comments of the Human Rights Committee", in: Torkel Opsahl (ed.), *Law and Equality, Selected Articles on Human Rights* (Oslo, 1996), pp. 403-17.

44. A general comment on the validity of reservations, for instance, has met with fierce resistance by the governments of the United States and the United Kingdom, because it concluded that "it necessarily falls to the Committee to determine whether a specific reservation is compatible with the object and purpose of the Covenant." HRC, CCPR General Comment No. 24, Issues Relating to Reservations Made Upon Ratification or Accession to the Covenant or the OPs Thereto, or in Relation to Declarations Under Article 41 of the Covenant, dated 10 November 1989, paragraph 18. Thus, the committee could declare a reservation to be null and void and undo a state's attempt to exclude the applicability of a particular provision. That is seen by some as a cause for concern that states willing to ratify the ICCPR with reservations and to accept the power of the committee to consider individual cases might abstain from doing so out of fear that their reservation might later be declared inapplicable.

45. See Nowak, "The International Covenant on Civil and Political Rights", at p. 93.

46. Niewerth, op.cit., at p. 197: "bedeutungslos".

47. See generally Norman Weiss, "Einführung in den Individualrechtsschutz nach dem Internationalen Pakt über bürgerliche und politische Rechte", 1 (1) *MenschenRechtsMagazin* (1996), pp. 7-11.

48. Article 1 of the OP to the ICCPR.

49. See P.R. Ghandhi, *The Human Rights Committee and the Right of Individual Communication* (Aldershot, 1998), p. 48.

50. See Elias Kastanas, "The Preventive Dimension of the Activities of United Nations Treaty Bodies", in: L.-A. Sicilianos (ed.), *The Prevention of Human Rights Violations* (The Hague, Boston, London, 2001), pp. 57-66, at pp. 63-4.

51. HRC, *1996 Annual Report to the General Assembly*, A/51/40 (Vol. I), 63 et seq., paragraph 419.

52. See Nowak, "The International Covenant on Civil and Political Rights", at p. 90 and, for a list of such opinions in recent cases, 2002 Annual Report I, 84, paragraph 100.

53. See generally United Nations High Commissioner of Human Rights, Overview of Procedure of the HRC, at http://www.unhchr.ch/html/menu2/8/over.htm

54. Christian Tomuschat, "Making Individual Communications an Effective Tool for the Protection of Human Rights", in: Ulrich Beyerlin, Michael Bothe, Rainer Hofmann and Ernst-Ulrich Petersmann (eds), *Recht zwischen Umbruch und Bewahrung. Völkerrecht – Europarecht – Staatsrecht. Festschrift für Rudolf Bernhardt* (Berlin, 1995), pp. 615-34, at p. 619.

55. HRC, 2002 Annual Report to the General Assembly, A/57/40 (Vol. I), 81, paragraph 89 (hereinafter: "2002 Annual Report I").

56. Ibid.

57. Ibid., paragraph 95.

58. Total number of all cases decided, whether by the adoption of views or inadmissibility decisions, and cases that were discontinued.

59. See HRC, 2002 Annual Report I, 83 et seq., paragraph 96.

60. See HRC, 2001 Annual Report I, 108, paragraph 101.

61. HRC, 1997 Annual Report I, 77, paragraphs 470–471.

62. HRC, 1999 Annual Report I, 76, paragraphs 394 et seq. The committee explained

that "[t]he essence of the problem" is (a) an increase in the number of communications, (b) a decrease of professional staff dealing with them, (c) consequently, despite best efforts, an increase in the backlog of unprocessed communications and, (d) the fact that "[a]n increasing number of cases are being submitted in languages which are not available among the available professional staff, in particular Russian", ibid.

63. See http://www.unhchr.ch/html/menu2/8/over.htm In Communication No. 78/1980, A.D. (The Mikmaq Tribal Society) v. Canada, decision on the admissibility of 29 July 1984, CCPR/C/22/D/78/1980, a complaint was declared inadmissible because of the "lack of standing" of the author, who is the Grand Captain of the tribe. It appears there was some internal fighting going on, because the Grand Chief of the Grand Council told the committee that he had not authorised A.D. to speak on behalf of the tribe. Soon thereafter the author claimed that the Grand Council had indeed entrusted him with the representation of the tribe before the committee. The Grand Chief apparently refused to sign the necessary document, however, since that bore the signatures of A.D. and the Assistant Grand Chief. The committee found that "it is not the Grand Council in its legal entity which authorises A. D. to act but that it is the author himself who confirms his self-authorization", and dismissed the case, ibid., at paragraphs 7.6. et seq.

64. HRC, 2001 Annual Report, A/56/40 (Vol. I), 111, paragraphs 115-116.

65. Ibid., paragraph 113.

66. Ibid., paragraph 118.

67. This rule as such only prohibits the *simultaneous* submission and consideration of the same matter (i.e. the same victims complaining about the same facts and alleging the violation of the same rights), but not *successive* complaints. However, "[u]pon becoming parties to the OP some States have made a reservation to preclude the Committee's competence if the same matter has already been examined elsewhere." HRC, 2001 Annual Report, 112, paragraph 120.

68. HRC, 2001 Annual Report, 114, paragraph 124.

69. Alexander H. E. Morawa, "The Individual as a Party to International Human Rights Litigation, With Particular Reference to the Issue of 'Abuse of the Right to Petition'", 4 *J. Int'l Rel.* (1997) pp. 11-28, at p. 21.

70. See the unconvincing opinion of a majority of committee members in Communication No. 787/1997, Vishwadeo Gobin v. Mauritius, decision on the admissibility of 16 July 2001, CCPR/C/72/D/787/1997, at paragraph 6.3. The majority held that in the absence of a reasonable explanation by the author a five-year delay in submitting a communication would qualify as an abuse of the right to petition. Five dissenters correctly pointed out that the committee was precluded from introducing a "preclusive time limit in the OP" (dissenting opinion of members Chanet, Henkin, Scheinin, Shearer, and Yalden). Mr Klein considered that the delay of five years should not be taken as a reason for shifting the burden of proof that it was (not) abusive from the government to the author and found that abuse was not shown in the given case.

71. Communication No. 30/1978, Eduardo Bleier v. Uruguay, views of 29 March 1982, CCPR/C/15/D/30/1978, paragraph 13.3.

72. Laurence R. Helfer and Anne-Marie Slaughter, "Toward a Theory of Effective Supranational Adjudication", 107 *Yale LJ.* (1997), p. 273.

73. HRC, 2001 Annual Report I, 114, paragraph 126.

74. See Communications Nos. 107/1981, Elena Quinteros Almeida v. Uruguay, views of 17 September 1981, CCPR/C/19/D/107/1981, paragraph 11, and 161/1983, Herrera Rubio v. Colombia, views of 2 November 1987, CCPR/C/31/D/161/1983, paragraph 10.5.

75. See Communication No. 194/1985, Jean Miango Muiyo v. Zaire, views of 27 October 1987, CCPR/C/31/D/194/1985, paragraphs 5.2 and 9.

76. HRC, 1999 Annual Report I, 81, paragraph 421.

77, Article 5(3) OP.

78. See HRC, 1997 Annual Report to the General Assembly, A/52/40 (Vol. I), 74, paragraph 456.

79. See HRC, 2001 Annual Report I, 105, paragraph 88.

80. HRC, 2001 Annual Report I,. 129, paragraph 167.

81. Nowak, op.cit., at p. 95.

82. Blumenwitz, *Internationale Schutzmechanismen zur Durchsetzung von Minderheiten- und Volksgruppenrechten* (Köln, 1997), at p. 101.

83. Ibid.

84. HRC, Summary Record of the 1719th Meeting, 30 October 1998, CCPR/C/SR.1719, paragraph 22.

85. Ibid., paragraph 49.

86. Ibid., paragraph 60.

87. Communication No. 489/1992, Peter Bradshaw v. Barbados, decision on the admissibility of 19 July 1994, CCPR/C/31/D/489/1992, paragraph 5.3.

88. HRC, Concluding Observations: Lithuania, CCPR/C/79/Add.87, dated 19 November 1997, paragraph 8 (emphasis added).

89. Communication No. 857/1999, Miroslav Blazek v. the Czech Republic, views of 12 July 2001, CCPR/C/72/D/857/1999, paragraph 7.

90. See, e.g., the Concluding Observations: Croatia, CCPR/CO/71/HRV, dated 26 April 2001, paragraph 11. Again, with respect to newly independent states the committee has taken note of "... the heritage of the negative aspects of the past ..." and has accepted that these "... could not be rectified overnight ...", adding that "...it also notes that the Government's efforts in restructuring the existing legal system have at times been hampered by certain lacunae in national legislation as well as by continuing resort to legislation of the former regime." Concluding Observations: Belarus, CCPR/C/79/Add.5, paragraph 5.

91. Blazek v. the Czech Republic, paragraph 7; see also Communication No. 402/1990, Henricus Brinkhof v. the Netherlands, views of 27 July 1993, CCPR/C/48/D/402/1990, paragraphs 9.3. et seq. See also Communication No. 965/2000, Karakurt v. Austria, views of 4 April 2002, CCPR/C/74/D/965/2000, paragraph 10, where the committee found that the proper remedy would include "modifying the applicable law so that no improper differentiation is made".

92. See Communication No. 839, 840, 841/1998, Anthony B. Mansaraj et al. v. Sierra Leone, views of 16 July 2001, CCPR/C/72/D/839/1998, paragraph 6.3.

93. See, on the other hand, Articles 41 ECHR and 63(1) ACHR.

94. HRC, 2001 Annual Report I, 130, paragraph 173.

95. "594. The Committee's recommendation in case No. 780/1997 (Laptsevich v. Belarus) is a new step towards more specific pronouncements on the remedy, in referring to the amount of compensation." HRC, 2000 Annual Report I, 90, paragraph 594. With respect to monetary compensation for the victims of breaches of the covenant the committee has also "... urge[d] States parties to consider the adoption of specific enabling legislation. HRC, 1996 Annual Report I, 68, paragraph 432.

96. HRC, 2001 Annual Report I, 131, paragraph 176.

97. HRC, 1996 Annual Report I, 65, paragraph 427.

98. HRC, 2001 Annual Report I, 131, paragraph 178.

99. Ibid., 131, paragraphs 178-179.

100. See HRC, 1996 I, 71, paragraph 437, where the committee lists, *inter alia*, separate chapters on follow-up activities under the OP in the Annual Reports to the General Assembly which "make clear which States have co-operated and which States have failed to co-operate with the Special Rapporteur for the Follow-Up on Views" as one of the publicity tools at its disposal and adds that it "welcomes information which non-governmental organisations might wish to submit on measures that States parties have taken, or failed to take, in implementation of the Committee's views."

101. See Thomas Buergenthal, *International Human Rights* (St. Paul, MN, 2nd ed. 1995) 40, and, for a review of the drafting history of Article 27, Patrick Thornberry,

International Law and the Rights of Minorities (Oxford, 1991) p. 149 et seq.

102. See Dieter Blumenwitz, op.cit., at p. 96.

103. Communication No. 167/1984, Chief Bernard Ominayak and the Lubicon Lake Band v. Canada, views of 26 March 1990, CCPR/C/38/D/167/1984, at paragraphs 31.1 and 32.2.

104. Communication No. 760/1996, J.G.A. Diergaardt et al. v. Namibia, views of 25 July 2000, CCPR/C/69/D/760/1996, at paragraph 10.3.

105. See Communication No. 932/2000, Gillot v. France, views of 15 July 2002, CCPR/C/75/D/932/2000, at paragraph 13.4.

106. Article 1 (1) ICERD.

107. Article 1 (4) ICERD.

108. Article 2 (2) ICERD.

109. See Article 6 ICERD.

110. General Comment No. 23, The Rights of Minorities (Article 27), dated 8 April 1994.

111. See Rainer Hofmann, *Minderheitenschutz in Europa – Völker- und Staatsrechtliche Lage im Überblick* (Berlin, 1995), pp. 22-23, and Kristin Henrard, *Devising an Adequate System for Minority Protection* (The Hague, Boston, London, 2000), p. 162.

112. Ibid., paragraph 1.

113. Ibid., paragraph 2.

114. Ibid. and paragraph 4.

115. Ibid., paragraph 4.

116. Ibid., paragraph 3.2.

117. Communication No. 197/1985, Kitok v. Sweden, views of 27 July 1988, [1988] Annual Report 221.

118. General Comment No. 23, paragraph 7, with reference to Communications Nos. 167/1984, Ominayak and the Lubicon Lake Band v. Canada, views of 26 March 1990, [1990] Annual Report 1, and 197/1985, Kitok v. Sweden.

119. General Comment No. 23, paragraph 5.1.

120. Ibid., paragraph 5.2.

121. Fourth Periodic Report of Germany, CCPR/C/84/Add.5, dated 22 February 1996, at paragraph 242, with reference to Doc. A/2929, 181, paragraph 184.

122. Concluding Observations of the HRC: Germany, CCPR/C/79/Add.73, dated 8 November 1996, at paragraph 13.

123. General Comment No. 23, paragraph 6.1.

124. Ibid., paragraph 6.2.

125. Ibid.

126. Ibid., paragraph 9.

127. Comprehensive reviews and excerpts from the jurisprudence of the past couple of years can be found in: Alexander H. E. Morawa, "The Jurisprudence of the United Nations Human Rights Committee and Other Treaty Monitoring Bodies", *European Yearbook of Minority Issues* 1 (2001/2), pp. 461-85, and Hannah McGlue's similarly titled report in *European Yearbook of Minority Issues* 2 (2002/3), forthcoming. See also Henrard, *Devising an Adequate System for Minority Protection*, pp. 157-185, Gaetano Pentassuglia, *Minorities in International Law* (Strasbourg, 2002), pp. 97-111 and, for the area of indigenous peoples, Patrick Thornberry, *Indigenous Peoples and Human Rights* (Manchester, 2002), pp. 116-181.

128. Communication No. 24/1977, Sandra Lovelace v. Canada, views of 30 July 1981, CCPR/C/13/D/24/1977, paragraph 14.

129. Concluding Observations of the HRC: Ukraine, CCPR/CO/73/UKR, dated 4 November 2001, at paragraph 23.

130. Lovelace v. Canada, paragraph 16.

131. Ibid., paragraph 17.

132. Communication No. 197/1985, Kitok v. Sweden, paragraph 9.8.

133. Communication No. 760/1996, Diergaardt et al. v. Namibia, paragraph 10.3. For a discussion see Alexander H. E. Morawa, "Minority Languages and Public Administration – A Comment on Issues Raised in Diergaardt et al. v. Namibia", ECMI Working Paper No. 16, at http://www.ecmi.de/doc/download/working_paper_16.pdf

134. Diergaardt et al. v. Namibia, at paragraph 2.1.

135. Ibid., at paragraph 10.6.

136. Ibid., paragraph 10.6.

137. Ibid., Annex.

138. Ibid., paragraph 10.10.

139. Communication No. 671/1995, Jouni E. Länsman v. Finland, views of 30 October 1996, CCPR/C/65/D/671/1995, paragraph 2.1; see also the earlier case of I. Länsman v. Finland, Communication No. 511/1992, views of 26 October 1994, [1995] Annual Report II, 66.

140. Jouni E. Länsman v. Finland, paragraph 6.10.

141. Ibid., paragraph 6.11.

142. See ibid., paragraph 6.12.

143. Ibid., at paragraph 6.14.

144. Ibid., at paragraph 7.3.

145. Ibid., at paragraph 10.4.

146. HRC, 1997 Annual Report to the General Assembly, A/52/40 (Vol. I), 86 et seq., paragraph 516.

147. Communication No. 779/1997, Anni Äärelä and Jouni Näkkäläjärvi v. Finland, views of 24 October 2001, CCPR/C/73/D/779/1997.

148. Communication No. 547/1993, Apirana Mahuika et al. v. New Zealand, views of 27 October 2000, CCPR/C/70/D/547/1993.

149. Ibid., at paragraph 9.8.

150. Communication No. 884/1999, Antonina Ignatane v. Latvia, views of 25 July 2001, CCPR/C/72/D/884/1999.

151. It appears that Mrs Ignatane was in fact dragged from her classroom where she was teaching German and made to take the Latvian spelling test right then and there.

152. HRC, 2001 Annual Report I, p. 126, paragraph 160.

CHAPTER 2

THE ROLE OF THE UNITED NATIONS WORKING GROUP ON MINORITIES

Asbjørn Eide*

Introduction

The United Nations Working Group on Minorities (WGM) was established in 1995 under the UN Sub-Commission on the Promotion and Protection of Human Rights (then called the Sub-Commission on Prevention of Discrimination and Protection of Minorities). By the establishment of the working group, minorities were empowered to bring to an international forum their grievances and concerns. It opened up the possibility for a dialogue with governments with the WGM as facilitator. It has a limited but important function in addressing the highly sensitive issues of peaceful and constructive group accommodation and pluralism inside states. Its normative basis is the United Nations Declaration on the Rights of Persons Belonging to National or Ethnic, Religious and Linguistic Minorities (UNDM). [1]

Establishment: background, mandate and composition

The establishment of the WGM was recommended by the sub-commission in its Resolution 1994/4, authorised by the Commission on Human Rights in Commission Resolution 1995/24 and endorsed by the Economic and Social Council in its Resolution 1995/31. Barely two years earlier, the General Assembly had adopted the Declaration on the Rights of Persons Belonging to National or Ethnic, Religious and Linguistic Minorities, which had spelled out in a non-binding document the rights members of minorities should enjoy and the commitments states should undertake to ensure the existence of minorities and promote conditions for the preservation and development of their identities.

The declaration had brought to a temporary halt a long-standing division of views among the members of the United Nations. From the UN's inception, the majority of member states had been reluctant to establish international standards on minority rights. Most western states were of the view that there was no need for such rights, since members of minorities would be protected by regular individual human rights – the principle of non-discrimination, the freedom of expression, freedom of religion, freedom of association and cultural rights. There is no reference to the rights of minorities or their members in the Universal Declaration of Human Rights, adopted in 1948. Not because it was overlooked: on the contrary, several proposals for inclusion of minority rights in the declaration had been presented by the UN Secretariat and by the delegations of Denmark, the former Yugoslavia and the Soviet Union. The majority of states were not in favour, however. Some of them thought that if human rights of every person were respected and protected, minority rights would be superfluous, while others had apprehensions about the possible negative consequences of minority rights for the integrity and stability of states. There was also a widespread fear that minority rights would be construed as group rights which could become the platform for fragmentation, secession or annexation of territories.

When the General Assembly on 10 December 1948 adopted Resolution 217 A (III), which contains the UNDM as an annex, it also adopted Resolution 217 C (III) which addresses the minority issue. The General Assembly stated in that resolution that while the United Nations could not remain indifferent to the fate of minorities, it had found it difficult to adopt a uniform solution for this "complex and delicate question, which has special aspects in each State in which it arises". The General Assembly had therefore decided not to deal in specific provisions with the question of minorities in the text of the UNDM, but turned the issue over to the Sub-Commission on Prevention of Discrimination and Protection of Minorities for proposals on how to deal with minority issues by the United Nations.

The divergences of views continued for many years thereafter. A modest compromise was found with the inclusion in the International Covenant on Civil and Political Rights (ICCPR) of Article 27, which simply states that "[p]ersons belonging to ethnic, religious or linguistic minorities shall not be denied the right, in community with other members of their group, to enjoy their own culture, to profess and practice their own religion or to use their own language". Read literally, it adds almost nothing to the individual human rights contained in the ICCPR: the right to profess and practise the minority religion follows already from the freedom of religion in Article 18 of the ICCPR, and the right to use one's own language, in relation to any willing listener or reader follows from the freedom of expression in Article 19. Its wording makes it clear also that the rights are held by individual persons, not by groups as such.

Following the adoption of the ICCPR in 1966, the sub-commission through its Italian member Francesco Capotorti initiated a comprehensive study on the situation of minorities throughout the world. He sought to give Article 27 a broader meaning than what the words literally say. His study nevertheless concluded with a proposal that a declaration spelling out the rights of minorities in greater detail ought to be adopted by the United Nations. In 1979 the Yugoslav delegation presented a draft declaration on the subject, and a working group under the Commission on Human Rights met annually to work on the draft. Nothing much happened for many years, however, due to serious divergences of views among members.

The attitudes changed only at the time of the fall of the Berlin Wall and the dissolution of the Soviet Union, former Yugoslavia and Czechoslovakia. Group conflicts caused severe turmoil. The urgency to ensure minority protection was recognised by a growing majority of states. In the sub-commission, a study was carried out from 1990 to 1993 with a somewhat different approach: by searching for ways to achieve peaceful and constructive solutions to situations involving minorities'[2] and in 1992 the General Assembly finally adopted the UNDM. As stated in its preamble, it is inspired by Article 27 of the ICCPR and maintains the individualistic language ("persons belonging to"), but is much more elaborate than Article 27 of the ICCPR and contains clear recommendations for positive measures by states to ensure the conditions for the preservation of minority cohesion and identity.

The establishment of the WGM in 1995 was the first mechanism to promote the implementation of the declaration and to facilitate peaceful accommodation of minorities within states. Its mandate, as set out in the enabling resolution by the Commission on Human Rights, is threefold:

— to review the promotion and practical realisation of the Declaration on the Rights of Persons Belonging to National or Ethnic, Religious and Linguistic Minorities;

— to examine possible solutions to problems involving minorities, including the promotion of mutual understanding between and among minorities and governments;

— to recommend further measures, as appropriate, for the promotion and protection of the rights of persons belonging to national or ethnic, religious and linguistic minorities.[3]

What makes the WGM almost unique in the United Nations system is that it has adopted a very flexible approach in order to encourage wide participation in its sessions, particularly by its openness to participation by representatives of minorities. The WGM proper consists of only five members, selected by and among the 26 members of the Sub-Commission on the Promotion and Protection of Human Rights, one from each of the five regions of the United Nations (Asia, Africa, Latin America and the Caribbean, eastern Europe, western Europe and others). Minorities, however, can also be represented, nominally as observers, but in practice the observers have full speaking rights and can submit proposals. Access is very informal. Any representative of minority groups can through a written request be given accreditation to participate in the sessions, and over the years they have participated in substantial numbers.

Similarly, non-governmental organisations (NGOs) concerned with minority issues can also participate as observers. All governments can also attend the WGM, and will have the same status as minority representatives: as observers with full speaking rights and rights to submit proposals. Usually, some fifty governments are represented during the sessions. UN bodies and specialised agencies, and other intergovernmental organisations including regional organisations, are also participating, some of them also submitting information on their activities regarding minorities, in line with Article 9 of the declaration. An even more special feature of the WGM is its openness to participation by scholars and researchers in the field of minority rights.

The annual sessions of the WGM last for one week and are usually attended by observers from a number of states (about 60 to 70 each year), some 60 to 70 NGOs and minority representatives, three or four United Nations organisations and specialised agencies, representatives of the Council of Europe, the OSCE and other intergovernmental organisations, and a varying number of scholars and graduate students from universities and research institutions.[4]

Functions and opinions

The WGM was established to explore constructive ways to deal with situations involving minorities, drawing on the guidelines contained in the UNDM. It is neither a monitoring body in a formal sense of the word, nor a mechanism for handling complaints. Minority issues are still far too sensitive at the global level to make such functions possible; regional mechanisms in Europe have far outpaced the United Nations in these regards.

It should not be overlooked, however, that the treaty bodies of the United Nations do have some monitoring possibilities in regard to minority protection. Based on a proposal by the WGM, the sub-commission has requested the respective committees to include in their reporting guidelines for states parties a call for information concerning the minority-related rights relevant to the treaty in question, and to pay particular attention to the question of the status of minorities during their consideration of states party reports.

The WGM has recommended that the Committee on the Elimination of Racial Discrimination (CERD) should discuss, *inter alia*, the matter of allocation of citizenship and its consequences with respect to indirect discrimination on grounds of race, colour, descent or ethnic or national origin; the Human Rights Committee should more actively pursue its analysis of Article 27 of the ICCPR; the Committee on Economic, Social and Cultural Rights, in its dialogue with reporting states, should focus on Articles 11, 12, 13, and particularly on Article 15 of the International Covenant on Economic, Social and Cultural Rights; the Committee on the Rights of the Child should pay particular attention to Articles 12, 29, and 30 of the Convention on the Rights of the Child; and that the Committee on the Elimination of Discrimination Against Women should, in its dialogue with governments, explore the relative situations of women belonging to minorities and those belonging to majorities, and make suggestions as to ways in which inequalities can be addressed.

The WGM itself can best be described as a forum. It serves as an ongoing workshop exploring ways to promote constructive group accommodation based on the UNDM, and plays an important role in creating awareness of problematic situations. Based on information presented to it and on available expertise it seeks to indicate policy options in conformity with the requirements of international human rights and minority law. The broad and general terms of its mandate allow considerable flexibility of approach.

The first part of its mandate – to review the promotion and practical realisation of the declaration – illustrates this: while the WGM has no formal monitoring function and states are under no obligation to report on their implementation of the declaration, the process of reviewing the practical realisation makes it possible in an informal way to discuss matters brought to its attention. Several governments, at their own initiative, present information on national constitutional and legal provisions and on general measures they have taken to protect the existence and identity of minorities in their country.

While the WGM has been given no authority to process complaints and adopt views or conclusions in specific cases, it is open for persons belonging to minorities to present their grievances, to which the state may respond, and some of them do. Over time, a number of governments have become more willing to meet some of the concerns of the minorities, while others are still rather reluctant to engage in the dialogue and caution the WGM not to become too activist.

The second part of the mandate of the WGM is to examine possible solutions to problems involving minorities, including the promotion of mutual understanding between and among minorities and governments. Taken literally this should authorise the WGM to examine in detail particular situations brought to its attention with a view to proposing appropriate policies and measures to the parties involved in these situations. This has not happened. Many governments are opposed to such a role for the WGM. It would also require substantially more resources than those presently available. As noted, the WGM meets only once a year, for five days, and it is serviced only by two professionals who also have other mandates and therefore can allocate only part of their time to the WGM.

It is doubtful that the group as such could go very far in this direction even when allowed by governments to do so. The five members of the group come from five different parts of the world, from different cultures and political systems, and might have difficulties in agreeing on detailed suggestions in particular situations. Mediation or good offices would probably need to be entrusted to single persons, not to a WGM composed in this way.

The very existence of the WGM as a forum nevertheless probably has some conflict-preventing impact in that it allows minorities to air their grievances at the international level, which may induce the governments concerned to take the grievances more seriously. Similarly, when governments can present to the WGM the positive measures they have adopted, this makes the government less vulnerable internationally to unfounded criticism.

Under the third element of its mandate, the WGM may recommend further measures to promote and protect the rights of persons belonging to minorities. The reference is to measures which can or should be taken by the international community, at the global and regional level. Under Article 9 of the UNDM, the specialised agencies and other organisations of the United Nations system shall, within their respective fields of competence, contribute to the full realisation of the rights and principles contained in the declaration. The WGM has sought to stimulate attention to this task from the agencies and other bodies. Two concerns have been in the forefront: on the one hand, international agencies providing technical or development assistance to governments should always make an impact analysis of its possible negative consequences for minorities; and on the other, agencies should encourage states to call for technical assistance specifically aimed at improving the minority protection in the country concerned. During its sessions, a number of international agencies have been represented and have provided information on their activities of relevance for minorities, and have also taken note of requests made by minority representatives, which they then have included in their dialogue with the government concerned. On behalf of the WGM, the chairman has prepared an interpretative commentary to the declaration.[5]

The WGM has, under this agenda item, also discussed whether international law or procedures for minority protection need to be strengthened. Suggestions have been made to explore whether a convention on minority rights should be drafted, in order to create more legally binding obligations for states willing to become parties to such a convention. The WGM is divided on this point. A convention would be useful mainly for non-European countries, since most European states are already parties to the European Framework Convention for the Protection of National Minorities. Proposals have also been made to establish a Special Rapporteur of the Commission on Human Rights on minority protection, or a Special Representative of the Secretary-General. The main purpose would be to prevent conflicts by improving implementation of the declaration, which is expected to be achieved through the efforts of such a rapporteur or representative. In this regard also, the greatest need exists in regard to countries outside Europe, since the European scene is fairly well covered by the work of the High Commissioner on National Minorities (HCNM) of the Organization for Security and Co-operation in Europe (OSCE).[6]

Major issues identified by the WGM

A major function of the WGM has been to list and discuss some of the main issues involved in constructive approaches to situations involving minorities. Functioning as a forum with wide participation it has explored the range of views on such issues between experts, minorities and governments. While the WGM has not always been able to form clear and consensual positions – based on the UNDM – on existing or potential policy options, it has at least identified major issues.

The challenge for the WGM is to discourage unacceptable policies and encourage and promote constructive ones, based on the requirements of human rights in general and on the rights and obligations set out in the declaration in particular. In so doing it is essential to take into account the context of each particular situation.

Whether one looks back on history or looks around at contemporary practices, one can observe that policies of governments towards minorities fall into three categories: assimilation, integration, or separation and exclusion. Policies of particular governments are often a combination of two and sometimes all three: assimilation of some groups, separation or exclusion of others, and constructive integration among yet other groups.

Options preferred by minorities can also be grouped into three: calls for equal treatment (non-discrimination), demands for respect and protection of their separate identity and conditions for the preservation of that identity in a multicultural setting, and demands for more or less comprehensive auton-omy, cultural or territorial. This may sometimes border on demands for full self-determination, ultimately by way of secession including territorial dis-memberment. The WGM has firmly resisted discussing claims of secession, pointing to the limits set in Article 9 of the UNDM.

The diversity of situations

Being presented with a great variety of different situations, members of the WGM have pointed to several historical stages which have given rise to dif-ferent categories of minority concerns. The European nationalist stage during the tumultuous dissolution of empires starting from the end of the Napoleonic wars and lasting for at least a hundred and fifty years gave rise to the concept of "national" minorities, particularly clearly articulated in the peace settlements after the First World War and still lingering on though with quite ambiguous meanings. The decolonisation which gathered momentum after the end of the Second World War was initially articulated as minority claims but gradually became reformulated as claims of peoples to self-determination, fully endorsed by the United Nations around 1960. From the 1970s, the concept of "internal colonisation" was taken up by indigenous peoples in their rejec-tion of assimilationist and even integrationist policies, and from the 1980s they started to formulate their claims as a right to self-determination. There is an ongoing controversy within the United Nations whether this should be understood as a claim for internal autonomy only, or as an ultimate claim of secession and independence. From the 1980s and gathering strength from 1990 onwards, three relatively new minority issues started to emerge: one was the increasing demand for autonomy and/or control over land and nat-ural resources by ethnic or religious groups within newly independent coun-tries which had been under colonial rule, and where the colonial borders had been drawn somewhat haphazardly so that quite different and unrelated ethnic groups had been included in the territory of the colony. A second set of issues are represented by the "new" minorities emerging in the older, established nation states of western Europe: groups of persons who have arrived as migrant workers or students are starting to articulate their rights as minorities. The third and more dramatic development were the ethnic ten-sions which came into the open as a result of the collapse of the Soviet Union and former Yugoslavia.

These different situations have given rise to their own separate problems and responses. The WGM has come to recognise fully the wisdom of the General Assembly in 1948 when it stated in Resolution 217 C (III) that "it is difficult to adopt a uniform solution for this complex and delicate question, which has special aspects in each State in which it arises...". Nevertheless, some guidance can be drawn from the UNDM as to those policies that are accept-able and those that are not. Within the range of the permissible, however, there must be a considerable margin of appreciation in each country, pro-vided appropriate consultations and effective participation in decision-making is ensured.

Existence and recognition

The core of minority protection is spelled out in Article 1 of the UNDM: "[s]tates shall protect the existence and the national or ethnic, cultural, religious and linguistic identity of minorities within their respective territories and shall encourage conditions for the promotion of that identity." The WGM has discussed this subject at some length.[7]

Protection of their existence requires, firstly, that the minority is recognised. The WGM shares the view of the Human Rights Committee in its general comment on Article 27 of the ICCPR[8] that "the existence of an ethnic, religious or linguistic minority in a given State party does not depend upon a decision by that State party but requires to be established by objective criteria". Nevertheless, recognition is essential in order for members of the group to enjoy their minority rights.

Prohibition of imposed assimilation

Recognition should include not only their physical existence, but should extend also to their identity, understood in the way the minority itself understands it. This means that states must abstain from deliberate assimilation policies. "Assimilation" is understood as a process by which homogeneity is obtained on the basis of a dominant culture, to which other groups are expected to conform by shedding their own cultural characteristics. The prohibition of assimilation is a central theme of the declaration. Article 1 is followed up, in this respect, by Article 4, paragraph 2 ("[s]tates shall take measures to create favourable conditions to enable persons belonging to minorities to express their characteristics and to develop their culture, language, religion, traditions and customs, except where specific practices are in violation of national law and contrary to international standards") and Article 4, paragraph 3 ("[s]tates should take appropriate measures so that, wherever possible, persons belonging to minorities may have adequate opportunities to learn their mother tongue or to have instruction in their mother tongue").

There is a broad area of non-intended assimilation, resulting from the necessities of interaction in the national market, where members of minorities for purely instrumental reasons are tempted to adopt the language, and to some extent the habits, of the majority. It is not the role of the WGM to prevent such processes from taking place, but it remains a controversial question how much should be expected from the government in taking countermeasures – for instance, by pursuing a policy of bilingualism at all levels of society. Factors to be taken into account are the size, strength and demands of the minority.

Minority representatives have brought to the WGM's attention several cases of enforced assimilation through denial of the right of members of the minority group to use their own language, prohibition of publication in the minority language, and prohibition of the conduct of meetings and organisations in the minority language. Such policies are obviously in violation not only of the UNDM and of Article 27 of the ICCPR, but also of the freedom of expression and information.

In practice, governments often pursue a selective policy, recognising the separate identity of some groups by facilitating the use of their own language and ensuring their effective social, cultural and political participation, while pursuing an active assimilationist policy towards others. While sometimes the policies towards old and well-established minorities are pluralistic, policies towards "new" minorities are often more assimilationist in nature. There may be several factors behind such differences in treatment. When there is a kin-state watching over the treatment of its "national" group in the neighbouring state, the home-state is less inclined to pursue an assimilationist policy than in regard to minorities which have no kin-state.

The unacceptability of enforced separation or exclusion

Protecting the existence of the minority requires, also, that governments are required not to engage in any form of ethnic cleansing, where members of certain minorities through threat or intimidation are forced to leave areas where they have traditionally lived. It implies that they have to be protected in the areas where they live; it would be a violation to displace them from their traditional settlement without their informed consent. The WGM has been provided with information about serious violations of this nature, where minorities have been physically removed from their traditional habitat due, for example, to the discovery of oil resources in their region.

It would also be a violation if members of a particular minority are systematically excluded from equal participation in the social, economic, cultural and political life of society (Article 2, paragraphs 2 and 3, of the UNDM).

The WGM has noted that exclusionism sometimes starts by denying or depriving persons belonging to undesired ethnic or religious groups of their citizenship. Controversies of citizenship are in many contexts closely related to minority issues. The dominant approach to citizenship in a given country is often influenced by the predominant nature of the state in question. It depends on whether the predominant self-conception of the state is based on ethnic, religious or territorial criteria. To illustrate: in many of the new states emerging out of decolonisation, the initial approach has been a territorial conception of the state, though this is now changing in some of the countries concerned. In many states of central and eastern Europe, on the other hand, the dominant conception is of the state as the homeland of a dominant ethnic group. This can lead to problems for ethnic and/or religious or linguistic minorities.[9]

Non-citizens cannot be excluded from minority rights simply on a basis of definition of minorities. In this respect, the WGM follows the approach of the Human Rights Committee, which in its General Comment No. 23 has made it clear that the minority status of a person under Article 27 of the ICCPR does not depend on her or his citizenship. But exclusion of residents belonging to minorities from participation in political life can still occur due to the limitation of political rights under Article 25 of the ICCPR. The WGM therefore has to watch over citizenship regulations to react to deprivation of citizenship or the use of excessively rigid criteria for obtaining it.

Integration and pluralism

A positive minority policy requires a combination of equal treatment and pluralist arrangements. Equality of treatment is required in the common domain. States must ensure that everyone, including persons belonging to minorities, may exercise fully and effectively all their human rights and fundamental freedoms without any discrimination, and in full equality before the law (Article 4, paragraph 1, of the UNDM). It requires sufficient integration to provide the government with the necessary authority and capacity to ensure equality before the law for everyone, whether members of majorities or minorities. This has to be balanced with the requirement to governments to encourage conditions by which the minorities can maintain their separate identity (Article 1 of the UNDM). The WGM has held extensive discussions on the appropriate balance in these regards, taking into account the provisions of the declaration and the different contexts in which the issues arise.

Language and education are among the most important issues determining the scope of pluralism in society. In these respects, the WGM has taken note of and generally endorsed the Hague Recommendations Regarding the Education Rights of National Minorities.[10] The main thrust of the recommendations is twofold: on the one hand, it spells out the importance that the education of minority children should ideally be in the language of the minority at kindergarten and in the first year of primary school, and that the official language should then be gradually introduced, but with many qualifications. The other main point is the right of members of minorities, like anybody else in society, to establish and manage their own private educational institutions.

The Hague recommendations include the encouragement of persons belonging to minorities to learn the official language of the state and to be able to function as citizens of the state, while states are obliged to ensure the equality of everyone within the state; the principle of non-discrimination based on language; the participation of minorities in the educational system; the provision of alternative forms of education for children belonging to minorities; the need for minorities and majority populations to learn about each other; and the need for a language mix in the programme at primary and secondary school levels, which would open the way towards a multilingual society.

The WGM is aware that these recommendations are suitable for some minorities, particularly the old and established groups living compactly together, and may be less appropriate in regard to other minorities and in other parts of the world, particularly where the minority language is only oral, not written, or when the minority is dispersed.

The WGM has also taken note of and generally endorsed the Oslo Recommendations Regarding the Linguistic Rights of National Minorities.[11] They deal, among others, with linguistic rights concerning names (personal names, names of associations, street and place names); with language in religious practices and religious documents; with language use in NGOs, associations and community institutions; language rights in the media (the right to establish media in the minority language and the right to demand some of the broadcasting of publicly funded institutions in the minority language); the use of language in economic life; and the use of minority language in relations with administrative authorities and public services.[12]

Multiculturalism, interculturalism and transculturalism

Respecting the existence and identity of the group requires recognition of the multicultural composition of society. A large part of minority rights focus on conditions for the preservation of multiculturalism. It is ensured, in particular, through the educational institutions and through the local use of local or minority languages.

But multiculturalism needs to be combined with interculturalism – the ability to interact constructively between members of the different cultures.

The WGM took the initiative to convene an International Seminar on Intercultural and Multicultural Education held in Montreal, Canada, at the end of September 1999,[13] together with the Centre d'études sur le droit international et la mondialisation at the University of Quebec.[14] The participants discussed the protection of the rights of minorities within the framework of the United Nations, the role of intercultural education in fostering social cohesion, education in the mother tongue, the right to manage educational institutions, and the principle of non-discrimination in the area of education.

The conclusions and recommendations of the seminar referred to the need to reflect in educational curricula the history and culture of all groups within society, the participation of all groups in educational policy and programmes, the teaching of the mother tongue, the need for recruitment of teachers from minority communities, the integration of intercultural education into mainstream programmes of initial and continuous education of teachers, and the role of reconciliation processes through education, as well as the establishment of government working groups in Canada to develop federal and provincial policy regarding educational policy, programmes and practices.

A fully harmonious integration also requires a degree of transculturalism involved, reciprocal learning from each other, shedding the more negative aspects of one's own culture and absorbing or developing the positive aspects of the culture of the other.

Integration and autonomy

Efforts are under way in the WGM to study the relative value of integrative and autonomous approaches to situations involving minorities, and a seminar on this topic was organised in Copenhagen in co-operation with the Danish Centre for Human Rights.[15] Clearly the choices depend on the particular circumstances of the special majority-minority relations, the settlement pattern of the minority group, the historical experience and future expectations. Regarding the settlement pattern, distinctions have to be made between groups living compactly together or dispersed, and whether they live in predominantly rural or urban areas. Territorial autonomies are particularly unsuitable where the different groups are coexisting within the same major cities.

Territorial autonomies are particularly well suited when the minority already lives compactly together in a particular region of the country and has a different way of using land and natural resources.

Territorial autonomies can function well as part of a historical process of aggregation, meaning that different ethnic groups living in separate territories gradually increase their co-operation in a federal system, as illustrated by the case of Switzerland. Territorial autonomies are much more problematic as a solution to ethnic conflicts where they have already been mixed together, and where therefore an autonomy would require a disaggregation and ethnic displacements. A factor to be taken into account is that the government is responsible, under international human rights law, to ensure the implementation of human rights for everyone within its territory and subject to its jurisdiction. It can therefore not negotiate away that responsibility by providing such extensive autonomy in legislative, policing and judicial areas that the government no longer can take care of its obligations for the human rights of those who live in the autonomous area.

Cultural autonomy can sometimes be a better option. It avoids the danger of discrimination inside the territorial autonomy, while allowing the minority group to manage its own cultural affairs, including linguistic and educational matters. Several examples of good practices concerning cultural autonomy have been brought to the attention of the WGM.

Minorities and development

Article 4, paragraph 5, of the UNDM calls on states to consider appropriate measures so that persons belonging to minorities may participate fully in the economic progress and development in their country. Article 5, paragraph 1, provides that national policies and programmes shall be planned and implemented with due regard for the legitimate interests of persons belonging to minorities, and Article 5, paragraph 2, that programmes of co-operation and assistance among states should be planned and implemented with due regard for the legitimate interests of persons belonging to minorities. The WGM has during the last two sessions started an intensive discussion on policy options concerning minorities and development. There are at least two sets of problems. One is that some minorities are excluded from development projects which are adopted by and pursued for the benefit of the dominant groups. A second set of problems is that the majority may have a conception of development which does not fit with the culture of the minority. As a result, there is a tendency to pursue a paternalistic approach by the dominant group, however well-intentioned, which alienates members of the minority group and leads to cultural disorientation.

These issues have been discussed at great length at recent seminars in which the working group has been involved, three of them in Africa (Arusha, Botswana and Mali) and the most recent one a seminar for Southeast Asia held in Chiang Mai, Thailand, in December 2002. The Minority Rights Group has been particularly active on this issue,[16] and recently it has been taken up also by the United Nations Development Programme (UNDP).

In Africa, the problem manifests itself particularly in the conflict between settled agriculturalists on the one hand and pastoralists on the other, and in the relations to the gatherers and hunters, in particular San and Pygmy peoples, who are experiencing serious discrimination as a consequence of processes of development. This is reflected in the seminars held, in co-operation between the WGM and the Working Group on Indigenous Populations, in Arusha[17] and in Botswana.[18]

The working group has also examined the particular problems of the Afro-descendants in the Americas.[19]

Conflict prevention

The preamble to the UNDM considers that the promotion and protection of the rights of persons belonging to national or ethnic, religious and linguistic minorities contribute to the political and social stability of the states in which they live. The assumption is that appropriate minority protection reduces the likelihood of group conflict. It is unrealistic, of course, to assume that even the best crafted minority regulation can prevent conflicts in all circumstances. The factors which cause ethnic conflicts are numerous and relate to external as well as internal developments, and can be quite unpredictable. Minority protection can contribute to stability, but cannot guarantee it.

The WGM has examined in more general terms the ingredients of appropriate conflict prevention in situations involving minorities.[20] It has recognised that there are many different situations to take into account and that there can be many different levels of conflict and tension inside a country. The relations between large groups may require different responses than the protection of small groups. Much depends also on whether the minority group lives compactly together or is dispersed. A large group living compactly together in a sizeable part of the country may require a substantial territorial autonomy which can be achieved through comprehensive decentralisation, while a large but dispersed group may be best served by cultural autonomy. When different groups live in the same city, territorial autonomy is probably not a good policy.

Conflict prevention also has to take into account whether there is a powerful neighbouring kin-state. In such cases, the risk of open conflict is substantial, and international mediation may be required. This is the typical function of the High Commissioner on National Minorities of the OSCE. Where no kin-state or other powerful supporters of the minority exist, there is a risk that minority rights will be neglected unless there is international attention through multilateral bodies.

In general terms, the search for stability requires respect for the equal dignity of everyone; effective participation by all in the economic, social and political life of the society as a whole and in particular in decisions affecting the minority itself. Presentations made to the WGM by governments have listed a wide range of good practices which often have worked well, including arrangements for consociational democracy, various types of decentralisation and autonomy, and a wide range of mechanisms for consultation with minorities.

Conclusions and prospects for the future

The WGM has its weaknesses and strengths. It has not been able to develop a fully-fledged monitoring function and even less a mechanism for processing and responding to complaints about violations of minority rights. But it has been able to develop a fairly penetrating examination of major issues which have to be addressed in developing constructive policies in the minority field.

Should a new mechanism be established, to supplement or replace the WGM? Proposals have been made in recent years for the appointment of a Special Rapporteur of the UN Commission on Human Rights, or a Special Representative of the Secretary-General of the United Nations. A special rapporteur would focus, in particular, on violations of minority rights, whereas a special representative would be focusing on conflict prevention.

Among considerations to be born in mind is that the European mechanisms are now well in place, both monitoring (Advisory Committee on the Framework Convention for the Protection of National Minorities – ACFC) and conflict prevention (High Commissioner on National Minorities – HCNM), and that there is very little that the UN can do in the European setting beyond what these mechanisms can achieve. The issue of indigenous rights is now well covered by the Permanent Forum on Indigenous Issues, established by the UN Economic and Social Council through its Resolution E/Res/2000/22, and the Special Rapporteur on the Situation of Human Rights and Fundamental Freedoms of Indigenous Peoples, appointed by the Commission on Human Rights in its Resolution 2001/57. There is a possibility that a separate mechanism will be established for the Afro-descendants.

Hence, the main issues now concern minority rights in Africa and Asia. In the case of Africa there is a chance, however slim, that some mechanism might be developed to deal with peaceful and constructive group accommodation. Such prospects do not yet exist for Asia or the Middle East.

It would be highly desirable if a special rapporteur or representative was appointed, in line with the role of the HCNM for Europe, but chances are at this stage very slim indeed; therefore the most likely prospect, is that the WGM will continue and give increasing attention to Africa (until the African Union establishes its own mechanism) and Asia.

The observer for the International Centre for Ethnic Studies, a south Asian regional research centre located in Colombo, Sri Lanka, described some recent activities undertaken by the centre at the regional level. They included the holding of a training workshop for NGOs from south Asia on minority rights and monitoring the implementation of such rights, as well as the organisation of a brainstorming session to discuss the question of the provision and development of advisory services to minorities in south Asia. These activities were aimed at enhancing the capacity of minorities to claim their rights and to bring violations of minority rights to the attention of the international community, in addition to strengthening the monitoring functions of human rights mechanisms. The observer highlighted the need to develop networks among NGOs working on minority issues in order to elaborate strategies for national and regional advisory services to protect the rights of minorities as a contribution to the prevention of ethnic conflicts. She stressed that initiatives on advisory services had to take due account of local needs and circumstances and should be developed in accordance with the provisions of the UNDM.

While it is essential that regional or sub-regional mechanisms are developed or strengthened to deal with the particular nature of the minority problems in different regions, it is also essential to maintain a global mechanism, for at least two reasons: one is to be an agent to push for and encourage the development of regional mechanisms, for which purpose the regional seminars have been very useful and hopefully will stimulate more sustained regional action; the second is that many minority problems are arising from or are intensified by present processes of globalisation of the market and the global reach of economic activities; it is therefore important that there exist mechanisms with a global reach which can address the consequences of those processes in an inclusive way. Whether the mechanism should be the existing UN Working Group on Minorities or whether it should be replaced or supplemented by other mechanisms, can be a matter of discussion. What is essential is that the existing working group must remain until something better is in place. It has already contributed substantially to the understanding of the major issues facing group accommodation in different parts of the world, and has thereby established a basis on which one can build in the future.

* Senior fellow of the Norwegian Centre for Human Rights; Guest Professor, University of Gothenburg and chairman of the UN Working Group on Minorities.

1. Declaration of the Rights of Persons Belonging to National or Ethnic, Religious and Linguistic Minorities, adopted by the UN General Assembly on 18 December 1992, GA Res. 47/135.

2. Report of the Special Rapporteur Asbjørn Eide on possible ways and means of facilitating the peaceful and constructive solution of problems involving minorities, E/CN.4/Sub.2/1993/34.

3. UN Commission on Human Rights Resolution 1995/24 on the rights of persons belonging to national or ethnic, religious and linguistic minorities, C.H.R. res. 1995/24, ESCOR Supp. (No. 4) at p. 92, U.N. Doc. E/CN.4/1995/24 (1995).

4. To date, reports on the first eight sessions of the working group have been published: Report of the WGM on its first session: E/CN.4/Sub.2/1996/2; second session: E/CN.4/Sub.2/1996/28; third session: E/CN.4/Sub.2/1997/18; fourth session: E/CN.4/Sub.2/1998/18; fifth session: E/CN.4/Sub.2/1999/21; sixth session: E/CN.4/Sub.2/2000/27; seventh session: E/CN.4/Sub.2/2001/22; eighth session: E/CN.4/Sub.2/2002/19.

5. Commentary to the Declaration on the Rights of Persons Belonging to National or Ethnic, Religious and Linguistic Minorities, E/CN.4/Sub.2/AC.5/2000/WP.2.

6. "Universal and Regional Mechanisms for Minority Protection", working paper prepared by Mr Vladimir Kartashkin, E/CN.4/Sub.2/AC.5/1999/WP.6.

7. Mr. José Bengoa, "Existence and Recognition of Minorities", working paper, E/CN.4/Sub.2/AC.5/2001/2.

8. General Comment No. 23, adopted by the Human Rights Committee at the 50th session, 1994.

9. Asbjørn Eide, "Citizenship and the Minority Rights of Non-Citizens" – working paper, E/CN.4/Sub.2/AC.5/1999/WP.3.

10. Foundation on Inter-Ethnic Relations, The Hague, 1997; prepared by a group of international experts in 1996 and presented to the WGM as a working paper, E/CN.4/Sub.2/AC.5/1997/WP.3.

11. Like the Hague recommendations, these were prepared by a group of experts under the auspices of the Foundation on Inter-Ethnic Relations and presented to the WGM in 1998, dealing with the linguistic rights of minorities.

12. Details about the Oslo recommendations can be found in 6(3) *International Journal on Minority and Group Rights* (1999) special issue on linguistic rights of national minorities.

13. The report is found in E/CN.4/Sub.2/AC.5/2000/WP.4.

14. The full report can be found in 12(1) *Revue Quebecoise de Droit International* (1999), special issue on Montreal International Seminar on Intercultural and Multicultural Education.

15. "Report of an International Seminar on Autonomist and Integrationist Approaches to Minority Protection", Danish Centre for Human Rights, Copenhagen, 3-4 April 2002, E/CN.4/Sub.2/AC.5/2002/WP.1

16. See Minority Rights Group International, "Minority rights and development: overcoming exclusion, discrimination and poverty", E/CN.4/Sub.2/AC.5/2002/WP.6.

17. "Multiculturalism in Africa: Peaceful and Constructive Group Accommodation in Situations involving Minorities and Indigenous Peoples", report on the seminar held in Arusha, E/CN.4/Sub.2/AC.5/2000/WP.3.

18. "Peaceful and Constructive Group Accommodation in Situations involving Minorities and Indigenous Peoples", report on the second workshop on multiculturalism in Africa, E/CN.4/Sub.2/AC.5/2001/3.

19. "Prevention of Discrimination", report of the regional seminar on Afro-descendants in the Americas, E/CN.4/Sub.2/2002/40 E/CN.4/Sub.2/AC.5/2000/CRP.3.

20. Fernand de Varennes, "Minority Rights and the Prevention of Ethnic Conflicts", working paper: E/CN.4/Sub.2/AC.5/2001/2.

CHAPTER 3

THE INTERNATIONAL COURT OF JUSTICE

Frank Selbmann*

Introduction

While the Permanent Court of International Justice (PCIJ) has played a significant role in minority protection and has rendered a number of important decisions in this field,[1] the role of the International Court of Justice (ICJ) in this area has been considered as limited for a long period. Thus, most scholarly publications about minority rights and rights of persons belonging to national minorities do not discuss the role of the ICJ.[2] However, as will be argued, due to developments in the last ten years, a handbook on the implementation of minority rights for practitioners must also address the proceedings before the principal judicial organ of the United Nations.

In 1993, Bosnia and Herzegovina initiated proceedings against the Federal Republic of Yugoslavia (FRY) before the ICJ where it sought to enforce the Convention on the Prevention and Punishment of the Crime of Genocide (hereinafter "Genocide Convention").[3] It was the first time that a case was submitted to the ICJ with the primary purpose of protecting human rights.[4] Today this case is the first in a row of cases where Article 9 of the Genocide Convention was invoked as the basis of jurisdiction of the ICJ. All of them are still pending. Nevertheless, it is now possible to draw the first conclusions for further submissions from the initial decisions in the said cases.

Compromissory clauses, which refer to the jurisdiction of the ICJ, might also be found in other multilateral and bilateral treaties. However, it will be shown that those treaties are less significant than the Genocide Convention.

Jurisdiction of the International Court of Justice

Jurisdiction clauses in the ICJ Statute

The ICJ is one of the principal organs of the United Nations and, according to Article 92 of the Charter of the United Nations, its principal judicial organ. First, it has to be established whether the ICJ has jurisdiction. Jurisdiction means that the court has the competency to decide a case.[5]

All member states of the United Nations are parties to the Statute of the ICJ, which is an integral part of the UN Charter.[6] Also, non-members of the United Nations can become a party to the ICJ Statute when they accept the conditions to be determined by the General Assembly based on recommendations of the Security Council.[7] In addition, the ICJ is open to states that are not members of the ICJ Statute when they accept the jurisdiction of the ICJ by a declaration made either particular or general.[8]

According to Article 34 of the ICJ Statute, only states can be parties before the ICJ. Thus, non-governmental organisations (NGOs), individuals and other non-state actors cannot initiate proceedings and litigate their own cases before the ICJ.

Furthermore, one of the fundamental principles of the ICJ Statute is that the court does not automatically have jurisdiction over legal disputes between states. It is necessary that states have given their consent in general or for an individual claim.[9] According to Article 36, paragraph 2, of the ICJ Statute, states may recognise the compulsory jurisdiction of the court.

In addition, according to Article 36, paragraph 1, of the ICJ Statute, "[t]he jurisdiction of the Court comprises all cases which the parties refer to it and all matters specially provided for in the Charter of the United Nations or in treaties and conventions in force". Treaties within the meaning of Article 36, paragraph 1, of the ICJ Statute can be general, bilateral or multilateral treaties of peaceful settlement of disputes or specific treaties.[10]

Multilateral treaties

a. Article 9 of the Genocide Convention

One treaty in the meaning of Article 36, paragraph 1, of the ICJ Statute is the Genocide Convention. The Genocide Convention, which entered into force on 12 January 1951, was designed to protect national, ethnical, racial or religious groups as such from physical destruction.[11] Thus, the Genocide Convention is not only a tool to protect minorities but also groups as such.[12] As of 9 October 2001, 133 nations were parties to the Genocide Convention.[13] It is therefore one of the most widely accepted treaties in the field of human rights law. Unlike more recent human rights instruments it contains no enforcement mechanism,[14] except for the compromissory clause in Article 9:

> Disputes between the Contracting Parties relating to the interpretation, application or fulfilment of the present Convention, including those relating to the responsibility of a State for genocide or for any of the other acts enumerated in article III, shall be submitted to the International Court of Justice at the request of any of the parties to the dispute.

According to Article 9, the ICJ has the subject matter jurisdiction to assess whether the Genocide Convention is applicable, to interpret the treaty terms and to examine whether a state party has fulfilled its obligations deriving from the convention and whether a state is responsible for genocide.[15] Thus the question as to whether a state party to the Genocide Convention has violated an obligation deriving from Articles 1 to 7 falls under the jurisdiction of the court.[16]

An applicant state, alleging that the respondent state is involved in acts of genocide, has to bring evidence that the claim falls within the scope of Article 2 of the Genocide Convention, which reads:

> In the present Convention, genocide means any of the following acts committed with intent to destroy, in whole or in part, a national, ethnical, racial or religious group, as such:
> (a) killing members of the group;
> (b) causing serious bodily or mental harm to members of the group;
> (c) deliberately inflicting on the group conditions of life calculated to bring about its physical destruction in whole or in part;
> (d) imposing measures intended to prevent births within the group;
> (e) forcibly transferring children of the group to another group.

The essential element of the crime of genocide is "the intended destruction of 'a national, ethnical, racial or religious group'".[17] Therefore the ICJ came to the conclusion that "the threat or use of force against a State cannot in itself constitute an act of genocide within the meaning of Article 2 of the Genocide Convention".[18] Intent to commit genocide is difficult to prove. The crime of genocide requires a specific intent or *dolus specialis*, which means that the perpetrator "seeks to achieve the destruction, in whole or in part, of a national, ethnical, racial or religious group, as such".[19] Thus, applications have to meet a very high threshold.

Although the convention does not explicitly allow reservations, many states parties objected to the jurisdiction of the ICJ. The question of the admissibility of reservations to the Genocide Convention was the subject of an advisory opinion of the ICJ, which accepted reservations compatible with the object and the purpose of the convention. According to the ICJ, the Genocide Convention was "adopted for purely a humanitarian and civilising purpose", which brings no individual advantages or disadvantages to states. Therefore, as many states as possible should become parties to the Genocide Convention.[20] Thus, Article 9 of the Genocide Convention cannot be invoked against states which made a reservation thereto.[21] Currently, there are 17 reservations to Article 9.[22] A further 11 states parties have withdrawn their reservations since 1989.[23]

Article 8 of the Genocide Convention according to which states parties can call upon the competent organs of the United Nations to take action appropriate for the prevention and suppression of genocide under the UN Charter gives no additional competence to the ICJ.[24]

b. Article 22 of the Convention on the Elimination of All Forms of Racial Discrimination

Another multilateral treaty relevant for actors in the field of minority rights law, which refers to the jurisdiction of the ICJ, is the International Convention on the Elimination of All Forms of Racial Discrimination (ICERD).[25] Article 22 of the ICERD reads:

> Any dispute between two or more States Parties with respect to the interpretation or application of this Convention, which is not settled by negotiation or by the procedures

73

expressly provided for in this Convention, shall, at the request of any of the parties to the dispute, be referred to the International Court of Justice for decision, unless the disputants agree to another mode of settlement.

It can only be invoked as a basis for jurisdiction of the ICJ against states parties of ICERD. If the respondent state has declared a reservation to Article 22, the proceedings are inadmissible.[26] Prior to the initiating of proceedings before the ICJ, states parties must make attempts to settle the dispute by negotiations or by the supervisory mechanism explicitly laid down in the ICERD. The court examines whether these preconditions are fulfilled.[27] Unlike the Genocide Convention, ICERD sets up a detailed supervisory mechanism, which also gives NGOs the possibility of providing information to the Committee on the Elimination of Racial Discrimination (CERD).[28] Since there exist other supervisory mechanisms, it is unlikely that proceedings before the ICJ under Article 22 of the ICERD will play an important role in protecting minority groups in the near future.

Bilateral treaties and the European Convention for the Peaceful Settlement of Disputes

Compromissory clauses, which refer to the jurisdiction of the ICJ might also be found in bilateral treaties. In the period of the League of Nations, bilateral treaties were one important pillar of minority protection.[29] The post-Second World War system of minority protection failed, and the idea to protect persons belonging to national minorities by bilateral treaties was then neglected for decades. It was in the 1990s when bilateral treaties with the aim of minority protection had a renaissance.[30] However, none of these new negotiated treaties makes reference to the jurisdiction of the ICJ. But even if a bilateral treaty does not explicitly refer to the jurisdiction of the ICJ, a European state might have the duty to bring an international legal dispute on minority issues to the ICJ. According to Article 1 of the European Convention for the Peaceful Settlement of Disputes (ECPSD),[31] contracting states undertake to submit to the ICJ all international legal disputes which arise between them and relate to the interpretation of a treaty, any question of international law, the existence of any fact constituting a breach of an international obligation, and the nature or the extent of compensatory claims to be made for the breach of such obligation. Unfortunately, the ECPSD is not widely accepted. As of January 2003, only 14 states – most of them western European – had ratified the convention.[32] In addition, the provisions of the ECPSD do not apply to disputes related to facts or situations prior to the entry into force of the convention in the parties concerned in the disputes (Article 27, paragraph a) and when the parties have agreed upon another procedure of peaceful settlement (Article 28, paragraph 1).

So far, only Austria and Italy have voted for a bilateral system, which explicitly gives the option of submitting a dispute concerning minority issues to the ICJ. Austria and Italy adopted a bilateral treaty, which modified Article 27, paragraph a, of the ECPSD and also allows the retroactive application of Chapter I of the convention.[33] Now claims arising from the bilateral

De Gasperi-Gruber Agreement on South Tyrol of 5 September 1946 and the South-Tyrol autonomy statutes can be brought before the ICJ.[34]

The proceedings before the ICJ

Proceedings

The proceedings before the ICJ consist of both written and oral parts.[35] Proceedings which will be initiated by applications shall specify the legal grounds upon which the jurisdiction is said to be based, the precise nature of the claim, and a statement of facts.[36]

The written proceedings consist of a memorial by the applicant, which shall contain a statement of facts, a statement of law and the submissions[37] and a counter-memorial by the respondent, which shall contain an admission or denial of the facts given in the memorial, observations regarding the statement of law, the respondent's statement of law and the submissions.[38] In addition, replies and rejoinders can be admitted, if necessary.[39] The court can fix time limits for the completion of the steps in written proceedings, which shall be as short as the character of the case permits.[40] The oral proceedings follow after the closure of the written proceedings.[41] Normally the hearings of the court shall be public.[42]

The respondent can object to the jurisdiction of the court or to the application within three months after the delivery of the memorial (preliminary objections).[43] Upon receipt of a preliminary objection, the proceedings on the merits will be suspended.[44] When the written and oral proceedings regarding the preliminary objections are finished, the court renders a judgment, by which it either upholds or rejects the objections. If the ICJ rejects the objections, time limits for the continuation of the further proceedings will be fixed.[45]

The indication of provisional measures

As has been outlined above, in the field of minority protection before the ICJ, the arbitration clause Article 9 of the Genocide Convention is the most relevant norm. In case of an alleged or an occurring genocide it is necessary to act very fast. Thus, the clauses in the ICJ Statute and the Rules of the Court regarding interim protection play an important role in this area.

According to Article 41 of the ICJ Statute, the ICJ has the power to indicate provisional measures. Decisions on interim protection can be taken, when circumstances in order to preserve the rights of the party so require.[46] Either the party concerned can make a written request for provisional measures[47] or the court can decide *propriu motu*, whether the circumstances of the case require the indication of provisional measures.[48] Requests for the indication of provisional measures have priority over all other cases.[49]

The ICJ has developed the criteria for the indication of provisional measures in the case of application of the Convention on the Prevention and Punishment of the Crime of Genocide and has referred to them in all similar cases. Before deciding upon a request for provisional measures the ICJ need not finally satisfy itself that it has jurisdiction on the merits of the case. But the provisions invoked by the applicant or laid down in the Statute must establish prima facie a basis for the jurisdiction of the ICJ.[50] Once the prima facie case of jurisdiction is established, the indication of provisional measures is limited to those which can also be made in a final judgment, that is, when Article 9 of the Genocide Convention is invoked as the basis of jurisdiction, the ICJ can indicate only those measures which fall within the scope of Articles 1 to 7 of the Genocide Convention.[51]

Relationship to other international judicial organs and to inter-state proceedings in other instruments

a. Relationship to the international criminal courts

There is no hierarchy between the ICJ and other judicial organs within the UN, namely the International Criminal Tribunal for the former Yugoslavia (ICTY) and the International Criminal Tribunal for Rwanda (ICTR).[52] However, it is expected that a final judgment of the ICTY against Slobodan Milošević would influence the outcome of the cases concerning the application of the Genocide Convention initiated by Bosnia and Herzegovina and Croatia against the FRY.

There is also no hierarchy between the ICJ and the new International Criminal Court (ICC), which was set up by a multilateral treaty. Unlike the ICTY and the ICTR, which are subsidiary organs of the Security Council, the ICC is a separate organisation which will be brought into a relationship with the United Nations by a special agreement.[53] While the ICJ gives states the opportunity to settle their legal disputes peacefully, the task of the three international criminal courts is different. The criminal courts have to prove individual criminal guilt for serious violations of humanitarian law, that is, "the most serious crimes of concern to the international community as a whole".[54]

b. Relationship to other inter-state proceedings

Neither the ICJ Statute nor the Rules of the Court preclude states from the initiation of inter-state proceedings under different systems of human rights protection. This conclusion can be illustrated with the following example.

In March 1999, the Democratic Republic of Congo (DRC) filed a communication under Article 49 of the African Charter on Human and Peoples' Rights to the African Commission on Human and Peoples' Rights.[55] The commission declared the application admissible.[56] Furthermore, in June 1999 the DRC initiated proceedings before the ICJ against Burundi, Rwanda and Uganda for alleged acts of aggression committed in breach of the UN Charter and the Charter of the Organisation of African Unity.[57] The proceedings against Burundi and Rwanda before the ICJ were discontinued in January 2001 when the DRC withdrew its applications. The proceedings against Uganda remained at the courts list.

In 2002, the DRC instituted new proceedings against Rwanda partly based on the same facts as given also in the application to the African Commission on Human and Peoples' Rights, alleging, *inter alia*, a breach of the Genocide Convention. In the ICJ's order concerning the request of the DRC for the indication of provisional measures, the issue of parallel proceedings was not addressed. Although the ICJ came to the conclusion that the court does not have prima facie jurisdiction, it decided that there is no manifest lack of jurisdiction and stayed in the proceedings.[58]

Relevance for NGOs in the field of minority protection

While Article 22 of the ICERD and bilateral treaties play a limited role, the relevance of Article 9 of the Genocide Convention must be examined in more detail.

In 1995, Payam Akhavan came to the conclusion that Article 9 of the Genocide Convention has never been an effective mechanism for preventing or punishing genocide.[59] Although since then the number of cases in which Article 9 has been invoked has increased, this conclusion has not yet been disproved. Over more than forty years after the entry into force of the Genocide Convention Article 9 has had no relevance. It was invoked for the first time by Pakistan in the trial of Pakistani prisoners of war in 1973, but the application was withdrawn before the court came to a decision.[60] As explained above proceedings before the ICJ can only be initiated by states. In the 1970s and 1980s NGOs unsuccessfully persuaded governments to initiate "altruistic" proceedings under Article 9 regarding crimes committed by the Khmer Rouge in Cambodia and regarding mass murder committed against Kurds in Iraq.[61] It is unlikely that states will give up their reluctance regarding "altruistic" proceedings under Article 9 of the Genocide Convention. But in the 1990s, the compromissory clause in Article 9 of the Genocide Convention gained a more important role because it was invoked by states which were directly affected by mass atrocities. The cases are in chronological order: Bosnia and Herzegovina against the FRY,[62] the FRY against Belgium, Canada, France, Germany, Italy, the Netherlands, Portugal, Spain, the United Kingdom and the United States of America,[63] Croatia against the FRY[64] and the Democratic Republic of the Congo against Rwanda.[65] All of these cases were brought before the ICJ in order to terminate ongoing armed conflicts and/or to make compensatory claims.

An analysis of the decisions rendered in the above-mentioned cases leads to a critical assessment. So far, the proceedings are not an effective tool for preventing genocide. As yet, the mechanism is also not sufficiently flexible to give victims and survivors of genocide, and their families, a chance to receive financial compensation without delays.

This conclusion can be illustrated with the case of Bosnia and Herzegovina against the FRY. The proceedings were initiated on 20 March 1993. Bosnia and Herzegovina alleged that the FRY was involved in violations of the Genocide Convention. In the same year, the ICJ rendered two decisions on requests for the indication of provisional measures,[66] which could not prevent further acts of violence.

In addition, up until now the proceedings have been excessively long. On 11 July 1996, the ICJ rejected the preliminary objections made by the FRY.[67] In 1997, the FRY filed counter-claims, which were declared admissible by the ICJ,[68] but eventually withdrawn. On 24 April 2001, the FRY requested the ICJ to revise the 1996 judgment in accordance with Article 61 of the ICJ Statute, according to which an application for revision of a judgment can be made after the discovery of a new fact that was not known at the time when the judgment was delivered. The application was based on the argument that the FRY became a member of the UN on 1 November 2001 and that in 1996 it was not a member of the UN, the ICJ Statute and the Genocide Convention, which is only open to UN members or to non-member states which have been invited to become parties to the convention. The application for revision was declared inadmissible on 3 February 2003.[69] Now 10 years after the initial application the case is open for a final decision.

Although the assessment of the current regime is very critical, the role of NGOs should not be underestimated. One important part of the work of human rights and minority rights organisations is the investigation of human rights abuses and their documentation. Firstly, NGOs can influence public opinion in order to persuade states to initiate proceedings under Article 9 of the Genocide Convention. Secondly, once a state party of the ICJ Statute has decided to initiate proceedings, NGOs can support the claims by providing documentation as evidence.

Besides the practical problems in current proceedings, which have arisen from the legal problems related to state succession, final judgments regarding the violation of the Genocide Convention are very important, since they are in general the legal basis for compensatory claims.[70]

*Dr. jur., Attorney-at-law, Leipzig. The author would like to thank Ms Emma Lantschner for her helpful comments.

1. Dieter Blumenwitz, *Internationale Schutzmechanismen zur Durchsetzung von Minderheiten- und Volksgruppenrechten* (Köln, 1997), p. 42. Iris Bils, "Internationale Schutzmechanismen zur Durchsetzung von Minderheiten- und Volksgruppenrechten", Ph.D. thesis, Bayerische Julius-Maximilians-Universität Würzburg (1995) on file at the Law Faculty of the University of Leipzig, compares the role of the PCIJ with the system in the Convention on the Elimination of All Forms of Racial Discrimination and the International Labour Organisation.

2. Exceptions are the above-mentioned publications and Patrick Thornberry, *International Law and the Rights of Minorities* (Oxford, 1991), pp. 81-5.

3. 78 UNTS 277.

4. Karin Oellers-Frahm, "Anmerkungen zur einstweiligen Anordnung des Internationalen Gerichtshofs im Fall Bosnien-Herzegowina gegen Jugoslawien (Serbien und Montenegro) vom 8 April 1993", 53 *ZaöRV* (1993), pp. 638-56, at p. 639; Bils, op.cit., p. 137.

5. Shabtai Rosenne, *The Law and Practice of the International Court: 1920-1996*, Vol. II: Jurisdiction (The Hague, Boston, London, 3rd ed. 1997), p. 536.

6. Article 93.1 of the UN Charter.

7. Article 93.2 of the UN Charter.

8. UN Security Council Resolution 9 (15 October 1946).

9. See, *inter alia*, Case Concerning Armed Activities on the Territory of the Congo (New Application 2002) (Democratic Republic of the Congo v. Rwanda), Request for the Indication of Provisional Measures, Order (10 July 2002), paragraph 57.

10. Rosenne, op.cit., p. 666.

11. See Daniel D. Ntanda Nsereko, "Genocide: A Crime against Mankind" in Gabrielle Kirk McDonald and Olivia Swaak-Goldmann (eds), *Substantive and Procedural Aspects of International Criminal Law, The Experience of International and National Courts*, Volume I, (The Hague, 2000) pp. 113-40, at p. 129.

12. Thus to narrow Partial Dissenting Opinion of Judge Wald, paragraph 2 in The Prosecutor v. Goran Jelisic, Appeal Judgment, ICTY-95-10-A (5 July 2001), who limits the scope of the Genocide Convention to "large scale state-sponsored campaigns to destroy minority groups". Wald overlooks that genocide can be directed also against majority groups.

13. UNHCHR, Status Report, at http://www.unhchr.ch/html/menu3/b/treaty1gen.htm

14. So far all proposals to amend the Genocide Convention in order to make it more effective failed. The most relevant proposals are outlined in Nicodème Ruhashyankiko, "Study on the Question of the Prevention and Punishment of Genocide" (4 July 1978), UN E/CN.4/Sub.2/416 and Benjamin Whitaker, "Revised and Updated Report on the Question of Prevention and Punishment of the Crime of Genocide" (2 July 1985), UN E/CN.4/Sub.2/1985/6.

15. Matthew Lippman, "The Convention on the Prevention and Punishment of the Crime of Genocide: Fifty Years Later", 15 *Arizona Journal of International and Comparative Law* (1998), pp. 415-514, at pp. 462-3.

16. See Case concerning the Application of the Convention on the Prevention and Punishment of the Crime of Genocide (Bosnia and Herzegovina v. Yugoslavia, Serbia and Montenegro), Preliminary Objections, 11 July 1996, ICJ Reports (1996), 595, paragraph 32-33.

17. Case concerning the Application of the Convention on the Prevention and Punishment of the Crime of Genocide (Bosnia and Herzegovina v. Yugoslavia, Serbia and Montenegro), Further Request for the Indication of Provisional Measures, Order, (13 September 1993), ICJ Reports (1993), 325, paragraph 42.

18. Case concerning Legality of Use of Force, Request for the Indication of Provisional Measures, Order, (Yugoslavia v. Germany), (2 June 1999), ICJ Reports (1999), 422, paragraph 27.

19. The Prosecutor v. Goran Jelisic, Appeal Judgment, ICTY-95-10-A (5 July 2001), paragraph 46. See also the detailed analysis in Selbmann, *Der Tatbestand des Genozids im Völkerstrafrecht* (Leipzig, 2002), pp. 165-70.

20. Reservations to the Convention on the Prevention and Punishment of the Crime of Genocide, ICJ Reports (1951), 15, at pp. 23-4.

21. See Case Concerning Armed Activities on the Territory of the Congo, op.cit., paragraphs 69-72.

22. These are Algeria, Argentina, Bahrain, Bangladesh, China, India, Malaysia, Morocco, Philippines, Rwanda, Singapore, Spain, USA, Venezuela, Vietnam, Yemen and Yugoslavia.

23. Namely Albania, Belarus, Bulgaria, the Czech Republic, Hungary, Mongolia, Poland, Romania, the Russian Federation, Slovakia and Ukraine.

24. Case concerning the Application of the Convention on the Prevention and Punishment of the Crime of Genocide, Provisional Measures, Order (8 April 1993), ICJ Reports (1993), 3, paragraph 47.

25. 660 UNTS 195.

26. See Case Concerning Armed Activities on the Territory of the Congo, op.cit., paragraph 67.

27. Ibid., paragraph 78-9 (regarding Article 29 of the Convention on the Elimination of All Forms of Discrimination Against Women , which can be compared to Article 22 of the ICERD).

28. See Cees Flinterman and Catherine Henderson, "Special Human Rights Treaties" in Raija Hanski and Marku Suksi, *An Introduction to the International Protection of Human Rights* (Turku, Åbo, 2nd ed. 2000), pp. 125-42, at pp. 127-8. Regarding the system of inter-state disputes in the ICERD, see Karl Josef Partsch, "Human Rights, Inter-state Disputes", in Rüdiger Wolfrum (ed.), *United Nations: Law Policies and Practice,* Vol. 1, (Munich, 1995), pp. 612-8.

29. See Kinga Gál, "Bilateral Agreements in Central and Eastern Europe: A New Inter-State Framework for Minority Protection", ECMI Working Paper No. 4 (May 1999), p. 3.

30. See ibid. and Emma Lantschner and Roberta Medda-Windischer, "Protection through Bilateral Agreements in South Eastern Europe", 1 *European Yearbook of Minority Issues* (2001/2), pp. 535-61.

31. Adopted on 29 April 1957, entered into force 30 April 1958, ETS No. 23.

32. These were: Austria, Belgium, Denmark, Germany, Italy, Liechtenstein, Luxembourg, Malta, the Netherlands, Norway, Slovakia, Sweden, Switzerland and the United Kingdom.

33. Vertrag betreffend die Abänderung des Art. 27 lit. a des Europäischen Übereinkommens zur friedlichen Beilegung von Streitigkeiten im Verhältnis zwischen Österreich und Italien, reprinted in: Karl Zeller, *Das Problem der völkerrechtlichen Verankerung des Südtirol-Pakets und die Zuständigkeit des Internationalen Gerichtshofs* (Wien, 1998), Document 16.

34. See Bils, op.cit., pp. 42-63 and Blumenwitz, op.cit., pp. 51-65.

35. Article 43 of the ICJ Statute.

36. Article 38 of the Rules of the Court (1978) as amended on 5 December 2000 (hereinafter "Rules of the Court").

37. Ibid., Article 45.1, 49.1.

38. Ibid., Article 45.1, 49.2.

39. See ibid., Article 45.2.

40. Ibid., Article 48.

41. The rules about the oral proceedings are laid down, ibid., Article 54-72.

42. See ibid., Article 59.

43. Ibid., Article 79.1.

44. Ibid., Article 79.5.

45. Ibid., Article 79.9.

46. Article 41.1 of the ICJ-Statute.

47. Article 73.1 of the Rules of the Court.

48. Ibid., Article 75.1.

49. Ibid., Article 74.1.

50. Case concerning the Application of the Convention on the Prevention and Punishment of the Crime of Genocide, op.cit., Order (8 April 1993), paragraph 14.

51. Ibid., paragraph 35.

52. Rosenne, op.cit., Vol. I: The Court and the United Nations, p. 142.

53. Article 2 of the Rome Statute of the International Criminal Court, UN A/CONF.183/9 (17 July 1998).

54. Ibid., Article 5.

55. OAU Doc. CAB/LEG/67/3 rev. 5. An overview of the regional system of human rights protection in Africa is given in Cees Flinterman and Catherine Henderson, "The African Charter on Human and Peoples' Rights", in Raija Hanski and Marku Suksi, *An Introduction to the International Protection of Human Rights* (Turku, Åbo, 2nd ed. 2000), pp. 387-96.

56. D.R. Congo v. Burundi, Rwanda and Uganda, Communication No. 227/99.

57. See International Court of Justice, Press Communiqué 99/34 (23 June 1999).

58. Case Concerning Armed Activities on the Territory of the Congo, op.cit., paragraphs 89-94.

59. Payam Akhavan, "Enforcement of the Genocide Convention: A Challenge to Civilization", 8 *Harvard Human Rights Law Journal* (1995), pp. 229-58, at p. 230.

60. Trial of Prisoners of War (Pakistan v. India), *ICJ Yearbook* (1973-4), pp. 123-4.

61. See the detailed analysis by Payam Akhavan, op.cit., pp. 247-9.

62. Filed on 20 March 1993.

63. Filed on 29 April 1999. Background of the case was the humanitarian intervention of Nato in order to stop the forced expulsion of ethnic Albanians in Kosovo. On 2 June the ICJ rendered in each of the cases a decision on the FRY's request for the indication of provisional measures. In all cases the court rejected the request. The cases against Spain and the USA, which made a reservation under Article 9 were removed from the list of the court. In the other cases the court stayed in the proceedings.

64. Filed on 2 July 1999.

65. Filed on 28 May 2002.

66. Case concerning the Application of the Convention on the Prevention and Punishment of the Crime of Genocide, op.cit., Provisional Measures, Order (8 April 1993) and Order, (13 September 1993).

67. Case concerning the Application of the Convention on the Prevention and Punishment of the Crime of Genocide, op.cit., Preliminary Objections.

68. Case concerning the Application of the Convention on the Prevention and Punishment of the Crime of Genocide, op.cit., Provisional Measures, Order (17 December 1997), ICJ Reports (1997), p. 243.

69. Application for Revision of the Judgment of 11 July 1996 in the Case concerning the Application of the Prevention and Punishment of the Crime of Genocide (Bosnia and Herzegovina v. Yugoslavia), Preliminary Objections, (Yugoslavia v. Bosnia and Herzegovina), Judgment, (3 February 2003).

70. See also Bils, op.cit., p. 139.

CHAPTER 4

USING THE EUROPEAN COURT OF HUMAN RIGHTS TO PROTECT THE RIGHTS OF MINORITIES

Fernand de Varennes[*]

Introduction

A large number of documents internationally and in Europe (Council of Europe, OSCE, European Union) acknowledge that minorities have rights – human rights – that must be respected. But in legal terms the protection offered by the specific rights that minorities can claim is far from comforting. Only the Council of Europe's Framework Convention for the Protection of National Minorities (FCNM)[1] and the European Charter for Regional or Minority Languages (ECRML)[2] create actual obligations on states which have ratified these instruments, but even these two documents are not as precedent setting as might have initially been presented. Both provide for supervisory mechanisms only rather than a more stringent judicial implementation system. Additionally, neither actually create directly enforceable rights for minorities: the ECRML explicitly denies any right for any individuals, since it only contains undertakings by states parties to provide certain benefits and usage for regional or minority languages, not any rights for individuals or groups as such. As for the FCNM, its explanatory report indicates the reason for the instrument's status as a "framework convention": it is based on "a choice … for a framework Convention which contains mostly programme-type provisions setting out objectives which the Parties undertake to pursue. These provisions, which will not be directly applicable, leave the states concerned a measure of discretion in the implementation of the objectives which they have undertaken to achieve …".[3]

This does not mean that there are no justiciable minority rights in Europe. As this chapter will attempt to outline, there are in fact many rights which minorities will find may be protected under the European Convention on Human Rights (ECHR).[4] Although not always well understood, there are a growing number of decisions – some emanating from other international or regional bodies – which are building up a framework which minorities may be able to use for their greater protection.

This chapter will in the first instance attempt to outline the essential features of the mechanism available to individuals under the ECHR and the European Court of Human Rights (ECtHR or "the Court"). It will then proceed to a description of the rights of minorities that could be protected by the use of this mechanism, including the various decisions of the ECtHR specifically dealing with minority situations, especially in the area of language. It will then seek to provide "guidance" to practitioners, pointing out some of the advantages of using the ECtHR mechanism.

The European Court of Human Rights mechanism

The history of the European Court of Human Rights

While the ECHR was drawn up within the Council of Europe in 1950 and entered into force in September 1953, the mechanism for the enforcement of the rights it contained has gone through a number of changes, culminating in 1998 with the establishment of the ECtHR as it is known today.

Initially, there were three institutions which dealt with the enforcement of the European Convention on Human Rights: the European Commission of Human Rights, the European Court of Human Rights (set up in 1959) and the Committee of Ministers of the Council of Europe.

States parties under the ECHR, as well as individuals, groups of individuals or non-governmental organisations when states parties had accepted the right of individual petition, could lodge a complaint for an alleged violation of any right contained in the ECHR or its optional protocols.

Because of an ever-increasing caseload in the 1970s and 1980s, it was agreed that the entire mechanism under the ECHR had to be streamlined and reformed. This led to an agreement on the creation of a single, full-time Court with a simplified structure in order to shorten proceedings. The reform also aimed at making the new ECtHR jurisdiction compulsory. This new European Court of Human Rights was set out on 11 May 1994 in Protocol No. 11 to the European Convention on Human Rights (ECHR Protocol No. 11).

The new European Court of Human Rights came into operation on 1 November 1998 with the entry into force of ECHR Protocol No. 11. On 31 October 1998, the old Court had ceased to function. However, ECHR Protocol No. 11 provided that the European Commission of Human Rights should continue for one year (until 31 October 1999) to deal with cases which had been declared admissible before the date of entry into force of the protocol.

The Court mechanism for human rights: an overview

The European Court of Human Rights,[5] based in Strasbourg, became the first permanent human rights court in the world in 1998. All member states of the Council of Europe are parties to the ECHR.

The Court is divided into four sections, with two of the sections presided over by the Vice-Presidents of the Court and the other two presided over by the Section Presidents. Each Section contains chambers of seven judges. There is also a Grand Chamber of the Court composed of 17 judges, who include, as *ex officio* members, the President, Vice-Presidents and Section Presidents.

The right of individual petition is inherent in the ECHR system since 1998, and all of the Court's judgments are legally binding on states parties.

The ECtHR can receive complaints from persons or organisations claiming that their rights under the ECHR and its protocols have been violated. The

Court can only deal with complaints relating to the rights listed in the ECHR and protocols. It is not a court of appeal from national courts and cannot annul or modify their decisions.

The Court can only receive complaints involving states which have ratified the ECHR, and it can only deal with complaints about events which have occurred since the ratification. It can only hear complaints about matters which are the responsibility of a public authority (legislature, administration, police, army, courts of law, etc.). It cannot deal with complaints against private individuals or private organisations.

Before an individual can submit a complaint, s/he must have exhausted all remedies – legal or administrative – in the state that is claimed to be in breach of the ECHR, before addressing a complaint to the Court. This includes bringing the complaint before the highest court of the state in question that can deal with it.

After decision of the highest competent national court or authority has been given, there is a six-month period within which an application may be made to the Court. If the complaint relates to a court conviction or sentence, this period runs from the final court decision in the ordinary appeal process and not from the date of any later refusal to re-open the case. If the details of the complaint are not submitted within this six-month period, the Court will not examine the case.

When ready to proceed with a complaint, a first letter should be sent to the Registrar of the ECtHR,[6] containing the following:

a. a brief summary of your complaints;

b. which Convention rights have been violated;

c. what remedies were used;

d. the list of official decisions in the case, giving the date of each decision, the court or authority which took it, and brief details of the decision itself;

e. a copy of these decisions (copies only, not the originals).

There will be a reply from the Registrar, who may ask for more information or documents or for further explanation of the complaint. There may be an indication of how the Convention has previously been interpreted in similar cases. If it seems that there is an obvious obstacle to the complaint, the complainant may be advised of this.

If a complaint can be registered as an application and the complainant accepts that this can be done, the Registrar will send the necessary document on which to submit the formal application. After this has been completed and submitted, it will be brought to the ECtHR.

Complainants will be informed by the Registrar of the progress of the case. The proceedings are in writing at the initial stage. A lawyer can be instructed by the complainant to present the case. At a later stage in the proceedings, if a complainant has insufficient means to pay a lawyer's fees, s/he may be eligible for free legal aid.

Not every application will necessarily make it to the ECtHR. Each application is subjected to a preliminary examination of the case, with a rapporteur deciding whether it should be dealt with by a three-member committee or by a chamber of the Court. A committee may decide for example, by unanimous vote, that the application does not involve any right or freedom contained in the ECHR, or that it does not comply with the time requirements and declare it inadmissible.

If admissible, the matter will then proceed to one of the chambers. Their decisions, which are made public, may conclude by majority vote that the application is inadmissible, or rule on the merits.

Once a chamber has decided to admit an application, parties can be invited to present further evidence and written observations. It is also possible for a chamber to hold a hearing on the merits of the case, though it is not obliged to do so, if none has been held at the admissibility stage.

It is not uncommon to have confidential negotiations – conducted through the Registrar – held during the procedure on the merits in the hope of reaching a friendly settlement.

The ECtHR does not reverse any decisions made by national courts. It can however indicate if there is a violation of the law, what this violation is, and even describe what should be done to correct that specific violation from continuing. It can also order a government to pay compensation to individuals whose rights have not been respected. However, the responsibility for supervising the execution of judgments of the Court is under the Committee of Ministers of the Council of Europe. The Committee of Ministers will check whether governments have taken the measures set forth in the Court's judgments.

The ECtHR has a busy workload: it receives approximately 200 international phone calls and almost 1000 letters a day. The number of cases it hears has also greatly increased in the last 10 years. This means that cases submitted to the Court can take a long time before a final judgment is handed down. It should be pointed out that most of the complaints it receives are rejected because they do not deal with rights guaranteed under the ECHR (they are inadmissible) or because there was a friendly settlement of the dispute.

The chambers decide by a majority vote. These judgments can be appealed, within three months of delivery, to the Grand Chamber only if a serious question of interpretation or application or a serious issue of importance is involved.

The request is examined by a panel of the Grand Chamber made up of five judges: the President of the Court, the Section Presidents (excluding the Section President of the original chamber that gave judgment) and another judge who was not a member of the original chamber. If the panel accepts the request, the Grand Chamber will issue a final judgment by a majority vote.

The rights of minorities and the ECHR mechanism

While the ECtHR is a well-developed and fully functioning mechanism for the protection of human rights, there is still the question of what this can do to ensure respect for the rights of minorities. Minorities are not mentioned in the ECHR – except for Article 14 which says that "the enjoyment of the rights and freedoms set forth in this Convention shall be secured without discrimination on any ground such as … association with a national minority". The ECHR contains no minority rights provision similar to Article 27 of the International Covenant on Civil and Political Rights (ICCPR).[7]

At first glance it would seem that since no specific rights for minorities are recognised, there is no direct way for members of a minority to claim "minority rights" before the ECtHR.

This is, however, a commonly held – though mistaken – view. A closer examination of the cases considered by the Court, especially in recent years, demonstrates that there are in fact many rights in the ECHR which minorities can use to protect their interests, including those involving their language, religion or culture.[8] In addition, many so-called minority rights are in fact based on general human rights standards, and can therefore also successfully be claimed and protected under the ECHR.

Protection of minorities in private activities under the ECHR

It appears that the rights of minorities in a number of private activities can be protected using provisions under the ECHR that deal with private activities, such as freedom of expression, freedom of religion, the right to private or family life, equality and non-discrimination, and freedom of association.

Under freedom of expression, for example, persons who are members of a minority (and all individuals) have the right to use their language among themselves in private activities. If public authorities forbid or prevent the use of a minority language in private, whether in written or oral forms, this would be a breach of freedom of expression under Article 10 of the ECHR. Many other international treaties and other documents dealing with human rights or the rights of minorities have a provision where this right is expressly recognised.[9]

As the following sections will show, minorities can invoke the Convention in a number of areas. Until now, it has been in the areas of religion, freedom of association and freedom of expression that many minorities have been able to use the ECHR and have their rights protected most effectively.

a. The ECHR and the existence or recognition of a minority

An increasing number of cases at the ECtHR have involved state authorities unwilling to acknowledge the existence or identity of certain minorities. In more extreme cases, state authorities have attempted to ban or prohibit organisations or activities of a particular minority on the basis that it involves activities likely to constitute a "separatist threat" or an "incitement to hatred or violence".

The jurisprudence of the ECtHR in this regard has been fairly consistent. Unless there is a clear incitement to violence or a clear necessity to restrict private activities for reasons of public safety, restrictions which affect a minority's identity and may be connected to the exercise of freedom of expression, freedom of religion or freedom of association have continually been found to be impermissible.[10]

This has meant in practical terms that certain minorities, previously frowned upon by state authorities, have begun to be more visible by asserting their existence and the right to certain private activities using the protection of the ECtHR.

In Sidiropoulos v. Greece,[11] the ECtHR in essence concluded that there was nothing objectionable in having a cultural organisation claim the existence of a Macedonian minority in that country, and in those circumstances to refuse to register such a private entity – with the subsequent limitations on their activities – was disproportionate and therefore a violation of freedom of association as guaranteed under Article 11 of the ECHR.

Additionally, even a minority holding separatist views – if held and advocated in a non-violent way – could not be prevented from gathering, since:

> ...the fact that a group of persons calls for autonomy or even requests secession of part of the country's territory – thus demanding fundamental constitutional and territorial changes – cannot automatically justify a prohibition of its assemblies. Demanding territorial changes in speeches and demonstrations does not automatically amount to a threat to the country's territorial integrity and national security.

> Freedom of assembly and the right to express one's views through it are among the paramount values in a democratic society. The essence of democracy is its capacity to resolve problems through open debate. Sweeping measures of a preventive nature to suppress freedom of assembly and expression other than in cases of incitement to violence or rejection of democratic principles – however shocking and unacceptable certain views or words used may appear to the authorities, and however illegitimate the demands made may be – do a disservice to democracy and often even endanger it.[12]

While it appears that the ECtHR is willing to admit that the existence of a minority is an objective, factual determination, it was less willing to admit to the existence of any special category of minorities which could bring about special legal entitlements in a state's domestic legal regime.

In Gorzelick and Others v. Poland,[13] for example, "registered associations of national minorities" were in parliamentary elections entitled to a number of privileges under the electoral law of Poland.

When members of the Silesian minority tried to register as a "national minority" association, it was claimed by Polish authorities that they would automatically have been afforded an unqualified and legally enforceable claim to special privileges granted to national minorities by the relevant legislation.

The Court decided that since it would have been simple to change a few words in order to be registered with no real consequences for the applicants, and without risking recognition of special privileges by using the words "national minority", there was no violation of freedom of association in not registering the association as a "national minority":

> 65. ... the applicants could easily have dispelled the doubts voiced by the authorities, in particular by slightly changing the name of their association and by sacrificing, or amending, a single provision of the memorandum of association... Those alterations would not, in the Court's view, have had harmful consequences for the Union's existence as an association and would not have prevented its members from achieving the objectives they set for themselves.

> 66. The Court accordingly considers that, in the particular circumstances of the present case, it was reasonable on the part of the authorities to act as they did in order to protect the electoral system of the state, a system which is an indispensable element of the proper functioning of a "democratic society" within the meaning of Article 11.

The Court was in other words acknowledging that the individuals were members of the Silesian minority, but unwilling to propose their registration as a "national minority" because of the legal consequences this might have had in Poland in relation to the electoral system.

In the increasingly numerous cases involving Kurds,[14] Roma/Gypsies,[15] Sorbs,[16] Russians,[17] Macedonians,[18] Basques,[19] Saami,[20] Jehovah's Witnesses,[21] Atheists,[22] Catholics,[23] Jews,[24] Muslims,[25] and other minorities (rather than the undefined category of "national minority"), there has never been a difficulty for the Court to acknowledge their objective, factual presence within a state, often referring to them specifically as minorities, regardless of their status or of a country's recognition, and regardless of the ECHR itself being quasi-silent on the existence or rights of minorities.

Even in the case of unacknowledged religious divisions, the Court has not hesitated to support a minority's right to pursue its own beliefs and activities, contrary to the position of state authorities.[26]

b. Names and surnames in a minority language

A state cannot prevent an individual from having a name or surname which is not in an official language or not contained on a prescribed list. The ECtHR concluded in the Burghartz v. Switzerland case that there was discrimination in the right to private life (Article 14 in combination to Article 8 of the ECHR) by Swiss rules in relation to the family name to use when a couple is married. The same reasoning would normally apply to the use of a minority's family name or first name.

However, it is not absolutely clear whether the right to private life necessarily means in itself, in the European context, that a state is obliged to officially recognise or use an individual's preferred name or surname. As long as individuals are not prevented by public authorities from using their preferred names or surnames privately, there may not be a violation of the right to private life.[27]

But it is still possible that the refusal of public authorities to officially recognise or use a minority's name could be discriminatory, in combination with Article 14.

c. Topographical indications in a minority language

It would also seem that public authorities cannot ban the private use of topographical or locality names in a minority language. Individuals have the right to designate and use privately local names and topographical designations in their own language. If public authorities were to ban such private use, this would constitute a violation of freedom of expression (Article 10), perhaps in combination with non-discrimination (Article 14), under the ECHR.

This right does not mean that public authorities must in all cases officially adopt the local names of towns or villages in minority languages. That involves the use of a minority language by public officials which would potentially involve the application of the general prohibition of discrimination under Protocol No. 12 to the European Convention on Human Rights (ECHR Protocol No. 12), which is not yet in force. There are consequently no cases from the ECtHR on this issue.

d. Public displays in a minority language

Since freedom of expression includes the right to linguistic expression, this means that every individual, including members of a minority, has the right to use his or her language of choice in private "expression" activities. This applies to the language used in the private display of signs, posters, etc. of a commercial, religious, social, cultural or even political nature which are in public view.[28]

Public authorities may require that an official language be used in addition to the minority language in some cases, but only if it does not exclude or interfere with the right to use a minority language in these displays.

As part of these rights, minorities have the right to use a particular script (such as Cyrillic, Greek, Latin, Hebrew, etc.) in their private signs, posters and documents. This is also protected under freedom of expression (Article 10), possibly in combination with non-discrimination (Article 14). No matter on this aspect of freedom of expression has yet been decided by the Court.

e. Private media and minorities

Individuals are free to publish books or newspapers privately in a minority language. If public authorities attempted to prohibit such activities because they are done in an unrecognised or banned language, this would be a violation of freedom of expression (Article 10) possibly in combination with non-discrimination (Article 14) of the ECHR.

At least one recent judgment of the ECtHR appears to confirm this. Ekin v. France[29] dealt with French legislation which permitted the Minister of the Interior to issue administrative bans on the dissemination of private publications of foreign origin or written in a foreign language (including apparently the Basque language). While this ban was seen as an infringement of freedom of expression since there was nothing in the book's content – including the language in which it was published – that demonstrated that the ban was based on any pressing social need or proportionate to the legitimate aim pursued, the Court also made it known how it generally felt about such restrictions:

> [The] application of those rules has, in certain cases, produced results that are at best surprising and in some cases verge on the arbitrary, depending on the language of publication or the place of origin.[30]

As for private broadcasting, it is generally guaranteed under freedom of expression and of the press. A prohibition on the use of a minority language in private broadcasting would therefore be a violation of freedom of expression.[31]

To force a private radio or television station to have a percentage of its broadcasts in the official language, and in effect limiting the use of a minority language in these private broadcasts, could also be a violation of freedom of expression (Article 10) in combination with non-discrimination (Article 14).

f. Use of minority languages in religious and cultural activities

Minorities have the right to use their language in their religious activities. If public authorities were to declare the use of a minority language illegal during religious practices or services, this would breach freedom of expression (Article 10), freedom of religion (Article 9), or in combination with Article 14 constitute discrimination contrary to the ECHR.

When a religious ceremony includes an official act, as often happens with marriage, public authorities cannot prevent the use of the minority language during the private part of the ceremony for the reasons described earlier, though they may require that the "official" part of the "private" rites be in an official language, in addition to but not excluding the minority language.

In the area of culture, a prohibition by public authorities making it illegal to play any song, theatre presentation, opera, etc., either in private or in public, in a minority language similarly would clearly be in violation of rights such as freedom of expression and non-discrimination.

A more difficult situation arises when these private events must be translated into the official language, so that there is not a direct prohibition of the use of a minority language. In this latter case, the requirement of a bilingual format for all private cultural activities could still be a violation of the ECHR if:

i.   The translation/bilingual requirement is so onerous that it in effect prevents the free use of a minority language in cultural events. This would violate freedom of expression and non-discrimination;

ii. While not preventing private cultural activities, the translation/bilingual requirement creates a disadvantage, and costs, which only the members of the minority are subjected too. This type of disadvantage could in many cases be a breach of non-discrimination, even if there is not a violation of freedom of expression under Article 10. In this last case, individuals would have to present a case based on Protocol No. 12 of the ECHR (not yet entered into force) instead of Article 14. This is because Protocol No. 12 is a general non-discrimination clause, while Article 14 can only be applied to other rights that are found in the ECHR.

g. Minorities in the context of private economic and employment activities

Public authorities cannot prevent minorities from using their preferred language in business activities. Legislation or restrictions that would prevent the use of a minority language between an employer and his or her employees, between a business owner and a client, or in writing in private commercial activities, would be a violation of freedom of expression.[32]

Public authorities could require that the official or other language also be used in addition to a minority language in private economic activities, but only if this does not constitute an actual obstacle to the use of the minority language.[33]

In situations where there are restrictions on the type of economic or work-related employment which individuals can occupy in private areas because of language requirements imposed by the government or public authorities, this could involve the prohibition of non-discrimination rather than freedom of expression.

This does not mean that governments cannot demand a degree of bilingualism in some areas of employment such as private transportation or health care. But, if the language requirements are disproportionate or unreasonable, given the impact they have on individuals who would be members of a minority, this could still be discrimination if it is too restrictive, if it greatly disadvantages large numbers of individuals, or if it is unreasonable or unjustified given the objectives sought and the means employed to reach these objectives. In other words, requiring that taxi drivers, doctors or other categories of private employees must all know an official language could constitute a violation of the right to non-discrimination under ECHR Protocol No. 12 (when it enters into force) if it is unreasonable or arbitrary.

Similarly, exclusion of individuals who are members of a religious minority from categories of private employment due to the proper exercise of their right to freedom of religion could constitute discrimination, as occurred in Thlimmenos v. Greece,[34] where a Jehovah's Witness was excluded from the profession of chartered accountant because of criminal convictions linked to his religious beliefs as a conscientious objector:

> ... a conviction for refusing on religious or philosophical grounds to wear the military uniform cannot imply any dishonesty or moral turpitude likely to undermine the offender's ability to exercise this profession. Excluding the applicant on the ground that he was an unfit person was not, therefore, justified. The Court takes note of the government's argument that persons who refuse to serve their country must be appropriately punished. However, it also notes that the applicant did serve a prison sentence for his refusal to wear the military uniform. In these circumstances, the Court considers that imposing a further sanction on the applicant was disproportionate. It follows that the applicant's exclusion from the profession of

chartered accountants did not pursue a legitimate aim. As a result, the Court finds that there existed no objective and reasonable justification for not treating the applicant differently from other persons convicted of a serious crime ...

In the present case the Court considers that it was the state having enacted the relevant legislation which violated the applicant's right not to be discriminated against in the enjoyment of his right under Article 9 [freedom of religion] of the Convention.[35]

h. Minority private organisations and language

Private organisations, such as cultural societies, minority associations, etc., have the right to use minority languages in their activities. This is protected under freedom of expression (Article 10, alone or in combination with Article 14). If public authorities attempt to prevent the use of a minority language, it would also constitute discrimination under Protocol No. 12 (when it enters into force).

While public authorities could require that a private organisation keep its financial records and other types of documentation in an official language, this must not prevent the minority organisation from also keeping these same documents in their own language.

In addition, individuals, as well as political parties or associations, have the right to use a minority language in their own affairs. Their activities are private by nature, even during elections. A prohibition on the use of a minority language in private political activities or during events with a political character would therefore be in violation, at the very least, of freedom of expression and non-discrimination under the ECHR.

Finally, public authorities cannot forbid individuals from occupying positions in non-governmental organisations, including political parties, because of insufficient proficiency in the official or state language, or of religious beliefs. Such interference by public authorities in organisations of a private nature would breach freedom of association, alone or in combination with the prohibition of discrimination under the ECHR.

i. Registration and operations of minority organisations

This is one of the areas where minorities have been most successful in seeking the protection of the ECHR.

The ECtHR has explicitly stated on a number of occasions:

The inhabitants of a region in a country are entitled to form associations in order to promote the region's special characteristics. The fact that an association asserts a minority consciousness cannot in itself justify an interference with its rights under Article 11 of the Convention.[36]

A refusal by public officials or government ministers to register a minority organisation, or to interfere in its operations has been deemed, for example, to be a violation of the ECHR if there is no law setting out clear criteria for registration and there are no procedural safeguards against arbitrary exercise of discretion, or if the interference is not one that can be prescribed by law.

In one case, while the Court was referring to a violation of freedom of religion, it also indicated, *inter alia,* that the same reasoning would be applicable to freedom of association.[37]

It would also be a violation of human rights if public authorities banned the establishment or operation of private organisations for their use of a minority language or identification of a minority religion or ethnic group. Governments cannot refuse the registration of such an organisation when this is required by legislation. If they did, this would be a violation of the ECHR's freedom of association (Article 11), perhaps in combination with Article 14, unless it is prescribed by law, in pursuit of a legitimate aim and necessary in a democratic society.

When the refusal also directly intervenes with the ability to conduct activities of a religious nature, the Court has tended to see this as an impermissible interference with the freedom of religion of minorities. In Metropolitan Church of Bessarabia v. Moldova,[38] failure to register the separate, minority church meant it could not hold property, receive legal protection as a religious denomination, or conduct some religious activities. This refusal directly impacted on the freedom to conduct religious activities for the minority, and therefore a violation of Article 9 of the ECHR:

> ... [T]he Court notes that in the absence of recognition the applicant church may neither organise itself nor operate. Lacking legal personality, it cannot bring legal proceedings to protect its assets, which are indispensable for worship, while its members cannot meet to carry on religious activities without contravening the legislation on religious denominations...

> As regards the tolerance allegedly shown by the government towards the applicant church and its members, the Court cannot regard such tolerance as a substitute for recognition, since recognition alone is capable of conferring rights on those concerned.

> The Court further notes that on occasion the applicants have not been able to defend themselves against acts of intimidation, since the authorities have fallen back on the excuse that only legal activities are entitled to legal protection (see paragraphs 56, 57 and 84 above).

> Lastly, it notes that when the authorities recognised other liturgical associations they did not apply the criteria which they used in order to refuse to recognise the applicant church and that no justification has been put forward by the Moldovan government for this difference in treatment.

> In conclusion, the Court considers that the refusal to recognise the applicant church has such consequences for the applicants' freedom of religion that it cannot be regarded as proportionate to the legitimate aim pursued or, accordingly, as necessary in a democratic society, and that there has been a violation of Article 9.[39]

Similarly, if a political party were banned for making demands for minority rights, this would normally be a violation of freedom of association, as the Court has just recently recognised.[40]

The ECtHR has also ruled that it is an impermissible interference in religious freedom for state authorities to impose on religious communities a particular form of centralised control and leadership. In one case involving members of the Muslim minority in Greece, it concluded that while the state only officially recognised a Mufti elected according to the provisions of the applicable Greek legislation, freedom of religion for members of the Muslim minority also included the right to have other individuals acting in purely religious matters as Muftis as part of the right inherent in freedom of religion to manifest their religion in worship and teaching in community with others and in public.[41]

Minorities have on occasion been able to successfully invoke the protection of non-discrimination (Article 14) to buttress their claims to the violation of other rights contained in the ECHR. This occurred in Greece where members of the Catholic minority found themselves disadvantaged because of a Greek court's determination that the Catholic Church had no capacity to take legal proceedings in order to protect its land and buildings, whereas the Orthodox Church and the Jewish community could do so without any formality or required procedure.

The ECtHR found that such a distinction clearly discriminated against members of the Catholic minority under Article 14 taken together with Article 6, paragraph 1, of the ECHR, since there was no objective and reasonable justification put forward for such a difference of treatment between the congregations of the Catholic and Jewish minorities, or between the Catholic and Orthodox majority.[42]

j. Respect of minority culture or lifestyle

Unless linked to religion or language, minorities have been far less successful in protecting aspects of their culture or lifestyle by using the ECHR. This has been particularly visible in a series of cases involving Roma/Gypsies in the United Kingdom (called "Gypsies" in that country) who sought "to follow a traditional gypsy lifestyle" which included living in a caravan.[43] Planning permission to live on the land in a caravan was refused on the basis that it conflicted with local and national planning policies for the protection of the environment.

The Roma/Gypsies in the United Kingdom argued that the refusal by planning authorities to permit the applicants to live in their caravans on land which they owned, and the insufficient availability of sites for their caravans, violated their right to private and family life contained in Article 8 of the ECHR. They also asserted that the use of the caravans as a lifestyle was intrinsically linked to their culture and traditions as Roma/Gypsies, and that the denial of permission therefore infringed on their right to private and family life.

The ECtHR was willing to accept that a minority's culture, ethnic identity and traditions could be protected under one's right to private and family life, "that the applicant's occupation of her caravan is an integral part of her ethnic identity as a Gypsy, reflecting the long tradition of that minority of following a travelling lifestyle",[44] and seemed to refer favourably to recent evolution of international law in this respect by mentioning the Council of Europe's Framework Convention for the Protection of National Minorities.

However, in the end the Court concluded in all cases that the interference in the life of the Roma/Gypsies was justified in the circumstances for the purpose of protecting the environment, although there appears to have been intense discomfort in the final outcome, with the Court majority seeming to say that it was not really in a position to decide in matters of planning.

Positive obligations of public authorities and the rights of minorities

The previous section dealt with the rights of minorities under provisions of the ECHR involving private activities. It could be argued that these are simply "negative obligations". Public authorities may however also have positive obligations: legal obligations to use minority languages, to accommodate religious preferences of minorities, and even to support the cultural and linguistic needs and preferences of minorities.

a. Language use by administrative and public authorities in general

When you have a sufficient number and concentration of speakers of a language at the national, regional or local levels, there is potentially a right under a general prohibition of discrimination on the basis of language to have public authorities provide an appropriate degree of service in this language. For example, in local administrative districts where speakers of a language are concentrated, local authorities should generally provide for an increasing level of services in their language as the number of speakers of a particular language increases. Basically, this means that the degree of use of a language must be "proportionate" to the relative importance of the numbers of people using a language. Proportionality means the more people speak a language, the more officials should provide public services in this language, as far as is reasonably possible.

The above situation would normally occur where state authorities refuse to use a minority language, and it is usually associated in various international instruments as a "minority right". However, there have been cases where state authorities refuse to use the language of a majority, though this would probably only occur where the linguistic majority has been excluded from political power, as occurred in Rhodesia and apartheid-era South Africa. It has also occurred in Europe, as is explained in the recent context of northern Cyprus described below.

This right is not a collective right: it is not a right that any group can assert successfully. It is in fact an individual right based on the application of non-discrimination on the ground of language. As indicated recently by the UN Human Rights Committee,[45] the exclusive use of an official language by public officials can be discriminatory towards minorities unless it is justified in the circumstances. Especially if it is simple to provide some degree of services in a language spoken by a substantial or territorially concentrated number of individuals, the refusal to do so could be deemed unreasonable and unjustified, and therefore discriminatory.

Currently however, the ECtHR mechanism is unlikely to be very helpful to individuals in this regard. The ECHR does not yet have a general prohibition of discrimination. Article 14 only prohibits discrimination "in the enjoyment of the rights and freedoms set forth in this Convention". In general therefore, most services handled by public officials do not involve any recognised right under the ECHR – with some exceptions such as education, elections, and the court system. This means that there are many areas involving public authorities which do not involve any entitlement under the ECHR, rendering unavailable claims of discrimination by minorities.

However, Protocol No. 12 of the ECHR is a general prohibition of discrimination which, once it enters into force, will mean that in any activities by public officials, not to provide for the use of a minority language where this would be justified or reasonable would possibly constitute discrimination as to language under the new protocol.

The following will try to show in more detail how minorities could seek to protect their rights, and in particular to enforce claims to "positive measures" by the state concerned, in specific areas by the use of the ECtHR mechanism, especially after Protocol No. 12 enters into force.

b. Public education and minority languages

Where "justified", "reasonable", or where the number of individuals in part of a territory is "substantial" or "sufficient", persons belonging to minorities have the right to be treated in a non-discriminatory manner in terms of language, and this would generally imply an appropriate degree of use of their language as a medium of instruction in public schools. This can range from perhaps only one or two courses taught through a minority language to complete instruction in such a language.

The exact degree of use of a minority language as a medium of instruction required will depend on the particular context of each situation: the extent of demand for such instruction, the degree of use of the medium of instruction, the state's ability to respond to these demands, etc.

A state which only uses an official language in public education could be acting in a discriminatory way under Article 14 of the ECHR in combination with Article 2 of Protocol No. 1 of the ECHR if the disadvantage suffered by some individuals as compared to the advantage received by others is deemed arbitrary or disproportionate given the circumstances and in light of the objectives sought.

Many practitioners and lawyers have mistakenly interpreted one decision of the ECtHR, the Belgian Linguistic Case,[46] as the basis for concluding that an individual cannot use the argument of discrimination in the language imposed on public educational facilities by government.

This is in fact a false reading of the decision, since what the Court actually said was that, given the social and political context at the time in Belgium, the overall linguistic regime which included – generally – monolingual Dutch- (and French-) language territories for purposes of public schooling was not arbitrary, and therefore was not discriminatory.

This meant that had some aspects of the linguistic regime been arbitrary, even if it involved an official language, then it would have constituted discrimination under Article 14 applied to Article 2 of Protocol No. 1 of the ECHR. In essence, this is the same reasoning recently used by the UN HRC.[47]

Interestingly, in a rather unusual case, the ECtHR seemed to indicate that public education may automatically be required in a particular language, in "unusual circumstances", even if at first reading Article 2 of Protocol No. 1 of the ECHR is silent on any linguistic dimension to the right.

In Cyprus v. Turkey,[48] the linguistic policies of the northern Cyprus authorities in the area of public education were essentially described as so inadequate in view of the circumstances as to constitute a violation of the protocol, even if it involved the official language.

The Court noted that children of Greek-Cypriot parents in northern Cyprus wishing to pursue a secondary education through the medium of the Greek language were obliged to transfer to schools in the south, while other children, on reaching the age of 12, could continue their education at a Turkish- or English-language school in the north.

Until recently, most experts on "minority rights" had assumed that this would be the end of the matter, since it was assumed on the basis of the Belgian Linguistic Case that there was no entitlement to an education in a particular language under the ECHR. The Court, however, went further:

> 277. In the strict sense, accordingly, there is no denial of the right to education, which is the primary obligation devolving on a Contracting Party under the first sentence of Article 2 of Protocol No. 1 ... Moreover, this provision does not specify the language in which education must be conducted in order that the right to education be respected ...

> 278. However, in the Court's opinion, the option available to Greek-Cypriot parents to continue their children's education in the north is unrealistic in view of the fact that the children in question have already received their primary education in a Greek-Cypriot school there. The authorities must no doubt be aware that it is the wish of Greek-Cypriot parents that the schooling of their children be completed through the medium of the Greek language. Having assumed responsibility for the provision of Greek-language primary schooling, the failure of the "TRNC" authorities to make continuing provision for it at the secondary-school level must be considered in effect to be a denial of the substance of the right at issue. It cannot be maintained that the provision of secondary education in the south in keeping with the linguistic tradition of the enclaved Greek Cypriots suffices to fulfil the obligation laid down in Article 2 of Protocol No. 1, having regard to the impact of that option on family life (see paragraph 277 above and paragraph 292 below).

> 280. Having regard to the above considerations, the Court concludes that there has been a violation of Article 2 of Protocol No. 1 in respect of Greek Cypriots living in

northern Cyprus in so far as no appropriate secondary-school facilities were available to them.

Admittedly, the logic used by the Court is not at first glance very satisfying. It admits on the one hand that Article 2 of Protocol No. 1 is devoid of a linguistic component, but then says there is a linguistic component for secondary education because authorities in northern Cyprus had in place primary education in the Greek language, and therefore not to offer it after primary school "negated" the right to education.

What the latter has to do with the non-existent linguistic component of Article 2 of Protocol No. 1 is never made explicit. The overall result would have made much more sense if the Court had stated more clearly what it possibly had meant, in line with its previous reasoning in the Belgian Linguistic Case, that in light of the circumstances, the restrictions on public education in the Greek language in northern Cyprus were unreasonable and unjustified because they were so blatantly inappropriate, and therefore discriminatory.

It is probably in this way that the judgment should be properly understood: otherwise, it would mean that the authorities of northern Cyprus could avoid a violation of the ECHR by simply abolishing primary education in Greek: this is unlikely to be the direction the Court had in mind.

It should finally be emphasised that public education in a minority language must not exclude instruction of the official or majority language. Members of a minority must be able to learn the official language to a reasonable degree of fluency, since to do otherwise would entail the risk of excluding minorities from employment or educational opportunities, as well as isolating them from participation in society. If minority students were prevented from learning the official language, this could also be considered discrimination under the ECHR.

c. Judicial and administrative proceedings

Members of a minority could under a general prohibition of discrimination have the right to use their language with judicial and administrative officials where this is appropriate given the number of speakers in a territory.

The language used during proceedings also brings up the issue of "disadvantage" when it affects individuals who are not perfectly fluent in the language of proceedings. In some situations, because of the scale of this disadvantage, it could be discriminatory under ECHR Protocol No. 12 (when it enters into force) not to provide for some appropriate degree of use of the minority language in these proceedings. Once again, what this implies is the application of proportionality.

This means that courts must hold hearings and operate in a minority language where there is a sufficiently high percentage or number of individuals who are concentrated in a locality or region to make this use appropriate and justified.

In addition, every accused person has the right to an interpreter in criminal proceedings, including translation of court documents, if s/he does not understand the language used in the proceedings. Public authorities must therefore provide for this use of a minority language when an accused is a member of a linguistic minority who does not understand the language used by officials during the proceedings. This right is universally recognised in international law and laid down in Article 6 of the ECHR.

This right does not depend on "practical" considerations, such as number of speakers of minority language or their territorial concentration in a state. It exists once it has been shown that an accused does not understand the language of proceedings.

All persons also have the right to be informed of the reasons for their arrest and/or detention and of the nature and cause of any accusation against them in a language s/he understands. In the case of a person who is a member of a linguistic minority, public authorities must therefore use the minority language in order to comply with this right. The right does not depend on the number of speakers involved or their territorial concentration, just as with the right to an interpreter in criminal proceedings. The ECtHR has also established in its jurisprudence the extent of the right to be informed promptly of the nature and cause of a criminal accusation.[49]

d. Official use of names and topographical designations

If public authorities refused to use or recognise an individual's name or surname in a minority language, this could be a violation of the general prohibition of discrimination under ECHR Protocol No. 12 (when it enters into force). It could also be a violation of the right to a private life (Article 8) in combination with Article 14 of the ECHR.

As for the official use of a commune, village, or town name in a minority language, to refuse to use the minority language name for localities in areas where there is a substantial or traditional minority population could constitute discrimination under ECHR Protocol No. 12.

e. Public media and the use of minority languages

Minorities have the right to have their language used by public media to the degree that it is justified and reasonable in light of the number of speakers of a minority language in application of the proportionality principle. This involves all types of public media, whether public authorities are involved in public radio or television broadcasting, printed or electronic media

This right involves the application of the right to non-discrimination: if public authorities control, operate or finance any media, they must do so in a non-discriminatory fashion and, at the very least, reflect in the time and resources allocated to its public media activities the relative demographic importance of its linguistic minorities, approximately in proportion. This is once again the application of non-discrimination, which means that if a government fails to broadcast in a minority language in a roughly proportionate way, it could be a violation of ECHR Protocol No. 12 (when it enters into force).

f. Political activities, electoral process and minorities

Minorities have the right not to be excluded from running or holding political office at the local, regional or national level because of unjustified language or religious requirements. A law or any other government measure which excludes individuals from being candidates or from holding an elected position because they do not speak an official language or refuse to swear a religious oath would generally be an arbitrary or unjustified restriction and therefore a violation of non-discrimination.

In Buscarini and Others v. San Marino,[50] individuals who as atheists were members of a minority because of their beliefs were prevented from sitting as elected members of the General Grand Council (parliament) of the country unless they took an oath on the Holy Gospels. They claimed that this infringed on their freedom of religion as it required them to publicly profess a particular faith. The Court agreed, concluding that the oath in question meant that the individuals who were atheists had to take an oath which was a limitation to their freedom not to hold religious beliefs and not to practice a religion, as enshrined in Article 9, paragraph 2, of the ECHR, and that "requiring the applicants to take the oath on the Gospels was tantamount to requiring two elected representatives of the people to swear allegiance to a particular religion, a requirement which is not compatible with Article 9 of the Convention".[51]

The Court was not willing to go quite as far in the case of the requirement to take an oath in a region's official language in order to take up an elected position in Mathieu-Mohin and Clerfayt v. Belgium,[52] though in that case members of the French-speaking minority in different parts of the country had in place legislation that guaranteed the use of their language, and that voters had to:

> ... vote either for candidates who will take the parliamentary oath in French and will accordingly join the French-language group in the House of Representatives or the Senate and sit on the French Community Council, or else for candidates who will take the oath in Dutch and so belong to the Dutch-language group in the House of Representatives or the Senate and sit on the Flemish Council. This is not a disproportionate limitation such as would thwart "the free expression of the opinion of the people in the choice of the legislature".[53]

More recently however, the ECtHR seems to have tempered its approach in the Mathieu-Mohin case. In Podkolzina v. Latvia[54] the applicant was a member of the Russian-speaking minority whose name as a candidate for a general election was removed for insufficient knowledge of the Latvian language. Though the Court concluded there was a violation of the applicant's right for mainly procedural reasons (there was no guarantee of objectivity in a second examination which resulted in her removal in a way which was incompatible with the requirements of procedural fairness), it also recognised that while it is a legitimate aim to require sufficient knowledge of the official language for candidates for election to the national parliament, such linguistic preference must still be proportionate to the aim pursued to comply with the right to stand as a candidate in an election, as guaranteed by Article 3 of Protocol No. 1.

In other words, language requirements which would be disproportionate, even if they involve the legitimate aim to require sufficient knowledge of the official language for candidates to the national parliament, would breach "the free expression of the opinion of the people in the choice of the legislature".[55]

Another right of minorities connected to the electoral process and language is the right not to be excluded from the right to vote by an official language requirement. Denying a person's right to vote because of insufficient fluency in the official or other prescribed language would be an "unreasonable restriction" to the right to vote and also amount to discrimination as to language, since it excludes individuals who are only or mainly fluent in a minority language from the right to vote. This would be a breach of Article 14 in combination with Article 3 of Protocol No. 1, or of Protocol No. 12 of the ECHR.

Election materials, voting ballots, and other documents and information linked to the holding of elections by public authorities must also be provided in minority languages where it is justified and reasonable, that is, where there are sufficient or substantial numbers of speakers of a minority language. This would fall under Article 14 in combination with Article 3 of Protocol No. 1, or of Protocol No. 12 of the ECHR.

It is important to distinguish here that what this right deals with is not an individual's private conduct, but a "service" or "benefit" from public officials. This has been highlighted in a number of European decisions, where it was correctly shown that neither freedom of expression nor the limited non-discrimination provision of the ECHR, guarantees a right to use a minority language in official activities connected to the electoral process. For example, the ECtHR has indicated that there is no unqualified obligation for public authorities to accept the registration of a political party in a minority language.[56]

Finally, there is a right to use a minority language during the activities of elected governmental bodies (commune, municipality, local or regional legislative body, etc.) although this right is not one which arises in every situation, as the ECtHR has previously shown.

It depends on what is justified and proportionate in each particular case. There must be a substantial, significant or sufficient number of speakers of a minority language for individuals to be entitled to use of their language in the activities of elected bodies. For example, to prohibit or prevent the use of a minority language during sessions of a municipal council (either by an elected politician or a member of the public) would violate non-discrimination under ECHR Protocol No. 12 (when it enters into force) if a significant proportion of the population of this municipality are members of a linguistic minority.

Especially in view of the fundamental role and prominence of political activities in a democratic setting, it would seem that in international law and treaties of the Council of Europe, political institutions must be very generous and flexible in accommodating as far as possible the use of a minority language in order to respect the rights of minorities and ensure their effective participation in public affairs.

Some practical guidance

From a practical point of view, the judicial mechanism provided by the ECHR is the most legally powerful mechanism at the international level for protecting the rights of minorities. It resembles a domestic court proceeding in both its sophistication and in the equality it maintains between the parties involved.

Using the ECtHR's system may be effective in obtaining a judgment where individuals have been unable to have their rights respected in their country's national legal system.

It is in fact more concrete and direct than the supervision systems that exist under both the Framework Convention for the Protection of National Minorities and the European Charter for Regional or Minority Languages. While these two last systems do impose "obligations" on governments of states parties, they only involve committees of experts who help "supervise" the application of the treaties with periodic reports, and do not issue any decisions on individual cases, nor are their reports legally binding. On the scale of impact, the ECtHR system is among the strongest mechanisms available, whereas the supervision mechanisms for the other treaties dealing with minorities or their languages are at the weaker end.

The mechanism under the ECtHR would therefore be a much more effective mechanism to use in support of the rights of minorities. But in practical terms there are a number of problems. One of these difficulties is the issue of delay. Though the streamlined mechanism after 1998 has reduced some of the delays that previously existed, the Court has become a victim of its own success, with the number of cases submitted to it continuously increasing. Using the ECtHR may therefore involve a long process. For purely practical reasons, it would strategically probably be better to combine this judicial approach with other practical attempts to have the rights of minorities respected, such as using other treaties and bodies of the Council of Europe, and lobbying and other efforts in combination.

In this regard, one should also keep in mind that using the ECtHR system should never be considered as the only option, nor perhaps even the preferable one. There should always be attempts to negotiate with public authorities some amicable settlement of matters. Public authorities often operate under the mistaken belief that their conduct is in full compliance with rights under the ECHR and international human rights standards. Patient lobbying, discussion, exchange of information and even education of public officials may sometimes be just as effective – and certainly less antagonistic or expensive – as bringing a case before the ECtHR in a confrontational battle of legal arguments.

In practical terms, the significance of traditional human rights in areas involving religion, culture or language has still not been addressed widely in the case-law of the Court. This means that there are still many areas of application which have not been clarified by the Court in earlier decisions and where there may be some hesitancy or confusion. Before bringing a case before the Court, the legal arguments would have to be well researched and fully developed, and the facts of the case clear and strong.

For example, in a number of previous decisions involving language use by public officials,[57] minorities presented their case as one involving freedom of expression (it should rather have been based on a general non-discrimination clause such as Protocol No. 12). The ECtHR (and the European Commission in one case) rightfully rejected these cases, but in failing to properly base them on the appropriate legal standards contained in the ECHR, these cases have left a trail which has led many governments, practitioners, and others to believe that the private use of language is not necessarily protected under freedom of expression. It may also have led to the assumption that there are no rights under the ECHR that may affect the language preferences of government officials. It is only with a few recent decisions of the ECtHR that these two views are beginning to appear erroneous, though it hasn't yet been directly and unambiguously addressed by the Court.

Individuals who decide to proceed to court in order to have their rights respected by their government should make sure they follow the steps listed below:

– identify clearly the specific rights which may be involved under the ECHR.

– consult with minority organisations or other interested NGOs (non-governmental organisations) in determining whether the case is a strong one and does indeed raise the legal arguments that are claimed. Many of these have expertise or contacts which may be able to assist individuals.

– internal remedies must be exhausted. It is very likely that individuals will lose court cases in their own country, so they should always keep in mind that years may go by before the matter can finally be submitted to the ECtHR and settled.

Conclusions

"A country should be judged on how it treats its minorities." Mahatma Gandhi

Minority rights are human rights. An individual is no less deserving of protection and respect by public authorities for being a member of a religious, cultural or linguistic minority. Individuals who believe their rights are not being respected need to consider whether they have the resources and time to bring a case all the way to the ECtHR. It is also true that the Court has only recently begun to hand down many decisions clarifying the impact of human rights applications on the situations of minorities. Because of a number of uncertainties and even confusion as to the effects of human rights standards, one needs to proceed cautiously and be extremely well prepared to present arguments that demonstrate clearly how human rights standards such as freedom of expression, religion or association, non-discrimination, and others can be used to ensure the respect of the inherent dignity of minorities and reasonably accommodate their preferences.

While the use of this mechanism means that in most cases individuals may have to spend years going through their national judicial system before being able to seek a decision from the ECtHR, it may still be the best hope for a favourable decision in countries where minority rights are misunderstood or denied. It is also a much stronger mechanism than those involving limited supervisory functions by committees of experts under the Framework Convention for the Protection of National Minorities and the European Charter for Regional or Minority Languages. All in all, it is an option worth considering, especially when used with other strategies and efforts to ensure governments fully comply with their human rights obligations towards minorities.

* Senior Lecturer LL.B LL.M Dr. Jur., Human Rights and International Law, Murdoch University, Perth, Australia; Senior (Non-Resident) Research Associate at the European Centre for Minority Issues, Flensburg, Germany; 2004 Linguapax Laureate.

1. Adopted on 1 February 1995, entered into force on 1 February 1998, ETS No. 157.

2. Adopted on 5 November 1995, entered into force on 1 March 1998, ETS No. 158.

3. Framework Convention for the Protection of National Minorities – Explanatory Report, ETS No. 157, paragraph 11.

4. Dated 4 November 1950, ETS No. 5.

5. Information on the procedures at the European Court of Human Rights and its decisions can be found at http://www.ECHR.coe.int/

6. The Registrar, European Court of Human Rights, Council of Europe, F-67075 Strasbourg CEDEX, France.

7. Adopted on 16 December 1966, entered into force on 23 March 1976, 999 UNTS 171.

8. See in general, Fernand de Varennes, *A Guide to the Rights of Minorities and Language* (Budapest, 2001), also available at http://www.eumap.org/library/datab/Documents/1018259824.56/7colpi4.pdf

9. These include, among others, Article 9.1 of the FCNM and Article 2 of the United Nations Declaration on the Rights of Persons belonging to National or Ethnic, Religious and Linguistic Minorities (UNDM), adopted by the UN General Assembly on 18 December 1992, GA Res. 47/135.

10. On the large number of cases involving Turkey and restrictions of freedom of expression in relation to the existence or demands of the Kurdish minority, only two were found not to involve a breach of the ECHR, and in both the Court found that there was in the publications an incitement to violence. ECtHR, Sürek v. Turkey (No. 1), Application 26682/95, judgment of 8 July 1999, and Sürek v. Turkey (No. 3), Application 24735/94, judgment of 8 July 1999.

11. Judgment of 10 July 1998, paragraphs 43-47.

12. ECtHR, Stankov and the United Macedonian Organisation Ilinden v. Bulgaria, judgment of 2 October 2001, paragraph 97.

13. Judgment of 20 December 2001. This decision has been referred to the Grand Chamber.

14. ECtHR, Özgür Gündem v. Turkey, judgment of 16 March 2000; ECtHR, Ceylan v. Turkey, judgment of July 1999; Gerger v. Turkey, judgment of July 1999; Karatas v. Turkey, judgment of July 1999; Polat v. Turkey, judgment of July 1999; etc.

15. ECtHR, Anguelova v. Bulgaria, judgment of 6 June 2000, ECtHR, Cyprus v. Turkey, judgment of 10 May 2001 (Grand Chamber).

16. ECtHR, Noack v. Germany, judgment of 25 May 2000.

17. ECtHR, Podkolzina v. Latvia, judgment of 9 April 2002.

18. ECtHR, Stankov and the United Macedonian Organisation Ilinden v. Bulgaria, judgment of 2 October 2001.

19. ECtHR, Ekin v. France, judgment of 17 July 2001.

20. ECtHR, Muonio Saami Village v. Sweden, struck out of the list because of friendly settlement 9 January 2001.

21. ECtHR, Thlimmenos v. Greece, judgment of 6 April 2000.

22. ECtHR, Buscarini and Others v. San Marino, judgment of 18 February 1999.

23. ECtHR, Canea Catholic Church v. Greece, judgment of 16 December 1997.

24. ECtHR, Cha'are Shalom Ve Tsedek v. France, judgment of 27 June 2000; Canea Catholic Church v. Greece, judgment of 16 December 1997.

25. ECtHR, Serif v. Greece, judgment of 14 December 1999; ECtHR, Hasan and Chaush v. Bulgaria, judgment of 26 October 2000; ECtHR, Agga v. Greece (No. 2), judgment of 17 October 2002.

26. ECtHR, Metropolitan Church of Bessarabia and Others v. Moldova, judgment of 13 December 2001.

27. See ECtHR, Guillot v. France, judgment of 24 October 1996, and Stjerna v. Finland, judgment of 25 November 1994, Series A No. 299-B.

28. HRC Communications Nos. 359/1989 and 385/1989, Ballantyne, Davidson and McIntyre v. Canada, views of 31 March 1993.

29. ECtHR, judgment of 17 July 2001.

30. Ibid., paragraph 60.

31. Confirmed in international law by the Human Rights Committee in HRC, Comments on Dominican Republic, CCPR/C/79/Add.18, dated 5 May 1993, paragraph 7.

32. Raimo Pekkanen and Hans Danelius, "Human Rights in the Republic of Estonia" 13 *HRLJ* (1991), pp. 236-256, at p. 241, and HRC Communications Nos. 359/1989 and 385/1989, Ballantyne, Davidson and McIntyre v. Canada, views of 31 March 1993.

33. HRC Communications Nos. 359/1989 and 385/1989, Ballantyne, Davidson and McIntyre v. Canada, views of 31 March 1993.

34. ECtHR, judgment of 6 April 2000.

35. Ibid., paragraphs 47-48.

36. ECtHR, Stankov and the United Macedonian Organisation Ilinden v. Bulgaria, judgment of 2 October 2001, paragraph 87.

37. ECtHR, Hasan and Chaush v. Bulgaria, judgment of 26 October 2000.

38. ECtHR, judgment of 13 December 2001.

39. Ibid., paragraphs 129-130.

40. ECtHR, Yazar, Karataş, Aksoy and the People's Labour Party (HEP) v. Turkey, Chamber judgment of 9 April 2002.

41. ECtHR, Agga v. Greece (No. 2), judgment of 17 October 2002, paragraphs 59-61.

42. ECtHR, Canea Catholic Church v. Greece, judgment of 16 December 1997, paragraphs 44-47.

43. ECtHR, Jane Smith v. The United Kingdom, judgment of 18 January 2001; ECtHR, Chapman v. The United Kingdom, judgment of 18 January 2001; Beard v. The United Kingdom, judgment of 18 January 2001; Coster v. The United Kingdom, judgment of 18 January 2001; Lee v. The United Kingdom, judgment of 18 January 2001.

44. ECtHR, Chapman v. The United Kingdom, judgment of 18 January 2001, paragraph 73.

45. HRC, Communication No. 760/1997, Diergaardt v Namibia, views of 25 July 2000.

46. ECtHR, Cases Relating to Certain Aspects of the Laws on the Use of Languages in Education in Belgium, judgment of 23 July 1968, Series A, No. 6.

47. HRC, Communication No. 760/1997, Diergaardt v Namibia, views of 25 July 2000.

48. ECtHR, Cyprus v. Turkey, judgment of 10 May 2001 (Grand Chamber).

49. ECtHR, Brozicek v. Italy, judgment of 19 December 1989, Series A, No. 167.

50. ECtHR, Buscarini and Others v. San Marino, judgment of 18 February 1999.

51. Ibid., paragraph 39.

52. In the situation where elected politicians were prevented from taking up their office for refusing to take a parliamentary oath in Dutch in ECtHR, Mathieu-Mohin and Clerfayt v. Belgium, judgment of 2 March 1987, Series A, No. 113, at 25, the European Court of Human Rights essentially concluded that such a linguistic requirement affecting the principles embodied in Article 3 ECHR Protocol No. 1 could not be deemed to be unreasonable, and therefore discriminatory, under Article 14:

> The aim is to defuse the language disputes in the country by establishing more stable and decentralised organisational structures ... In any consideration of the electoral system in issue, its general context must not be forgotten. The system does

not appear unreasonable if regard is had to the intentions it reflects and to the respondent state's margin of appreciation within the Belgian parliamentary system – a margin that is all the greater as the system is incomplete and provisional.

53. Ibid., paragraph 57.

54. Judgment of 9 April 2002.

55. Ibid., paragraph 33.

56. ECommHR, Fryske Nasjonale Partij v. Netherlands, (1986) 45 Decisions and Reports 240, at p. 243.

57. ECommHR, X. v. Ireland, 13 *Yearbook of the European Convention on Human Rights* (1970) p. 792 ECtHR; ECommHR, Inhabitants of Leeuw-St. Pierre v. Belgium, 8 *Yearbook of the European Convention on Human Rights* (1965) p. 338; ECommHR, Fryske Nasjonale Partij v. Netherlands, 45 Decisions and Reports (1986) p. 240.

THE FRAMEWORK CONVENTION FOR THE PROTECTION OF NATIONAL MINORITIES (FCNM)

Alan Phillips*

Introduction

This chapter, like the Framework Convention for the Protection of National Minorities (FCNM) itself, is a dynamic document that can be used in a variety of ways to protect and promote the rights of minorities. The convention contains programme-type provisions, setting objectives, giving states a measure of discretion on the implementation thereby enabling them to take specific circumstances into account. Similarly the advice that follows is not prescriptive, it is descriptive, showing opportunities for advocacy programmes, and suggesting a variety of opportunities for the implementation of the FCNM depending on local circumstances.

This chapter begins with a description of the FCNM, though it is recognised that international standards are not frozen in time and develop as they are used and interpreted in practice. This is followed by a section on achievements, where possible outputs and outcomes are described, even though it is often the case that processes, for example, the building of good will and trust, are as important as specific results. Consequently, the new relationships that the FCNM has helped flourish are a distinct and unique achievement. The third main section concerns practitioners and the FCNM, as the convention is of little value unless it is owned, used and celebrated by national minorities and the wider society.

Description of the FCNM

The Framework Convention for the Protection of National Minorities, which entered into force on 1 February 1998, is the first ever legally binding multilateral instrument devoted to the protection of national minorities. It is one of the most comprehensive treaties designed to protect the rights of persons belonging to national minorities. Parties to this convention undertake to promote the full and effective equality of persons belonging to minorities in all areas of economic, social, political and cultural life together with the conditions that will allow them to express, preserve and develop their culture and identity.[1]

Framework

The word "framework" highlights the scope for states to translate this convention's provisions to their situation in a specific country through national legislation and appropriate governmental policies. Nevertheless this in no way detracts from its legally binding character, but it does allow for the incremental development of policies and programmes over time recognising that the FCNM shall be applied in good faith, and in a spirit of understanding and tolerance.[2]

The FCNM clearly shows the objectives of those who drafted the instrument and why the application of good faith is needed.[3] It states that the protection of national minorities is essential to stability, democratic security and peace on this continent.

It continues by assuming that there will be a pluralist and democratic society creating appropriate conditions enabling national minorities to express, preserve and develop their identity.

This is followed by two considerations. Firstly, the creation of a climate of tolerance and dialogue is necessary to enable cultural diversity to be a source and a factor, not of division, but of enrichment of each society. Secondly, the realisation of a tolerant and prosperous Europe depends on co-operation between states but also requires transfrontier co-operation between local and regional authorities.

In 1992, the Council of Europe (CoE) decided to examine the possibility of agreeing legal standards for the protection of national minorities with options including a European convention for the protection of national minorities and an additional protocol to the European Convention on Human Rights (ECHR).[4]

At the First Summit of Heads of State and Government of the Council of Europe in October 1993 it was agreed that a framework convention should be drawn up in preference to an additional protocol to the ECHR. The approach led to mainly programme-type provisions setting out objectives for states to pursue but which would not be directly applicable. Consequently the FCNM does not allow for the possibility of individual petitions and findings on individual cases.

Protection offered by the FCNM

The provisions of the FCNM[5] cover a wide range of issues, including, *inter alia*:

— non-discrimination;
— promotion of effective equality;
— promotion of conditions favouring the preservation and development of culture, religion, language and traditions;
— freedom of assembly, association, expression, thought, conscience and religion;
— access to and use of media;
— linguistic freedoms;
— use of the minority language in private and in public as well as its use before administrative authorities;
— use of one's own name in the minority language;
— display of information of a private nature in the minority language;
— topographical names in the minority language;
— education;

- learning of and instruction in the minority language;
- freedom to set up educational institutions;
- transfrontier contacts;
- international and transfrontier co-operation;
- participation in economic, cultural and social life;
- participation in public life;
- prohibition of forced assimilation.

States ratifying the FCNM[6]

It is the responsibility of all states that ratify the FCNM to ensure that the provisions of the FCNM are in force in their country. Any state that ratifies the FCNM does so completely of its own volition both in recognition of the importance of this norm within their own state and within the Council of Europe.

The importance of the FCNM is widely recognised today and its geographic scope has expanded rapidly. By April 2003, it had been ratified by the following 35 states: Albania, Armenia, Austria, Azerbaijan, Bosnia and Herzegovina, Bulgaria, Croatia, Cyprus, Czech Republic, Denmark, Estonia, Finland, Germany, Hungary, Ireland, Italy, Liechtenstein, Lithuania, Malta, Moldova, Norway, Poland, Portugal, Romania, Russia, San Marino, Slovakia, Slovenia, Spain, Sweden, Switzerland, "the former Yugoslav Republic of Macedonia", Ukraine, the United Kingdom, as well as Serbia and Montenegro.

A further seven states have signed but not ratified the convention: Belgium, Georgia, Greece, Iceland, Latvia, Luxembourg, and the Netherlands.

National minorities

The FCNM does not contain a definition of the concept of national minority, as there is no general definition agreed upon by all Council of Europe member states. Each party to the convention is therefore left room to assess which groups of persons are to be covered by the convention within their territory. This selection must, however, be made in good faith and in accordance with general principles of international law and the fundamental principles set out in Article 3 of the FCNM.

In its opinions, the Advisory Committee on the Framework Convention (ACFC) examines this issue. It consistently emphasises that the implementation of the Framework Convention should not be a source of arbitrary or unjustified distinctions.[7]

For the ACFC, the FCNM is not an "all-or-nothing" instrument. The ACFC has therefore adopted an article-by-article approach to the question of the groups covered by the FCNM, recognising that some of its articles have a larger scope to include a wide range of groups than others.

For example, Article 6, paragraph 1, states:

> Parties shall encourage a spirit of tolerance and intercultural dialogue and take effective measures to promote mutual respect and understanding and co-operation among all persons living on their territory, irrespective of those persons' ethnic, cul-

tural, linguistic or religious identity, in particular in the fields of education, culture and the media.

Article 6, paragraph 1, thus lends itself to including within its scope a broader range of groups, while Article 10, paragraph 2, which concerns the use of language in relations with public authorities has much more limited application and is circumscribed with many caveats:

> In areas inhabited by persons belonging to national minorities traditionally or in substantial numbers, if those persons so request and where such a request corresponds to a real need, the Parties shall endeavour to ensure, as far as possible, the conditions which would make it possible to use the minority language in relations between those persons and the administrative authorities.

Certain groups of persons may therefore benefit from some articles, but not necessarily all.

Individuals are free to decide whether or not they wish to be treated as belonging to a national minority. This does not mean that each person can arbitrarily choose to belong to any national minority (see Article 3, paragraph 1). An individual's choice must be based on objective criteria connected with that person's identity, such as language, religion and culture, that are specified in Article 5, paragraph 1, while states must interpret this convention in good faith (see Article 2).

Monitoring state compliance with the FCNM

The Committee of Ministers, composed of ministers of foreign affairs, usually represented by ambassadors as their deputies, and the ACFC, composed of 18 independent experts nominated by states, are both involved in the monitoring of the FCNM. They evaluate the adequacy of the measures taken by states that have ratified the FCNM to give effect to the principles set out in it.[8]

The monitoring procedure requires each state to submit a first report within one year of entry into force of the convention and additional reports every five subsequent years, or upon a specific request of the Committee of Ministers. Where it requires specific additional information, the ACFC also sends states written questionnaires.[9]

The style of these state reports differs in the first and second round of reporting, as the ACFC takes advantage of the information and the views formed in the first round of reporting. The first round of reporting demands a comprehensive set of data on the situation within a state, its policies, programmes, constitution and legislation as well as a report on each relevant article of the convention. In the second round of reporting states must provide information under three main headings:[10]

- practical arrangements made at a national level for following up the results of the first monitoring cycle on the implementation of the FCNM;
- measures taken to improve the implementation of the FCNM in response to the resolution adopted by the Committee of Ministers in respect to a specific country;
- specific questions to each state party to the FCNM.

The drafting of state reports often involves a process of consultation with minority and non-governmental organisations, which are also encouraged to submit alternative reports or information.[11] The ACFC was empowered to seek information from a variety of sources including international organisations, ombudsmen, national institutions for the promotion and protection of human rights, as well as from civil society and non-governmental organisations. This would of course also include members of national minorities.

These reports are examined by the ACFC, which makes use of a wide variety of written sources of information from state and non-state actors. The ACFC has also developed the practice of carrying out country visits where it meets with government officials, parliamentarians, representatives of minorities, NGOs, specialised bodies and other relevant interlocutors.[12] During the author's term in the Advisory Committee every country has offered an invitation when the ACFC has indicated that it would welcome a visit. They usually last four days and often include a specific visit to an area where a minority community is concentrated. (The stages of monitoring and the opportunities for civil society organisations and others to make a contribution are shown in the brochure on the FCNM.)[13]

Opinions, comments and resolutions

Following its examination of a state's report, the ACFC adopts an opinion that is transmitted to the state concerned, which has an opportunity to make a comment on this opinion. These opinions on the implementation of the FCNM include some general remarks, an article-by-article evaluation of Articles 1 to 19, main findings and a set of concluding remarks. Their length varies but is often 20 to 30 pages of typed script.[14] The comments made by states vary considerably and may include annexes with information on recent developments.

It is open to states to make public the ACFC's opinion at this stage – a possibility a number of states have taken up – or when they first receive the opinion. In preparing their comment,[15] some states parties have also chosen to benefit from further consultations with minority and non-governmental organisations.

The Committee of Ministers considers the opinion and the comments and adopts a resolution containing conclusions and recommendations to the state on the implementation of the FCNM.[16] This resolution is made public together with the comments by the state party and the ACFC opinion, if the latter has not been made public at an earlier stage.

Follow-up action

The resolutions adopted by the Committee of Ministers have followed a common format. Section 1 adopts conclusions concerning the implementation of the FCNM by the state concerned.

It is followed by a recommendation in Section 2 that the state take appropriate account of the conclusions set out in Section 1 together with the various comments in the ACFC's opinion.

It continues in Section 3 by inviting the governmênt, in accordance with Resolution (97) 10:[17]

> ... to continue the dialogue in progress with the ACFC; to keep the ACFC regularly informed of the measures it has taken in response to the conclusions and recommendations set out in sections 1 and 2. Once again this can be seen on the Council of Europe minorities web page for every State.

A wide range of actors are encouraged by the Council of Europe to undertake ongoing follow-up activities in order to promote effective implementation. In a number of countries there have been follow-up meetings to consider the resolution of the Committee of Ministers involving a one-day meeting with ministers, government officials, national minorities, civil society and the ACFC. Furthermore, monitoring the effective follow-up of previous resolutions will be an important aspect of the second round of reporting and monitoring.

Achievements of the FCNM

Ratifications

The Council of Europe (CoE), with its high reputation for human rights conventions, has achieved a considerable success with the FCNM. In less than five years, 35 of its 45 member states have ratified the convention. Since 1995 all CoE applicant states have been obliged to ratify the FCNM, while the EU considers states implementation of the FCNM as an important factor in its accession criteria on minority rights. The EU stipulated that "[a]ccession will take place as soon as an applicant is able to assume the obligations of membership by satisfying the economic and political conditions required".[18] At the same time, the member states designed the membership criteria, which are often referred to as the Copenhagen Criteria. As stated in Copenhagen, membership requires that the candidate country has achieved:

- stability of institutions guaranteeing democracy, the rule of law, human rights and respect for and protection of minorities;
- the existence of a functioning market economy as well as the capacity to cope with competitive pressure and market forces within the Union;
- the ability to take on the obligations of membership including adherence to the aims of political, economic and monetary union.19

Additionally, some states have ratified the convention, but have failed to make this widely known domestically. However, Belgium, France, Greece, Luxembourg and the Netherlands have not ratified the convention, while some countries such as Germany and particularly Denmark have done so, while entering declarations attempting to limit the potential beneficiaries. The prospect of the FCNM being accepted as part of EU law, or *acquis communautaire* is far away.

These double standards have been justified by a narrow interpretation of the purposes of the convention; they emerge from a failure of some EU states to use the FCNM to celebrate pluralism and to promote the culture of those communities that have lived in these particular states' territory for several decades. With good will in all states, it would be possible to implement key elements of the convention de facto before legislative changes take place, as the protection offered is largely through policies and programmes.

State reporting and comments

The state reports so far submitted did largely follow the proposed structure but were mixed in their breadth and depth. Most concentrated on the first two categories – narrative and legal – with some limited reflections on state infrastructure and policy, but there was usually insufficient evidence of the factual situation. States were invited to highlight measures, practices and policies, which they considered to have worked particularly well, but such value judgments were rare. Similarly, states were invited to indicate issues on which they would particularly welcome the support and the advice of the ACFC. In most cases this did not happen. However, the Czech Republic's report was a commendable exception. More positively, many states did indicate the measures they had taken to promote awareness among the public and the relevant authorities about the convention. Although the procedures do not specify this, most states consulted a range of minority groups before submitting their report, and this was encouraged informally as a model of good practice. Nevertheless, some minorities are unaware of the FCNM. The Slovak Government suggested that its report was also the work of civil society organisations, but the ACFC rejected this suggestion. In Romania, the Constitutional Court made a judgment, being unaware that Romania had ratified the FCNM, and denied its applicability, while other ministries, including their Office of National Minorities, had not been consulted in the drawing up of the report.[20] A significant number of governments have convened conferences to discuss the convention and to engage minorities in the preparation of the state report, and have reflected the views expressed by minorities. It is important that this becomes custom and practice in the next round of reporting, and that there is widespread involvement of minorities throughout the state. States are invited to comment on the ACFC opinions within four months of the opinion being distributed to the Committee of Ministers. Almost all states have provided such comments, and their substance and tone have varied considerably. Most address the key issues but other interesting aspects have emerged. The comments on some occasions have emphasised new measures adopted since the ACFC made its findings; these have included new legislation and new strategies (for instance Croatia and Hungary). A few pointed to areas where it was suggested that the opinion was, in part, inaccurate (for instance Slovakia), and some have sought to rebut criticism by implying that other international monitoring bodies had accepted their behaviour (for instance Estonia). Most have been complimentary about the ACFC work (for instance Italy), although the Danish Government reacted negatively to the opinion. The Finnish and the Hungarian comments, two of the first states to provide a comment, were significantly more helpful in promoting the FCNM and minority protection than those of Denmark and Slovakia. The constructive approach of Finland, which also published its opinion and comments early, has set the scene for the future.

States' comments have gradually become more constructive and accepting of the opinions, and many states have agreed to publish opinions and comments early. In the next set of opinions on Croatia, Cyprus, the Czech Republic and Romania some serious outstanding issues were identified and the response of the states has been constructive. Civil society has an important role to play in following the outcome of the monitoring, and continuing the dialogue and debate domestically and internationally.

Many states agree to the publication of opinions, once they have submitted the state comments on the opinions. This has been a valuable innovation, avoiding the delay before the adoption of a resolution by the CoM. The Minority Rights Group (MRG) argues that all states should be pressed to follow this good practice and should consider going one step further by agreeing to the publication of the opinion once it is received by the CoM, its 46 ambassadors and the observers to the CoM. The MRG points out that this could ensure that opinions would become available some seven months earlier than at present.[21]

Visits to states

The custom and practice has gradually developed of states parties inviting the ACFC to visit. Although this was not referred to in CoM Resolution (97) 10,[22] via the ACFC openness to invitations alongside lobbying by NGOs, every state to date has invited the ACFC when a visit has been thought to be valuable. These visits have become central in monitoring the FCNM and have transformed the methodology into a process of engagement of government and civil society, including national minorities. During the visits a range of meetings are held with many actors, particularly governments and minority organisations. This methodology has been warmly welcomed by all parties and has played a significant part in confidence-building.

At its meeting in February 2002 the ACFC considered an evaluation paper prepared by the author and concluded that country visits had become one of the most valuable parts of monitoring the implementation of the FCNM. Visits have helped to ensure that the convention and its implementation could become a process that is used and owned locally. The visits, including visits to minority areas, have not only opened up many new sources of information and understanding, but have led to a much deeper appreciation of the situation of national minorities and provided a framework for dialogue on contentious issues. It is argued by the MRG that no other human rights treaty monitoring body has enjoyed such discussions and meetings with governments and civil society.[23]

ACFC opinions

The opinions on the implementation of the operative articles of the FCNM are described above. The language is carefully chosen with a commentary on the implementation of each appropriate article of the FCNM. Good practice is recognised and welcomed while the ACFC does not fail to criticise, where necessary, its heaviest criticism being to stipulate that an activity is not compatible with the FCNM. This paper does not seek to make a judgment on those opinions, although initial surveys indicate that all the key issues raised by more than one reliable NGO have been examined and referred to in the opinions. The ACFC has been careful to adopt the same standards of scrutiny in all countries, although its opinions will naturally vary, reflecting different situations across states. The ACFC votes on each opinion, with a majority of members needing to be present and voting for it to be adopted. In practice, opinions are often adopted unanimously.

The independent expert nominated by the state concerned, whether a member of the ACFC or not, only takes part in the final discussion on the opinion, where misunderstandings can be corrected. However it is deliberate that these experts do not play an important part in formulating the opinion and they are excluded from voting on their own state.

In the future, it will be important to look at thematic issues and develop a commentary on each article of the FCNM[24] to help guide states and minorities on good practice. This could take a similar course to the approach adopted in the General Recommendations of the UN Committee on the Elimination of Racial Discrimination[25] and could be assisted by scholarly papers.

Comments made by states

Every state has been asked to provide their comment on the opinion of the ACFC, within four months of the opinion being made available to them and other member states of the Council of Europe. These are eventually made public together with the opinion and are not available to national minorities of the state concerned or to the wider public. In general, state comments have been provided on time and have usually been constructive, often highlighting recent developments and offering additional data.

To date, they have not contested the main findings of the ACFC, but sometimes sought either to add to the interpretation or to reduce the strength of criticism.[26]

The Committee of Ministers' Deputies and their resolutions

At the outset, considerable concern was expressed by some academics over the role the CoM would play in the implementation of the FCNM, as the CoM is a political body composed of foreign ministers (normally represented by ambassadors as their deputies) from each of the member states, often taking instructions from governments. The CoM has the power under the convention to control and politicise the monitoring process and restrict the independent role of the ACFC.[27]

In general, a constructive, trusting relationship has developed between the ACFC and the CoM. This can be seen by the way the CoM has endorsed, without amendment, the ACFC proposals on:

— rules of procedure of the Advisory Committee;
— outline for state reports both in the first and second round of reporting;
— information from sources other than the state concerned;
— mandate for the ACFC to hold meetings;
— role of additional members;
— non-referral of issues to the European Court of Human Rights.

The CoM initiated its own resolutions on:

— written comments by states on ACFC opinions;
— early publication of opinions;
— involving the ACFC in the follow-up to opinions;
— invitations to the ACFC to observe meetings of the CoM and the Rapporteur Group on Human Rights (GR-H), when FCNM opinions, comments and resolutions are discussed.

These followed consultation with the ACFC and its secretariat and have met with satisfaction in the ACFC bureau (composed of the president and two vice-presidents). This success story has been achieved by good co-ordination within the FCNM secretariat and by the ACFC bureau cultivating good relationships with ambassadors at the CoM and with the chair of the GR-H. Confidence has been built on both sides, which has enabled the system to cope with individual states that objected to the opinions. Additionally, some states, particularly Finland, have set good precedents on inviting the ACFC to visit, and publishing opinions early; this has encouraged other states to adopt similar approaches so that it is becoming customary and practice. It will be important that this good practice continues.

While the first four opinions were being considered, the CoM recognised how complex and controversial it would be to reopen substantial debate on the monitoring. Consequently, it delegated discussion to the GR-H that invited the ACFC bureau to introduce opinions, and states to comment. Both the ACFC and CoM appear happy with this mechanism. Nevertheless, this mechanism is open to criticism by civil society as it lacks transparency.[28]

Differences in interpretation

When the rules of procedure were adopted by the CoM, there was considerable concern that the ACFC and the CoM would take fundamentally different approaches. Some five years after these debates, it is interesting to examine if this is the case, and compare the operative paragraphs in the CoM resolutions with the ACFC concluding remarks.[29] The style of language and the format of the concluding remarks in the opinions and the resolutions of the CoM differ, the resolutions drawing on the substance of the opinions but expressed in modified language. Consequently, a direct comparison is made more difficult and a close examination is needed to see if issues are obscured or excluded. Many of the resolutions faithfully reflect the key issues included in the concluding remarks of the opinions – notably for Cyprus, Denmark, Finland, Liechtenstein, Malta and San Marino. However, the resolutions on

Croatia, the Czech Republic, Hungary and Slovakia have one and sometimes two notable omissions from the concluding remarks in the opinions. These came about through a desire to accommodate representations from the state and a desire to reach a consensus.

These changes do not alter the main sentiment of the concluding remarks, but may represent a disturbing trend. However, the CoM resolutions always make a specific reference to the ACFC opinion.[30] Consequently, the fact that the whole opinion is published and a constructive reference is made to it in the CoM resolution is crucial. Civil society can monitor developments to ensure that states do not delay resolutions and do not seek to dilute criticisms. This dilution is easy to identify by examining the timing and content of opinions and resolutions. It will be important for civil society to publicise any dilution of the ACFC opinion, and lobby domestically and internationally on the excluded issues. Civil society can press the CoM to be more transparent, and to allow representatives of relevant Parliamentary Assembly committees and accredited NGO observers to listen to the debate at the GR-H on the ACFC opinions and disseminate their written comments.

Following up specific country issues

It is beyond the scope of this paper to analyse the issues that have emerged in more than 20 opinions that have been formed. The ACFC has sought to encourage local mechanisms for taking the issues forward, recommending the establishment of follow-up meetings.

In the second round of reporting it has asked states[31] to identify:

– practical arrangements made at a national level for following up the results of the first round of the monitoring cycle on the implementation of the FCNM;
– measures taken to improve the implementation of the FCNM in response to the resolution adopted by the Committee of Ministers in respect of their country; and
– specific questions to each state party to the FCNM.

Challenges of obtaining good programme data

Where data was provided in reports[32] by states on their implementation of the FCNM it was rarely disaggregated by age, gender or location; economic data on employment or access to land was weak, both at the macro and micro level, while there were few qualitative assessments of the data that was provided. This was notable in the area of unemployment, where some minorities identified much higher levels of unemployment in their communities than in society as a whole and made representations on the need for the government to address this issue. This indicates that a new approach will be needed to data collection, analysis and policy implications in the next round of monitoring.

In recent opinions the ACFC has recommended that governments should seek means of obtaining more reliable statistics on national minorities. If, in view of the historical context and the particularly sensitive nature of this information for persons belonging to national minorities, exhaustive statistical data pertaining to national minorities cannot be collected, it suggests that other methods should be used, with the co-operation of the national minorities, such as estimates based on ad hoc studies, special surveys, polls or any other scientifically sound method. This data should be broken down by age, gender and location.[33]

At an EU sponsored conference convened by the German organisation Inwent on Statistics and Human Rights on 27 to 29 November 2002 a set of proposals were made that are relevant to the monitoring of human rights instruments:[34] civil society should enter into dialogue with NGOs and governments to encourage them to collect relevant economic, social and cultural data on vulnerable groups in an appropriate manner; civil society should be encouraged and supported by governments and donors to undertake quantitative and qualitative studies that may be used to develop new policies and programmes for women, children, minorities, disabled and other groups.

Progress can be made by giving more attention to analysing existing data from the rights perspective rather than exclusively developing new ways of collecting data.

Processes of engagement

If international law is to be effectively implemented, like domestic law, it needs both political and moral support for its values and it needs knowledge of its substance. Mechanisms of monitoring are important but they need to be supported by a genuine commitment to make them work. Much international human rights law fails as it is treated as something that states wish to be seen to support in international fora, but may not be so enthusiastic about domestically, as it may be seen as an external imposition and not necessary to implement effectively. Monitoring can be seen as a nuisance or even a threat to both politicians and officials, as they see their actions criticised.

Work has been done by NGOs to address this dilemma and to encourage a constructive and inclusive ownership of the convention. However, more initiatives are needed.

It has been a considerable achievement that all states to date have invited the ACFC to pay a visit when this was thought necessary by the ACFC. Furthermore, in many cases there was a continuing dialogue between governments and members of national minorities around the implementation of the convention. On most occasions it happened at the stage of preparing the state reports, as recommended by the ACFC, and continued throughout the monitoring process including during in-country follow-up meetings after the opinion, comment and resolution had been published.

Although there is a need to improve transparency in the discussions of the Committee of Ministers and to make opinions available immediately after their adoption, the information provided on the CoE minorities' webpages is comprehensive and available in English and French.

Examples of positive action following ACFC opinions

It is often difficult to show that the ACFC opinions have led to specific outcomes and to be confident that these would not have happened without the opinions of the ACFC and resolutions of the Committee of Ministers. However the following outcomes were proposed by the ACFC and implemented by states:[35]

- as a step towards addressing the concerns of Roma/Gypsies in a more comprehensive manner, the Croatian authorities are designing a new strategy on the protection of Roma/Gypsies;
- the Croatian government has adopted a new Constitutional Law on National Minorities;
- in order to better protect minorities, the Czech Republic has adopted a law on national minorities;
- in order to eliminate the legal impossibility for a Greek and Turkish Cypriot to conclude a civil marriage in Cyprus, the Cypriot authorities decided to draft a law granting all persons this legal right irrespective of their race or religion;
- in order to bring legislation concerning the use of language into line with European standards, Estonia has amended the language proficiency requirements for electoral candidates;
- in order to improve norms and practices pertaining, *inter alia*, to the use of the Swedish language, a new language law is being developed in Finland;
- as a step towards addressing the problem of the over-representation of Roma/Gypsies in "schools with special curricula", Hungary has adopted a decree guaranteeing that pupils, including Roma/Gypsies, are placed in such institutions only in justifiable cases, on the basis of an aptitude test at the request and with the consent of the parents;
- in order to better reflect ethnic diversity in history teaching, Romania has started to review the curricula and examine the possibility of producing new textbooks;
- in order to strengthen their efforts aimed at protecting Roma/Gypsies, the Slovak authorities are reinforcing the office of the government's Plenipotentiary for Roma/Gypsy Communities;
- in order to strengthen the legislative framework to protect persons who may be subject to threats or acts of discrimination, hostility or violence, the United Kingdom has strengthened provisions concerning incitement to racial hatred and provided cover for religiously aggravated offences.

Practitioners and the FCNM

Minority rights practitioners

There are a range of ways that minority rights practitioners can engage themselves to help forward the effective implementation of the FCNM. At the outset, civil society, including national minorities, can encourage a government to sign and then ratify the FCNM without any declarations or reservations. They can work with the government or separately to promote knowledge and understanding of the convention to facilitate its effective implementation. This may involve a wide range of actors (see the brochure on the FCNM). They can participate in helping to realise projects and programmes to implement the policies adopted to support the FCNM and help with training and advice on the implementation of relevant domestic legislation.

The report demanded of states is complex and many governments want information and advice from civil society on the situation of national minorities before the government submits its report. Governments can also encourage a dialogue with national minorities to help understand their perceptions and to advance further action. Furthermore, the CoE has made it clear that it wishes to encourage information from a wide variety of sources when it evaluates how effectively the FCNM has been implemented by a state. Minority rights practitioners can submit evidence to the ACFC at the time of the state report or take the opportunity to produce their own shadow report on the implementation of the various articles of the FCNM.[36]

Once again practitioners including minorities and civil society organisations can have face to face conversations with the ACFC during its visit, help explain issues *sur place*, and help organise visits to minority communities. Once the opinion is available they may encourage early publication of the opinion and of the comment and hold meetings with government officials to help implement some of the recommendations emerging from the CoE resolution. These may be private meetings or public ones with the CoE as part of the follow-up process. Thereafter, practitioners can help by continuing to keep the government and the CoE informed on how far the CoE resolution has been implemented.

One of the most important aspects of the FCNM has been the way that civil society organisations have used the convention. International NGOs, working with local partners, have played a major role in publicising and promoting the convention internationally. A number of local NGOs have used the FCNM to promote minority rights in their countries. This has included:

- lobbying for FCNM ratification;
- local and Europe-wide training workshops on the convention;
- translation of the convention;
- publication of a training manual in many languages;
- organisation of local workshops and conferences to publicise the convention;
- supporting projects locally to submit alternative reports to the ACFC;
- encouraging specialist NGOs to present evidence on topics to the ACFC;
- meeting the ACFC and helping set the agenda during visits;
- providing extra data identified as important by the ACFC;
- lobbying governments to publish opinions and comments early;
- attending follow-up meetings to help implement the findings; and
- organising working groups to promote the findings of opinions locally.

There have been both individual initiatives and collective approaches by a wide variety of NGOs in many countries of Europe. However, funding is essential for this independent, participative work to continue. The EU, the CoE and some other donors have been supportive, yet much more work is needed to transform the analysis into action and much of this support is ending. Continuing resources are needed for local and international NGO practitioners, with an emphasis on the effective participation of minorities in such programmes.

Academics have played their part in offering reviews and criticisms of the convention and can continue to help by reviewing the opinions for consistency, and for the way they have taken forward international law and its application.

ACFC accessibility

The ACFC meets in camera although for specific general items it may invite outside experts to present papers to help stimulate a well-informed debate on complex issues such as the declarations and improvements in the reporting procedures.

During visits of its working groups to states as part of the monitoring cycle, it usually spends one day early on meeting minority groups and civil society groups individually and collectively, without the presence of any government officials. It also makes a point of meeting key parliamentary groups and state institutions such as ombudspersons.

The ACFC has taken part in training and information sessions organised by the CoE and by civil society organisations both in Strasbourg and locally.

At an early stage it was agreed to add to the rules of procedure[37] the authority of the ACFC to seek information from a wide range of sources and ensure through custom and practice that visits were paid to each appropriate state.

The minutes of the ACFC are published within a year of the meetings; this constraint is needed to retain confidentiality while the Committee of Ministers deliberates. However, there has been no desire to establish open meetings, as there is the danger that attendance at such meetings would be dominated by those based in Strasbourg, and the ACFC's deliberations and debate might be influenced by a skewed audience.

However, a strong case can be made that when the opinion and state comment are presented to the Committee of Ministers through its sub-committee, the GR-H, chairs of the relevant parliamentary committees and members of national minorities should be present as observers. This remains to be debated by those parties.

Training programmes

A range of training programmes have been organised by various organisations within states, in regions and internationally. Since 1998, the Minority Rights Group International (MRG) with the support of the Council of Europe has organised a major four-day training event in Strasbourg each year for 25 to 30 members of civil society organisations and many of the participants are members of minority communities. The MRG also organises an annual regional training event in Budapest on minority rights instruments and mechanisms with a similar audience, in which the FCNM plays a prominent role. In addition, there have been similar in-country training events.

The CoE also organises annual meetings of government offices on minorities and once again the FCNM is given an important place. The CoE also holds in-country seminars with host governments helping to promote the FCNM and helping to follow up the resolutions of the Committee of Ministers.

Early on, a number of Helsinki Committees were very active in a project co-ordinated by the Greek Helsinki Monitor in providing training and going on to produce a set of "shadow reports" on states' implementation of the FCNM for the ACFC.

The Danish Institute for Human Rights, through its Balkan Human Rights Network has held training seminars on the FCNM. Last, but by no means least, the European Centre for Minority Issues (ECMI) has embarked on a comprehensive programme of research, analysis, discussion and publications on the FCNM.

Links to CoE programmes

The secretariat of the FCNM promotes the objectives of the FCNM through a wide range of bilateral and multilateral co-operation activities that aim to:
- prepare states for ratifying the FCNM and submitting reports;
- ensure compatibility of legislation;
- assist in the implementation of the FCNM's provisions;
- contribute to dialogue and raise awareness about minority issues.

These activities take a wide variety of forms, such as workshops, seminars, legal and policy expertise, publications and study visits, and involve an array of actors from both the governmental and non-governmental sectors. Furthermore, a special meeting of government offices in the field of national minorities is organised regularly in order to provide a forum for countries to share information and experiences.

The Stability Pact for South Eastern Europe has also made possible a signifi-cant number of additional activities furthering the goals of the FCNM in countries covered by this pact. One example is a "non-discrimination review" project in which locally based expert groups are carrying out an extensive analysis of problems of discrimination and of the legislative framework aimed at combating such problems, as well as suggesting and developing effective responses and measures to promote full and effective equality. Another example is a Council of Europe project promoting a review and development of bilateral agreements as a mechanism to protect minorities.

Monitoring cycle crisis

The first twelve opinions, comments and resolutions took on average 31 months to produce. The ACFC itself took on average 20 months to formu-late its opinion. In a survey of minority-based and other human rights NGOs attending a practical training course on the convention (sponsored by the MRG and the CoE), over 75% of the participants stated that an opinion should be published within a year of the state report being submitted. Similarly, the meeting of government offices for national minorities called for speedier responses to their reports. The efficiency and effectiveness of the convention encouraging processes of dialogue and ensuring that data is up-to-date makes the suggested 12 months a good target.

It has been proposed that a set of measures is needed, and in the next round of reporting some obvious improvements can be made, without additional resources.[38] However, unless there is a radically new approach, which seems unlikely, the desired 12-month reporting cycle is unlikely to be achieved even within the ACFC. In addition, there will be further delays in the CoM unless states agree for opinions to be published immediately when they are available. Under present conditions, the best that may be hoped is that the ACFC agrees its opinions in 12 months and the CoM agrees its resolutions in a further six months.

Developing the process

Many challenges lie ahead, a serious one for civil society being to ensure that there is no complacency after an opinion is published, and as the convention is no longer new. Local involvement will be more important than ever to ensure that appropriate measures are taken to strengthen FCNM implementation and to maintain a dialogue between governments and minorities, as well as between the ACFC and CoM.

Civil society can encourage the CoE, the Organization for Security and Co-operation in Europe and the EU to maintain a determination to focus on the FCNM, as a practical way to promote stability and participative democracy that is crucial for peace and prosperity in Europe.

Academics and civil society can review what aspects of the FCNM implementation have worked well or not so well in practice, when, where and why. No two situations are the same but lessons of principle can be learnt and shared. International NGOs can help with strategies adapted or re-defined, and joint action promoted at local, sub-regional or regional levels as part of a rights-based approach to the full and effective participation of minorities.

Civil society can encourage and assist the CoE in publishing information on its range of work on minorities and in establishing a strategy for its work with minorities. These could draw together many competences to help reduce discrimination and to advance the implementation of minority rights and of the FCNM.

Relationship to other CoE monitoring mechanisms on minorities

The FCNM is one of the major CoE human rights conventions and it is unique in being the only comprehensive convention devoted to national minorities. The ACFC is a totally independent body, composed of independent experts whose task is exclusively devoted to monitoring the implementation of the FCNM. In its monitoring work, it takes account of a wide range of information in the public domain, including the outcomes of the monitoring of the European Charter for Regional or Minority Languages, the reports on individual states by the European Commission against Racism and Intolerance and those of the Commissioner on Human Rights. Evidence may also be received from bodies of the Council of Europe including the Venice Commission. In a similar way the opinions of the ACFC, once published, may be a source of information to other monitoring bodies that are reporting at a later stage.

The judgments of the European Court of Human Rights do influence the ACFC on how aspects of the FCNM are implemented in specific states. Similarly the opinions of the ACFC may be of assistance to the Court in understanding the circumstances in a state before a judgment is made on a case.

Conclusions

Practitioners and academics can work together to judge how far the FCNM has promoted the protection of national minorities through the principles set out in its preamble. Consequently, a key question is how far the application of the FCNM has increased stability, democratic security and peace in Europe. This needs a practical perspective for finding ways of assessing whether the FCNM has helped to promote the needs of a pluralist and genuinely democratic society, and the realisation of a tolerant and prosperous Europe. All those who are practitioners in the field of human rights know that such broad, long-term outcomes are immensely difficult to monitor and measure, even in a single state. Judgments may be made by looking at the outputs that this chapter has, in part, measured; and experience can be used to make future predictions. However, this cannot be a precise science.

The first round of monitoring has been largely successful. The reporting has been taken seriously by states, while NGOs have contributed significant additional information that has given a vitality to the process of dialogue. All states have of their own volition encouraged visits, placed no obstacles whatsoever in the way of meetings with NGOs, and often encouraged visits outside the capital. The ACFC has acted coherently and in unison to adopt substantial and constructive opinions that do not fail to criticise where necessary, while listening carefully to governments and minorities. The CoM has not been the *bête noire* painted by some early critics; rather it has developed confidence and trust in the ACFC, has worked in concert to strengthen the FCNM's mechanisms, and has largely worked as a team to achieve the convention's objectives. Some of the perceived weaknesses of the convention have often been its strength, over three quarters of the CoE member states have ratified the FCNM, while the flexibility of its language has allowed for practical interpretations by the ACFC, and an opportunity to persuade states to continue to improve their protection of minorities and the progressive realisation of their rights and responsibilities. Major difficulties remain, however, as the CoE has allocated inadequate resources for the development of the ACFC work, while there are unacceptable delays in the monitoring cycle that both the CoM and ACFC could address by streamlining procedures.

On the substantial issue of the application of the convention in states, it is too early to judge what changes it has contributed to although such work is now needed. There have been many cases where the protection of minorities has improved but there are many factors in play, and to isolate the FCNM as the primary cause would be premature. Some substantial research is needed on this. Nevertheless, in the MRG's dialogue with representatives of minorities, a good number have stated that the FCNM has contributed to significant gains, and that many want to continue to work with the FCNM as an important tool for furthering minority protection.

One key element in intercommunity relations is the prevailing atmosphere, which includes how far different communities and sectors of society (government/civil society) are in substantial dialogue on difficult issues, and how far there are serious attempts to seek common ground. It is clear that the process of alternative reports, consultations by governments, meetings during visits, state comments and follow-up meetings have all helped in this regard. Here, process is an essential prerequisite for product, and the development of action plans to implement the findings of the ACFC. The integration of the FCNM's standards and resolutions into governmental human rights strategies can be useful, and this offers the prospect that the application of the FCNM will be raised in discussions between governments. Civil society can encourage this to be done in a constructive manner.

Governments, officials and minorities need motivating to work together to protect minorities, and to ensure that the FCNM is properly used. When that motivation exists, the FCNM can be a useful objective tool to help encourage real material gains over time. The issues are often complex and controversial, especially when there has been deep distrust or violence. Nevertheless many opportunities exist for committed people from all parts of society to use the FCNM to strengthen the foundations of good interethnic relations on the basis of mutual respect, a celebration of rights and a real commitment to state responsibilities towards minorities.

* Alan Phillips was Vice President of the Council of Europe Advisory Committee on the FCNM 1998-2002 and Director of Minority Rights Group International 1989-2001. He currently acts as an adviser on human rights issues, including supporting training programmes on the FCNM.

1. Articles 4 and 5 of the FCNM.

2. Article 2 of the FCNM.

3. See preamble of the FCNM.

4. The history is outlined in the negotiated explanatory report to the FCNM published by the CoE under *FCNM Collected texts*, Council of Europe Publishing (2nd edition, August 2001).

5. The text of the FCNM is also published in FCNM Collected texts and on the CoE website www.coe.int.

6. For the most recent listing of signatories, ratifications, and the status of reporting, see the CoE web pages on minorities at http://www.coe.int/T/e/human_rights/ Minorities/2._FRAMEWORK_CONVENTION_(MONITORING)/2._Monitoring_mechanism/

7. Ibid.

8. This is specified in Articles 24 to 26 of the FCNM.

9. For a description of the monitoring mechanism and related texts, see CoE minorities website: www.coe.int/minorities

10. Ibid.

11. See Decision of the Committee of Ministers, Council of Europe, 19/20 May 1999.

12. See the Decision of the Council of Europe (CoE), Committee of Ministers, 3 May 2000 published in the *Collected texts* and on CoE minorities web pages.

13. See CoE web pages on minorities.

14. These are published by the CoE on its minority web pages once the Committee of Ministers' Deputies has adopted a resolution. However states may choose to publish them earlier.

15. Ibid, state comments are also published here.

16. Ibid.

17. This original resolution is also included in the *Collected texts*.

18. http://europa.eu.int/comm/enlargement/intro/criteria.htm

19. Ibid.

20. See Council of Europe minorities web pages, opinion on Romania paragraph 8, at http://www.coe.int/T/e/human_rights/Minorities/2._FRAMEWORK_CONVENTION_ (MONITORING)/2._Monitoring_mechanism/4._Opinions_of_the_Advisory_Committee/ 1._Country_specific_opinions/ACFC_INF_OP_I(2002)001

21. A substantial policy analysis was written by the author and published by Minority Rights Group, Alan Phillips, "The Framework Convention for the Protection of National Minorities: A Policy Analysis", MRG policy paper, (London, 2002).

22. See *Collected texts*.

23. Phillips, op.cit., paragraph 3.4.

24. As part of its project "Advancing the Efficiency of the Global Structures of Minority Rights Protection on the Basis of the Framework Convention for the Protection of National Minorities", the European Centre for Minority Issues (ECMI) has begun to develop such a commentary.

25. At www.unhchr.ch/html/menu3/b/d_icerd.htm

26. The comments are published in due course on the Council of Europe web pages on minorities. The Advisory Committee opinions and the state comments on Slovakia and Estonia provide interesting examples when the opinions and comments are compared.

27. Article 24 of the FCNM clearly places the monitoring responsibility with the CoM.

28. Alan Phillips, op.cit., paragraph 3.6.

29. Opinions and resolutions are easily compared on the CoE minority web pages.

30. Ibid.

31. CoE Rapporteur Group on Human Rights, 7 October 2002, Doc ACFC/INF (2003)001.

32. These are also published on the CoE web pages on minorities.

33. These can be accessed at on the CoE web pages on minorities.

34. The report may be found at http://cdg-fz.de/workshop3/

35. Details can be obtained from the CoE FCNM secretariat.

36. This is carefully explained in the valuable training courses the CoE FCNM secretariat and MRG organised together and outlined below.

37. 97 (10).

38. This is argued in the MRG FCNM policy analysis referred to earlier, see Phillips, op.cit., paragraph 4.2.

CHAPTER 6

THE EUROPEAN CHARTER FOR REGIONAL OR MINORITY LANGUAGES

Stefan Oeter*

Introduction

The European Charter for Regional or Minority Languages (hereinafter ECRML)[1] is a treaty of the Council of Europe dealing specifically with the question of international standard setting for language policy. The drafters of the ECRML deliberately avoided any formulation which might be read as granting individual or collective rights to minorities as collective entities or to individual members of linguistic minorities.[2] Instead, the ECRML uses the terminology of "objective" standards, binding the member states in its formulation and operation of language policies in sectors like education, administration, judiciary, media and cultural affairs. Nevertheless, the drafters of the ECRML could not avoid creating substantive obligations which might give rise in consequence to subjective rights in the internal legal sphere. The process of formulation thus could not insulate the instrument from the context of minority protection of which the original draft had been a part. The creation of the treaty had always formed part of the political discussion in Europe on the formation of an international regime of minority protection.[3] The first draft of the treaty, however, is much older than the recent discussion of the 1990s. In the early 1980s, a committee had already been instituted in the Council of Europe in order to draft a "European Charter of Minority Languages".[4] The work of drafting such an instrument went slowly, however, until in 1989/90 the Iron Curtain fell and the member states of the Council of Europe began to feel the need to come up with some instruments concerning the protection of minority cultures and languages.

The emphasis in these years was clearly put on the protection of minorities and/or their members. Explicit legal guarantees enshrined in a multilateral legal instrument should guarantee a series of rights granting minority members protected areas in education and other fields. Several draft conventions were prepared by various organs of the Council of Europe, such as the Venice Commission draft, with a proposed treaty body formed according to the model of the UN Human Rights Committee, and the proposed additional protocol to the European Convention on Human Rights codifying the rights of linguistic, cultural and ethnic minorities.[5] But such high-flying dreams of a "progressive" scheme of minority protection proved as illusionary as ever.

One after the other, the ambitious projects of "progressive" minority rights instruments ended in crash landings. Lacking the necessary political backing, they proved to be unachievable. The draft European charter for regional or minority languages is one of the two elements that survived the failure of more far-reaching ambitions. Compared to the instruments most international lawyers had struggled for, it constitutes a very peculiar regime, due to its so-called "menu approach".[6] Such a "menu" construction is not a complete novelty – the European Social Charter, the Council of Europe instrument attempting to codify economic and social rights, follows a comparable model. The ECRML was obviously inspired in its construction by this example. Most observers were afraid that the resulting tendency of selective ratification of arrangements of legal obligations might lead to the missing of any normative ambition.[7] States would tend to use such menu constructions as an invitation to ratify only the standards which they already apply in their previously existing legislation. International treaty law in this form would only consolidate the current state of national policies and legislation rather than contributing seriously to their development.

The construction of the mechanism

The process of ratification and implementation of the ECRML has proved, however, that this perception was exaggerated. Admittedly, states had a tendency to take the existing state of internal legislation as a basis for their instrument of ratification. At the same time, however, in order to constructively involve the minority communities, every member state integrated a considerable portion of normative ambition into its instrument, that is, promised certain reforms in its language policy through the obligations accepted under the ECRML. Another issue also proved to be of much more significance than originally expected: the ECRML contains an abstract definition of the term "minority languages", thus bringing under the charter languages that traditionally had not been given any attention and protection.[8] When fulfilling their reporting duties, states were realising this and beginning to deal with the deficient position of these neglected languages.

In order to understand the problems of implementation which arise after ratification of the charter, one also has to bear in mind another important point. The ECRML does not protect minorities as such, namely groups with certain characteristics that make them a specific community distinct from the majority population of a state. It also does not directly envisage the protection of individual rights. It is not conceived as a human rights treaty, but as a treaty on cultural matters creating a series of "objective" standards and obligations for member states, standards which have to be observed when states design their language policy.[9] The primary object of protection is "languages". Admittedly, the protection of languages in practical terms also means that people's linguistic rights are being protected. Indirectly, the ECRML thus also defines the legal status of individuals as far as measures of language policy are concerned.[10] But the political understanding upon which the draft charter was based had a specific direction: the political actors involved always stressed the question of language maintenance, hence the "objective" character of the instrument, linked with an attempt to taboo all connotations of group rights and the protection of minorities as collective entities. The ECRML thus only speaks of "languages" and of "speakers" of such languages, not of "minorities" or "linguistic communities". Despite this clear understanding, it is not always easy to respect such "political correctness". By protecting "languages", as an emanation of culture which is dependent upon communicative arrangements, the charter as a result undoubtedly also protects "linguistic communities", or – if one wants to use the word – "minorities". The ECRML, however, decidedly avoids any use of such collective concepts as "minorities", which also takes into consideration the fact that in some states speakers of a regional or minority language do not want to be considered as a "national minority" though they may want their language to be protected. The ECRML thus protects members of a linguistic minority only in a rather indirect way. Nevertheless, it is beyond doubt that the charter in its legal details, although not an explicit human rights instrument, contains a series of guarantees of individual rights of a human rights character. One only has to read commitments such as those under Article 8, paragraph 1.b, which provides for various schemes of guaranteed primary school education in minority languages – education in the relevant minority language, a substantial part of education in the language or the teaching of the language as an integral part of the curriculum – with a final option "to apply one of the measures provided for under i to iii above at least to those pupils whose families so request and whose number is considered sufficient". It is difficult to interpret such a clause without arriving at some kind of "subjective" right in substance.

The ECRML has two operative parts: Part II and Part III.[11] Part II contains a "minimum code" of elementary standards that must be observed in relation to all minority and regional languages which exist upon the territory of a member state. There is no "menu" concerning Part II – the (programmatic) standards laid down in this part are binding in all aspects and apply to each minority language covered.[12] The standards in its normative construction, however, are rather vague and are formulated more as policy objectives than as concrete legal standards that could be applied immediately by administrative authorities and courts. The "chapeau" of Article 7, the standard provision of Part II, accordingly requires that: "[i]n respect of regional or minority languages, within the territories in which such languages are used and according to the situation of each language, the parties shall base their policies, legislation and practice on the following objectives and principles: ..."

There follows a list of elementary objectives and principles of protection of minority languages, phrased in rather abstract terms, such as "the recognition of the regional or minority languages as an expression of cultural wealth", "the need for resolute action to promote regional or minority languages in order to safeguard them", "the facilitation and/or encouragement of the use of regional or minority languages, in speech and writing, in public and private life", and "the provision of appropriate forms and means for the teaching and study of regional or minority languages at all appropriate stages".[13] At first reading, these "objectives and principles" seem to be formulated so vaguely that one might question the usefulness of such a provision. This would misjudge, however, the genuine relevance of Part II. Admittedly, the provision does not give a set of clear and unconditional standards capable of being applied with "direct effect" by national authorities and judges. But, despite its open formulation, Article 7 with its set of "objectives and principles" gives a legal yardstick for measuring the compatibility of national policies with the charter. In fixing specific objectives of a "sensible" language policy concerning minority languages, it imposes an obligation to pursue such objectives, and not to pursue contradictory goals. Even more, it establishes certain principles, like "the respect of the geographical area of each regional or minority language in order to ensure that existing or new administrative divisions do not constitute an obstacle to the promotion of the regional or minority language in question". Since the aim of effective protection of minority languages is far from dominating the practical arrangements of language policies in most European states, the "objectives and principles" laid down in Article 7 are of much more practical relevance than one might think. They may be relevant in three different dimensions. Firstly, Part II offers a basic degree of protection where states have largely opted out of a certain section when selecting their menu.[14] Secondly, there are some "objectives and principles" in Article 7 that cover issues not raised under Part III, such as the previously mentioned principle relating to the geographical area of a language when designing administrative divisions.[15] Thirdly, they provide a basic standard of protection for minority languages that hitherto have been neglected in a member state, and which accordingly have not been included in the set of languages protected under Part III. This is not necessarily always the case for a small language. The Romany language, for example, falls under Part II in all the member states of the ECRML, although people of Roma/Gypsy origin in some of the states constitute by far the biggest minority.[16] Part II here safeguards an elementary protection of such languages. This might induce the state to develop a policy of language maintenance and development in cases where such languages traditionally were excluded from protection, but it may also serve as a catalyst to acknowledge the existence of hitherto "unknown" or repressed minority languages that might warrant such protection. The Netherlands, for example, during the preparation of its initial periodical report, detected that Lower Saxonian and "Limburgish" might qualify as minority languages in the sense of the charter, a learning process which started a debate as to whether and how these languages might be protected in future.[17]

Part III then contains the specific "menu" of protection for minority languages with options of a much more concrete nature. The ECRML in its Part III contains a list of nearly 100 proposed obligations, under which a state has to select 35 options as a minimum.[18] States "are free, within certain limits, to determine which of these provisions will apply to each of the languages spoken within their frontiers".[19] The flexibility thus granted to member states when tailoring their set of obligations "takes account of the major differences in the de facto situations of regional or minority languages (numbers of speakers, degree of fragmentation etc.). It also has regard to the costs entailed by many of the provisions and the varying administrative and financial capacity of the European states".[20]

Despite the flexibility, or perhaps even as a result of it, the individual oblig-ations contained in the menu are rather precise. In Article 8 on education, for example, taking the set of options for primary education as an exemplary case: every sub-paragraph contains the option "to make available primary education in the relevant regional or minority languages"; the option "to make available a substantial part of primary education in the relevant regional or minority languages"; the option "to provide, within primary edu-cation, for the teaching of the relevant regional or minority language as an integral part of the curriculum"; or fourthly, the possibility "to apply one of the measures provided for under i to iii above at least to those pupils whose families so request and whose number is considered sufficient". The example given here demonstrates the rationale of the menu approach. The various options are alternative instruments for fostering minority languages in school education. A state cannot apply all four forms of protection at the same time, but has to choose one of these possibilities when designing its language policy in the education field. By making the choice explicit, and asking the state which choice it has made or wants to make, the provision becomes much more concrete than an abstract, all-embracing formula cov-ering the whole field of primary education in one obligation.[21] The attempt to draft an overall formula, as was done in the Framework Convention for the Protection of National Minorities (FCNM), and also in the Venice Commission draft and in the draft additional protocol, cannot avoid hiding the inherent choice under an open and vague wording covering all the dif-ferent options. The charter thus manages to become extremely technical in its construction, formulating very precise and concrete obligations. States have a choice as to which commitments they want to make, but if they have undertaken a set of obligations, they have much less leeway in arguing that a certain policy conforms to these than they have under the FCNM, for example.

This makes compliance control under the ECRML an easy and a difficult task at the same time: easy, since the interpretation of the individual options is not a very complex task – most specific options are clear and precise in their content and do not need much interpretation; difficult at the same time, however, because it is a challenging task to keep an overview of the concrete menu of obligations of each member state. No one state has an identical set of obligations to another; the rationale of each menu is different, and calls for differentiated analyses of law and facts. Each menu is understandable only on the basis of the socio-linguistic situation of the languages in ques-tion and of the fundamental structures of national legislation. Menus of fed-eral states tend to be extremely complex, whereas centralised states tend to grant each language the same protection, irrespective of its situation, the number of its speakers and its geographical roots. Due to the complexity of the menu, state authorities are in an obvious danger of losing an overall view; sometimes it is evident from the information given in the reporting procedure that the competent state organs misunderstood the meaning of certain options, selected the "wrong" options if you link it up to the concrete situation in practice, or selected almost randomly certain options in order to fill up the menu, hoping that they would not be criticised for doing nothing towards implementing certain standards. The menu is not completely left to the discretion of the contracting states; a contracting state has to choose 35 options as a minimum, and has to subject itself to at least three obligations both in education and in the cultural field, and to one obligation at least relating to official use in administration, before the courts, in the media field and in economic and social life.[22] This sounds minimal, but Germany, for example, has found that such a straitjacket of minimum obligations can be rather challenging – attempts to increase the formal protection of the Romany language up to the level of Part III have proved to be extremely difficult.

How does one monitor the implementation of such a complex arrangement of different obligations selected from a broad range of options? The drafting committee – and behind it the member states of the Council of Europe – opted for an approach well-known in the United Nations context but rarely used by the Council of Europe. They combined the menu of substantial obligations with a standard reporting procedure.[23] Member states have to submit reports on their policies pursued in accordance with Part II of the charter and on the measures taken in application of those provisions of Part III which they have accepted, in a format which is prescribed in a standard form adopted by the Committee of Ministers.[24] The first periodical report is due one year after the charter has entered into force for a state A specific state authority determined by the government collects all the information necessary to report on the charter's implementation and puts the bits and pieces of information together in a comprehensive report. In contrast to the FCNM, the responsible ministry is not the Ministry of Foreign Affairs, but a ministry dealing with minority language issues inside a specific state, such as the Ministry of the Interior, of Education or of Culture. This ministry consults the other ministries and government offices whose competences are affected by the charter; it often also consults with non-governmental organisations representing the speakers of minority languages or working in the field of minority languages. In federal states or states with structures of regional autonomy, the member state bureaucracies and the regional authorities also have to be consulted. Such consultation procedures may be rather time-consuming, as in the case of Germany, where the federation has very few legislative and administrative competences appropriate for implementing the charter. Here the co-ordinating body in the Federal Ministry of the Interior instituted a whole scheme of co-ordination meetings with the *Länder* bureaucracies and the minority organisations in order to collect the information which is needed to draw up a useful report.

The reports are presented to the Secretary General of the Council of Europe. At the same time, the reports must be made public in the country concerned, usually by printing it as a government paper distributed publicly, and also often through the government's website.[25] The Secretary General forwards the reports to the committee of experts established under the ECRML, which has the responsibility of examining the reports in detail.

The committee of experts, a body provided for under Article 17 of the ECRML, is composed of one member per contracting party, appointed by the

Committee of Ministers for a term of six years "from a list of individuals of the highest integrity and recognised competence in the matters dealt with in the Charter, who shall be nominated by the Party concerned".[26] This formula sounds like legal poetry, but its observance is of extreme importance. This is particularly true for the required competence in minority language issues. Fortunately, member states have respected the competency requirement up to now. The committee now (September 2003) has 16 members. Nearly half of the members are law professors or scholars with a particular expertise in international law, social rights and minority rights; the other most important group comprises linguists, sociologists and journalists specialised in sociolinguistic issues. The rest of the members consist of administrators in the fields of education or media and legal practitioners (advocates or judges). Roughly half of the committee's members have a minority language as their mother tongue. To sum up: all members have been working for quite some time in the field of minority (language) protection – a common basis which creates a very specific atmosphere in the committee. It is a closed community of professionals with a common experience, a group of persons which may easily be described as an "epistemic community".

Another point is also important: the ECRML itself invites "bodies or associations legally established in a Party", which means primarily bodies or associations representing the speakers of minority languages, to "draw the attention of the committee of experts to matters relating to the undertakings entered into by that Party under Part III of this Charter".[27] Associations or bodies representing minorities or struggling for the rights of minorities thus may not only brief the committee's members behind the scenes, as is done in the UN, but are also allowed to act openly, to submit formal statements and information, or to add critical comments to the state reports. The committee is explicitly authorised by Article 16, paragraph 2, of the ECRML to make use of such information, after consulting the party concerned, thus giving the respective state a right to be heard. The committee may "take account of this information" in the preparation of its report, may include it in its factual statements and may openly refer to it. The information given in the state's periodical reports are thus balanced by information submitted by minority associations or bodies and by human rights organisations.

The procedural details for examining the reports are provided for in the rules of procedure adopted by the committee. Here we find a difference between the advisory committee under the FCNM (ACFC) and the committee of experts. While states were rather cautious in the case of the ACFC, reserving the Committee of Ministers the right to decide upon the rules of procedure, this competence has been delegated to the committee itself under the charter.[28] The rules of procedure contain nothing sensational, but offer certain mechanisms that allow fairly intense and effective monitoring of national implementation. As the Secretary General of the Council of Europe stated in his report to the Parliamentary Assembly on the application of the charter:

> It rapidly became clear that when examining the national reports the Committee of experts needed to enter into a dialogue with the national authorities concerned in order to clarify some aspects of the report and obtain additional information. This

dialogue is carried on in the first place in the form of written questions and answers. However, the Committee has normally found it necessary to follow up this written correspondence by sending a delegation, consisting of three members of the Committee, on an "on-the-spot-mission" to the country concerned. These visits provide an opportunity for a more intensive exchange of information with the governmental authorities, other public bodies (such as ombudsmen), parliamentarians and representatives of the speakers of the various regional or minority languages.[29]

One could also phrase it quite differently: reports are often rather deficient. Sometimes one has the impression that the state organs concerned did not really understand the meaning of the obligation selected by them, which later leads to inadequate information concerning such obligations. Sometimes the reporting organ has misunderstood the option in question, sometimes the relevant authorities have difficulty in obtaining the necessary information as to what is really happening "on the ground", and sometimes authorities are also simply trying to hide deficits in implementation behind a veil of irrelevant remarks or by remaining completely silent on certain delicate points.

According to the experience of the committee, there is no report which does not raise a whole series of additional questions. After a first, provisional examination, the committee accordingly draws up a questionnaire addressed to the competent authorities, asking for further information and clarification. Remaining gaps in information, open questions and doubts as to the adequateness of certain pieces of information must then be reserved for the final "on-the-spot visit".[30]

The procedure is mainly driven by the work of the "country rapporteur" appointed by the committee in advance, and by the lawyer from the secretariat responsible for the report. The committee's secretariat, by the way, is extremely small. For the first two years, the committee of experts had only one young lawyer from the Council's secretariat and a secretary. After a while, a second lawyer was attributed to the secretariat. With more and more states ratifying the ECRML, and thus more and more reports that have to be progressed at the same time, the small size of the secretariat is going to become a serious shortcoming that threatens to obstruct the efficiency of the committee's work.

The country rapporteur and the staff member prepare the first examination of the state report, draw up the questionnaires and prepare the "on-the-spot visits". The examination itself, as well as the drafting work for the questionnaires during the first years used to be done in plenary sessions of the committee. But since the number of reports simultaneously being in process of examination is increasing, the committee has had to change to a kind of "chamber procedure". Members of the committee are split up into various working groups where they deal with the details of checking the information given in the state reports and with drafting the committee's evaluation report. The proposed draft, however, must finally always be discussed by the whole committee, giving each member a chance to talk about any detail.

At the core of every working group is a small group of three members consisting of the "country rapporteur", the national member from the country
concerned and a third expert appointed by the committee. The core working
group prepares the draft documents for discussion in the "chambers". The
three-member core working group, together with the responsible secretariat
lawyer, also forms the delegation travelling to the state concerned. These
"on-the-spot visits" have proven to be an extremely valuable tool, which is
why they have become a standard part in practically any examination of a
country report (with the exception of Liechtenstein, where there are no
minority languages in the sense of the charter).[31] The "on-the-spot visits"
usually start with a round of discussions led by representatives of minority
language bodies and associations. These sessions are always extremely infor-
mative, since here one really meets the people concerned by the intricacies
(and deficiencies) of a specific national policy – people who give their opinions as to what is happening in everyday life with minority languages, which
constitutes the "real" practice of language policy. In addition, the working
group usually also travels to a region where there is a resident minority language community in order to visit kindergartens, schools, local administrations and courts.

In a second (and final) round of talks, the working group usually meets with
government officials and representatives of the various ministries involved
in implementing the charter. One might assume that the latter round is a
waste of time, since the group of actors concerned here has usually already
produced several written statements which gave them enough opportunity
to express their views. But this is not true. Reports are usually written by one
or two bureaucrats in a government office, who have to collect all the information. The same is true for the answers to the questionnaires from the committee
of experts. According to general experience gained during the "on-the-spot
visits", it makes quite a difference whether various government offices co-
ordinate themselves using a uniform reporting procedure or whether there
is direct discussion with officials from the various ministries and public
bodies. Different ministries usually have quite different perspectives, experiences and viewpoints, and you get a totally different picture depending
whether one office is harmonising these different views or whether you communicate directly with the different specialists. The value of such discussions
is further enhanced if they are informed by previous information delivered
during the first round of talks with minority representatives. In addition to
administrators from the relevant ministries, the working group often also
meets with other public officials, such as ombudspersons, parliamentarians,
regional and local administrators. In particular, talks with local politicians
and administrators can contribute a lot to the understanding of existing
problems that the implementation of the ECRML has had to face; local "nota-
bles" usually know well the problems "on the ground" and have a habit of
speaking rather openly.

The talks often have more the character of joint, co-operative meetings in
matters of compliance management than that of pure control inspection.
Although the mechanism of "on-the-spot visits" reminds one very much of
"inspections" similar to those in other fields of international law,[32] the technical character of the ECRML and the spirit of co-operation underlying the

whole enterprise tend to create an atmosphere of openness and trust. State officials usually do not hesitate to admit openly the problems and deficiencies in implementation, and the debates are often less centred upon the detection of "hidden" deficiencies but on an open discussion of the reasons underlying the problems and what could be done to cope with remaining deficiencies in policies and measures of implementation.

On its return from the visit, the working group (together with the responsible staff member from the secretariat) prepares a draft committee report on the results of the examination and on the state of implementation in the country concerned. This draft report is then discussed in a plenary session and is finally adopted by the committee, after resolving existing differences in perception and trying to reach a consensus on the formulation of the report. Formal voting is usually avoided; the committee of experts rarely decides by majority, but seeks (and reaches) a consensus.

As stipulated in Article 16, paragraph 3, the adopted report, with the suggestions for recommendations to the Committee of Ministers is submitted for comment to the state party.

The evaluation report of the committee of experts and the comments from the state party are then presented to the Committee of Ministers of the Council of Europe, the main decision-making organ of the Council. As Article 16, paragraph 4, of the ECRML provides, the report for the Committee of Ministers shall contain "proposals of the Committee of Experts to the Committee of Ministers for the preparation of such recommendations of the latter body to one or more of the parties as may be required". Accordingly, the Committee of Ministers takes note not only of the committee of expert's report, but also decides upon "recommendations" addressed to the state concerned. Up to now, the Committee of Ministers has always adopted the proposed recommendations annexed to the report of the committee of experts. Their report is made public after its adoption by the Committee of Ministers, unless the state party in question specifically objects.[33] Fortunately, all states parties up to now have consented without any hesitation to publication, which has set a valuable precedent for future practice.

Every three years a new periodical report is due to be presented by the member states. Taking into consideration the time needed to examine a country report in accordance with the procedure explained above, this is a relatively short time span. Usually it takes one and a half to two years before a country report is examined and the Committee of Ministers has adopted its recommendations. This means that soon after finishing one round of examination, the respective state has to start anew its internal procedure of collecting information for its next periodical report, thus giving the whole reporting procedure the character of a constant dialogue concerning questions of implementation.

The main results of the monitoring scheme

When the ECRML entered into force in March 1998, only eight states had ratified the treaty, namely Norway, Finland, Hungary, the Netherlands,

Croatia, Liechtenstein, Switzerland and Germany.[34] It took two years until the next states (Sweden, Denmark and Slovenia) ratified. This meant that the committee was relatively small at the beginning, consisting of only eight members, and could concentrate its efforts on the examination of a small number of country reports. This gave enough time to proceed carefully and to discuss all the issues of a precedential nature in the necessary detail, while at the same time developing the practical details of the examination procedure in an experimental process. The first "on-the-spot visits" were undertaken in late 1999 and early 2000, and the first draft reports to be submitted to the Committee of Ministers were discussed in 2000.

The committee has now developed a standard format for its evaluation reports, with a thorough analysis of the factual situation at the beginning, that is, an analysis of the socio-linguistic situation of the languages concerned. Then follows a legal analysis of the state of implementation article by article.[35] In this legal evaluation the committee usually includes specific observations relating to various points in the legal assessment. The "main" recommendations are put forward at the end of the report, after a general assessment of the situation in the country concerned.[36] The concluding part thus serves as a kind of reasoning for the "formal" recommendations, that is, the important points of a certain political profile. These recommendations serve as a proposal for the Committee of Ministers' final resolution on implementation. This format has met widespread support in the Committee of Ministers. At the beginning of 2001, the committee of experts submitted a first set of five evaluation reports to the Committee of Ministers, after giving the states concerned a certain time span to react and to annex their comments to the report. The reports were largely welcomed by the states concerned, although they contained quite a large degree of criticism, pointing to severe deficiencies in the national policies and measures intended to implement the charter. One or two states concerned were obviously not completely content with the treatment of their efforts, but finally accepted the report and the recommendations. Interestingly enough, these states were not the usual suspects, but states that used to perceive themselves as vanguards of minority protection. The reports went through the Committee of Ministers relatively smoothly, within a period of two to three months.

The Committee of Ministers finally succeeded in gaining consensus for a necessary additional step not predetermined in the charter itself – the regular publication of the reports by the committee of experts. The ECRML itself, in its Article 16, paragraph 3, only provides that the report "may be made public by the Committee of Ministers", a step requiring in practice the consent of the party concerned. There is a certain indirect pressure to publish, since the state concerned cannot escape criticism by keeping the report confidential. According to Article 16, paragraph 5, of the ECRML, the Secretary General of the Council of Europe shall make a two-yearly "detailed report to the Parliamentary Assembly on the application of the Charter", a report which inevitably would mirror the major points of criticism contained in the committee of experts' report.[37] Nevertheless, direct publication of the report is important for making the whole mechanism transparent and for exercising a certain public pressure upon states to reform deficient policies. By publishing the first set of reports immediately after acceptance and adoption of the proposed recommendations in the Committee of Ministers, an important precedent was established, and the later set of reports were published right after their adoption by the Committee of Ministers.

To date, 15 country reports have been presented to the committee of experts.[38] Of these, nine have been already examined, and evaluation reports have been presented to the Committee of Ministers (Croatia, Finland, Germany, Hungary, Liechtenstein, the Netherlands, Norway, Sweden, Switzerland). Another five reports have already been presented by states parties and are at different stages of being examined (Austria, Denmark, Slovakia, Slovenia, Spain, the United Kingdom). The first set of second periodical reports was due in 2002. Several of these second reports were presented in 2002 and early 2003; one, the Norwegian report, has been examined and was adopted in March 2003.

Although the time span for full operation of the implementation mechanism has thus been rather short, considerable experience of its operation and initial results has been gained already. It is not easy to give a general picture, however, since (due to the menu approach) the sets of obligations are relatively diverse, as a result of very different political, social and linguistic conditions under which the various language communities covered by the ECRML live. The range of situations covered extends from situations of "post-conflict peace-building" in cases such as the Serbs in Croatian eastern Slavonia, scattered urban minorities (like the Russians and the Tatars in Finland), endangered regional languages in remote rural areas where extinction of the language seems imminent (Lower Saxon in the Netherlands, Lower German in northern Germany, Bable and Aragonés in Spain), the various Roma/Gypsy communities, an "indigenous people" such as the Sami in Norway, Sweden and Finland (enjoying a limited autonomy) to "nation states" such as the Italians in the Swiss canton of Ticino or the Catalans and Basques in Spain (all three possessing their own state structure with a very rigorous language policy in favour of their language).

Despite these huge discrepancies in socio-linguistic conditions and international legal obligations under the charter, the examination of nearly a dozen reports has revealed a number of similarities in the deficiencies and problems of implementation of the ECRML. This begins with the problematic position in national language policies of the so-called "Part II languages", that is, the minority or regional languages where the states have not entered into specific obligations under Part III of the ECRML, but which are covered by the minimum standard of Part II. The languages that only receive protection under Part II usually lack a coherent territorial basis or are spoken by a very small number of speakers thereby making it very difficult and sometimes impossible to provide the kind of protection that is provided for in Part III. Often the languages are not even standardised, which makes it even more difficult to provide certain services, such as to produce documents, encourage various literary works, to provide education in the language, etc. These "repressed" or at least "neglected" languages usually enjoy no specific protection whatsoever, which means that there are no specific arrangements in the public education system for maintaining the language, they are completely excluded from official use, there is practically no media coverage and virtually no support in official schemes of cultural policy. The extremely asymmetric situation of "diglossy" normally means that there is a clear danger of extinction of these languages. The provisions of Part II of the ECRML, which are mainly of a programmatic character, call upon states to develop a policy of language maintenance in favour of these languages as well.[39] The vague and open nature of the objectives set in Article 7 means that there are no clear and precise measures required under the charter for these languages. Continuing to do nothing in favour of these languages, however, as was the traditional pattern of most member states in these cases, violates the normative programme laid down in Part II. A number of member states of the ECRML have discovered in the course of drawing up their report that certain languages fall under this category, and accordingly have begun to question what to do in these cases. This implies recognition of these languages and is a step towards accepting that something has to be done to support them. It is obvious that formulating a sensible policy for these languages needs considerable effort, and it would be unrealistic to expect a sudden change of policy that would solve all the problems at once. Official recognition of the problem and the start of a constructive dialogue with representative speakers of these respective languages is, however, a considerable progress that should not be underestimated.

A particular problem under Part II is the position of Roma/Gypsies. Practically all the member states have Romani-speaking communities living under problematic conditions, and are faced with largely similar problems arising from policies aimed at improving their living conditions, as the committee of experts has learned in the course of its first round of examination of country reports. There is a widespread understanding, among researchers as well as responsible bureaucrats, that more has to be done in favour of these communities. There is also a certain perplexity, however, as to what exactly should be done. To a large degree, the problems of Roma are problems of social marginalisation and of discrimination falling beyond the scope of the charter. Traditional "affirmative action" policies that mainly try to improve the social integration of people of Roma background are not easy to combine with measures of language maintenance relating to Romani. Strengthening a separate "Roma/Gypsy identity" is often seen as consolidating the social "ghetto" in which Roma all too often are entrapped.[40] The success of traditional assimilation policies, on the other hand, is not very convincing either, as examples like Hungary demonstrate.[41] Even if states parties decide to strengthen the cultural identity of Roma by specific measures in favour of Romani as a medium of communication, such a policy is difficult to implement. It needs the co-operation of Roma communities; but Roma communities are reluctant to co-operate with states in these matters and to "publicise" their language, which traditionally served as a kind of "secret code" reserved to members of the community. Nevertheless, some states are experimenting with practical measures in this direction.

As far as languages explicitly protected under Part III are concerned, the set of provisions on education in Article 8 of the ECRML is probably the most decisive part of the package if the survival of minority languages is to be ensured. As the second biennial report of the Secretary General on the application of the ECRML phrased it: "Education is a crucial and challenging field, in which it appears that similar problems exist in several States Parties, i.e. inadequacy of the conceptual and organisational framework for minority language education (at pre-school, primary school, secondary school), inadequate or even non-existent specific training for regional or minority language teachers and a serious lack of training materials."[42] This sentence expresses in a very abbreviated form the experience of minority languages in most member states and shows their deplorable (or perhaps difficult) state. Even if states are proud of their efforts, these efforts often remain fragmentary, leaving it to the local school authorities to decide whether they want to offer any education in or of the minority language. Since resources are usually scarce in the education sector in general and local authorities prefer to follow the wishes of the majority, minority language education is usually underfinanced, has to cope with a shortage of teachers and finds itself shifted to marginal hours. Despite some well-developed models of minority language schools run by minority organisations and also an impressive commitment by individual teachers in ordinary state schools, the lack of a systematic scheme of minority language education which covers all the places where parents might wish their children to receive this education, is extremely hampering. As a consequence, even if their parents wish such an education for them, children are denied the chance to get a minority language education – and this despite the clear and unconditional obligation resulting in that sense from all the options under Article 8, paragraph 1, subparagraphs a, b and c. The sets of options for pre-school education in Article 8, paragraph 1.a, primary school education in Article 8, paragraph 1.b, and secondary school education in Article 8, paragraph 1.c, distinguish various forms of minority language education – complete education in the minority language, making available a substantial part of education in the minority language, the teaching of the minority language as an integral part of the curriculum or the granting of such a possibility "at least to those pupils whose families so request and whose number is considered sufficient". One may discuss the minimum threshold required for the creation of such an educational offer. However, Article 8 places beyond doubt the necessity for states to offer such an option to all parents "within the territory in which such languages are used".

Even if some form of minority education is offered – and this is usually done only in the minimum form of some teaching of the minority language as subject matter in school, not with the minority language as medium of instruction – this provision is often limited to some stages of education, such as primary schools or secondary schools.[43] If minority language education shall serve as a tool of language maintenance, however, this education should be continued throughout the whole school career. Only under this condition does the minority language have a chance of becoming consolidated as an additional means of communication which can be used by its speakers in all spheres of life. Some two or three years of language education, in contrast, tends to serve as a "folkloristic" alibi, but does not play a useful role in

144

consolidating the communicative reach of a language. The ECRML is again relatively clear on that point – but common practice in a number of states shows a completely different picture. The committee has pointed out these weaknesses in most of its evaluation reports and will also emphasise these structural deficiencies in future rounds of reporting.

In some states, such as Germany, there is also a lack of ways of systematic monitoring of the efforts undertaken in minority language education.[44] Despite its very detailed regulatory framework for school education, there is only scarce control of what school establishments are really doing in practice. The fragmentary and unsystematic nature of the whole educational structure finds its expression here. The same is true for teacher education in a number of states, one of the crucial bottlenecks of any reform of minority language education. The committee has all too often found a situation where the state on the one hand makes serious pledges to improve minority language education in schools, while on the other hand there is an insufficient supply of minority language teachers, due to shortcomings in teacher training. In some situations, like Northern Frisian and Lower Sorbian in Germany, teacher education in minority languages is even cut back as a result of budgetary reallocations although even more teachers would be needed than were originally trained.[45] Some parts of the country are pursuing contradictory policies in these cases and the committee must highlight such contradictions in state policies and must point to the serious setbacks this might create in the implementation of the charter, giving the minority language communities concerned a better chance to attack such phenomena of ignorance towards international legal obligations politically.

Structural deficiencies of a comparable nature can be found in other fields. The use of regional or minority languages before the courts, for example, is a very difficult area. The legal provisions concerning regional or minority languages normally guarantee the possibility for their use, but in practice this possibility is made use of only in exceptional cases. Frequently, inadequate language skills on the part of the judicial personnel are compounded by a lack of qualified interpreters to whom recourse can be made in cases where a regional or minority language is used.[46] Speakers of minority languages accordingly are afraid of being perceived as "trouble-makers" and thus prefer in practice to use the majority language. If states really tried to take seriously the project codified in Article 9 of the ECRML, namely the effort to upgrade the social standing (and the communicative reach) of minority languages by giving them a place in judicial proceedings, they would have to create an organisational infrastructure which could make this a reality. Only if minority language speakers know that there are judges and clerks trained to use their language in proceedings and court matters, will they dare to use the formal rights granted to them. The committee has consistently pointed to this problem and its repercussions in the organisation of the judiciary in a number of reports – and states are learning, it seems, to take the point more seriously than they used to do until recently.

Similar problems are often found in the administrative authorities, where there is sometimes a serious lack of knowledge on the part of the officials about the obligation to produce or accept documents in a regional or minority language.[47] Despite such forms of resistance or at least ignorance towards the implementation of the obligations under Article 10 of the ECRML, local administrations are usually better equipped (and more willing) to make use of minority languages in their dealings with clients than central state administrations. Irrespective of the obligations undertaken by states under Article 10, paragraph 1, of the ECRML, central state bureaucracies regularly react with indulgence towards the idea of using more than one language in their transactions – with the exception of multinational states like Switzerland or Finland. In most other states, it seems to be a horrifying vision for centralist bureaucrats to come across a file in another language than the official language. Admittedly, files would have to be translated in such cases. But apart from the file problem, there are few problems of extra expenses for administrations in accepting minority languages as[48] means of communication and interaction. It is more a problem of adequate use of personnel than a question of big translation services, since in most minority territories there will be enough minority language officials among the staff to man specific contact offices for minority language speakers. An administration must simply feel the need to create such a structure. There are positive models demonstrating how easy such a change might be. The committee routinely points to these models in order to convince administrations to take their obligations under Article 10 of the ECRML seriously and to make them a reality.

In general, one might say that the effective protection and promotion of regional or minority languages often requires a change of attitude, on the part of both the speakers of these languages and the representatives of the public authorities.[48] This may be linked to the broader need to raise awareness among the majority language community of the existence of regional or minority languages and their place in the national cultural heritage. Here the media are of utmost importance. Being largely absent from the media is a serious handicap to the maintenance and development of a language in modern society. This is particularly a problem for the smaller language communities, that do not represent an audience big enough to be of interest to commercially based media. The state therefore has a responsibility to make sure that the special needs of regional or minority languages are sufficiently catered for especially in media with a public service mission.[49] The extent to which it does so seems to vary considerably from one state party to another. In general, even where there is a comprehensive legal framework for fulfilling a state's undertakings under the charter, the committee of experts has observed that concrete regulations capable of being applied by individual officials are often lacking, making the specific objectives difficult to attain. It has also concluded in several cases that there is a lack of a coherent policy for the protection and development especially of the weaker minority languages covered by Part III of the ECRML. States tend to hide themselves behind the "independence" of public service media. For this reason, they sometimes opted only for the obligations directed towards the regulatory framework for private media. But, left alone, private media will usually not adequately serve the needs of minority language speakers, at least in the case of smaller language communities. These groups do not form a commercially viable audience, at least in television. If states want to fulfil their obligations in this respect, they must operate with "must carry" obligations (agreed pre-determined minimum requirements) in their regulatory schemes, a possibility most regulatory arrangements provide for in principle. States are reluctant, however, to burden private stations with such "must carry" obligations, and even if they include them in the licensing requirements, they tend to neglect enforcement of such requirements. As a result, implementation in this field is somewhat lacking in a number of member states of the ECRML, a point which has been stressed in the committee's evaluation reports.

Another point has proven to be of crucial importance. The committee of experts has confirmed in its reports that the role of local and regional authorities in protecting and promoting regional or minority languages is essential. This can especially be noted in fields such as education, local and regional administration, transfrontier exchanges, media, culture or – to give another example – health care services for the sick and the elderly, where the provision of services in the minority languages needs a strong commitment from local authorities. The committee, however, has noted in many cases that local and regional authorities have not been informed adequately of the international commitments the state party has undertaken by ratifying the charter.[50] The key authority in the fulfilment of some of these commitments is therefore not always aware that it is obliged to arrange for certain services in a regional or minority language. The committee has therefore insisted on a more effective information flow down to the local level and on the need to involve local authorities better in the whole process. The principle of local autonomy is intended to ensure considerable manoeuvring space for local politicians, to allow local politics to pursue their own ends and to bring their specific preferences to bear, but considerations of local autonomy cannot legitimately be put forward as a reason for leaving it to the discretion of local authorities to determine how far the state's undertakings under the charter will be fulfilled in practice. The legislative, regulatory and organisational framework in which local authorities operate must safeguard the observation and implementation of the obligations of the charter at local level.

The main points of concern mentioned in this brief survey of the committee of experts' findings from the evaluation reports demonstrate that the implementation of the charter is an open enterprise where many problems still remain to be solved. One might put this in rather negative terms by saying that the standard of implementation of the charter's obligations is deficient. The ECRML, however, is a new (and ambitious) instrument that has come into force only some five years ago – and for most member states even much more recently. It would be unrealistic to expect a perfect state of implementation; this would be possible only if states simply had mirrored their pre-existing minority policy in a set of international legal obligations. But fortunately enough they have not done this in the case of the ECRML, despite the "menu approach" of the instrument. In another perspective, the huge amount of deficiencies in implementation discovered by the committee of experts during its examination of state reports proves the impressive amount of "normative ambition" built into the state's instruments of ratification. Member states want to improve their record in minority language maintenance, and implicitly have made a lot of ambitious pledges in order to improve their language policies towards minority languages.

These pledges are not that easy to fulfil – most of the deficiencies observed by the committee of experts are structural deficiencies which are difficult to overcome, even with a high level of political good will. The improvement of the standard of implementation will thus take considerable time. In the meantime, the committee of experts has to remind states again and again of the pledges they have made towards the Council of Europe member states – and implicitly also towards their own communities of minority language speakers. States do not always like such insistence – some of the promises made within the ECRML are rather painful to implement. But here we are at the essence of international law – states may make political promises and may a day later forget about these promises; if you transform such promises into an international legal obligation, however, it is no longer that easy to get rid of the promise once made. It has become part of the legal framework in which state authority is embedded, and the people concerned will be glad to come back to such obligations as often as the reference might help them in getting their points through. If the international legal instrument is accompanied by a mechanism of institutionalised "compliance control", this adds even more of a burden for the states concerned. States have to report periodically on how they implement their pledges. They have to give account of what they are really doing in practice in order to fulfil their promises. And if they are not doing enough, or are brushing aside some commitments in favour of other political objectives, they know that they will be criticised on an international level by the treaty bodies responsible for the monitoring of the relevant treaty.

The experience of the first years of operation of the ECRML's mechanism is encouraging. The specific points of criticism that were raised in the evaluation reports of the committee and which have been adopted by the Committee of Ministers have been given quite positive resonance. There was some critique by governments concerning specific points, but in general the evaluation of the committee was accepted as being balanced and to the point. In a series of cases governments concerned have taken measures to remedy certain deficiencies in implementation that were raised in the reports and to improve the standard of implementation. This was clearly visible in the second periodical reports which are now being examined by the committee of experts (one second report, the Norwegian one, has already been examined and a report by the committee adopted; three others, the Finnish, Hungarian and the Swiss, are in the process of being examined).[51]

What are the possibilities under the ECRML for minority rights practitioners?

The political (and practical) relevance of the criticisms voiced in the course of the international monitoring procedure depends very much on the resonance which such critique finds in the internal political process (and in the relevant civil society). The more the credibility of a government depends on its sincere implementation of legal standards, the more vulnerable a government will be towards the kind of criticism voiced in the evaluation reports of international treaty bodies like the committee of experts. This committee (and the entire Council of Europe) have no formal sanctions which could force a government to take seriously the recommendations voiced in an evaluation report (and in a recommendation of the Committee of Ministers). It is the internal political process (and the sincerity of a government's respect for the law) which gives such forms of impartial, international monitoring its relevance. Only where a society expects its government to abide by the rules, to take its legal obligations seriously, and where violations against such obligations are sanctioned politically (or even legally), does the mechanism gain real relevance. This means that the success of international monitoring in cases like the ECRML depends on the extent to which the actors in civil society take note of the results of international monitoring. The mechanism will only have an influence upon internal political actors when the network of national NGOs takes up the criticism voiced by international organs regarding deficiencies in implementation and puts pressure upon the governmental system to remedy such deficiencies. In other words, the practical relevance of international legal obligations depends strongly on the internal political relevance of international commitments. They will only be taken seriously when the perceived sincerity of a government depends on its attempts to implement international legal commitments. This places a huge burden upon NGOs as the primary actors of civil society. The actors of civil society must follow the monitoring process at international level and must transmit the critique voiced by international treaty bodies into internal critique, a critique which gains its strength from the demand that international obligations should be taken more seriously. Critical monitoring at international and internal levels must therefore work hand in hand.

The ECRML is relatively well construed for bringing about this kind of division of labour. It gives NGOs in the field of minority rights a formal role to play in the monitoring process. Article 16, paragraph 2, of the ECRML provides:

> Bodies or associations legally established in a Party may draw the attention of the Committee of Experts to matters relating to the undertakings entered into by that Party under Part III of this Charter. After consulting the Party concerned, the Committee of Experts may take account of this information in the preparation of the report specified in paragraph 3 below. These bodies or associations can furthermore submit statements concerning the policy pursued by a Party in accordance with Part II.

States parties have thus explicitly conceded that the functioning of the monitoring mechanism needs to rely upon critical material delivered by bodies or organisations representing minorities or struggling for minority rights. This is not a new insight; practically all the monitoring mechanisms, even at UN level, depend on such NGO-based material.[52] States have tended, however, not to admit this formally. Article 16, paragraph 2, of the ECRML in this sense is a breakthrough, since states now formally acknowledged the de facto role played for a long time by NGOs. NGOs may, according to Article 16, paragraph 2, of the ECRML, submit formal comments towards the information given in state reports. These comments will usually be critical towards the image given by the state authorities in the official country report, because otherwise it would not be worth NGOs investing time and energy in the process. These comments are brought to the attention of the respective government, which may react to them, and are formally integrated into the information material used for examination purposes by the committee of experts. But even beyond this formal mechanism, the committee inevitably uses information given by national minority rights NGOs and by public bodies representing minority language communities. Public sources, as well as information gained from such organisations and bodies during the "on-the-spot visits", form the necessary information base needed if one has to critically cross-check the information given by states in their official country reports.

National minority rights organisations as well as bodies representing minority communities are not yet exploiting these opportunities to the desired extent. For the treaty bodies administering the monitoring mechanism, such as the committee of experts, it would be extremely helpful if the competent organisations and bodies would invest more effort in countering the information given by states in their country reports. The optimal solution would be some kind of "shadow reporting", as has been established by human rights organisations in the framework of the UN monitoring mechanisms. Admittedly, the production of a "shadow report" costs time and resources – and minority organisations are often short on resources as well as professional expertise capable of producing such reports. But even partial "shadow reports", limited to some crucial issues, would be of great help to the committee of experts. The role of national NGOs active in the field of minority rights should be much more active in that regard, since the monitoring process gives a good opportunity for one's concerns to be heard on an international stage – and indirectly also at the level of government decision-making.

After the Committee of Ministers has made public the evaluation report and in particular the recommendations, the ball is thrown back into the national arena. Then national organisations and bodies with the responsibility of improving the standard of protection of minority languages in national practice must take up the ball and must exert pressure upon governments to deal with the problems raised in the monitoring report. This firstly requires that the report be clearly read and understood. National associations and bodies should check the Internet website of the ECRML where the reports are made public as soon as possible.[53]

Where there are also internal conflicts within the state authorities, such international documents may offer good arguments relating to internal competence and resource management if bureaucratic and political obstacles to improved protection of minority languages must be overcome. There are always some offices more favourable to the protection of minority languages and other offices and ministries less favourable to it. International monitoring mechanisms and the documents resulting from this clearly strengthen the authorities fighting for an improved standard. The "international obligation" argument grants a certain preference to the objectives enshrined in international treaties, since it is difficult for competing bureaucratic interests to argue openly that other objectives should prevail, when this would clearly entail violating international legal obligations.

Something comparable might work in internal political discourse. Minority rights associations should attempt to use the monitoring documents with their "official" critique as a "trump card" in public discourse. As explained above, the value of such a "trump card" depends very much on the specific political culture of a country. Certain political publics are much more susceptible to the "international legal obligation" argument than others, but to a certain degree minority and human rights associations may always play this game. One cannot say that the potential for building up pressure, which lies in these mechanisms, is used in the best way. Pressure groups and non-profit organisations, not just ministries and government offices, must learn to make the most of this instrument. This needs much better use of the press and of mass media than has been the norm in minority rights matters up till now. The topic needs improved media coverage – and the report of the committee of experts and the recommendations of the Committee of Ministers could be a valuable "event" worth being exploited in a media campaign, since the points of criticism contained in the report and the recommendations may highlight some of the main concerns of speakers of minority languages.

The construction of the ECRML mechanism gives a good basis for the described division of labour. It not only openly integrates minority rights associations and bodies representing minority language communities in the monitoring scheme, but – due to its relatively short interval of periodical reports – puts the governments in a process of permanent scrutiny. A three-year period of reporting is short. If one bears in mind that the process of examining the country reports takes a lot of time, usually between one and a half and two years, this mechanism brings governments to a situation where they must constantly deal with the ECRML. Immediately after learning the results of one round of monitoring, the relevant government offices must begin to prepare the next country report. This leaves little time to set in motion improvements to the standard of implementation, and makes it difficult to demonstrate achieved improvements in the next report – if such improvements have not been started long before the end of the monitoring process. But progress in reaction to a monitoring report may be reported some years later, with the successive periodical report. Readiness to improve the situation must not be proven at once.

On the other hand, the short interval of reporting gives organisations of minority language speakers a good chance to enter into a permanent dialogue with the responsible government offices. During the monitoring process, these organisations are part of the process anyway. If the government has to start with a new round of reporting soon after the end of the previous monitoring round, an incentive exists to put the contacts between responsible government officials and civil society organisations on a firm and permanent basis. In some states, like Germany, such contacts have nearly been institutionalised. Due to the complex federal structure of state organisation, the ministry responsible for the state report, the Federal Ministry of the Interior, had to set up a scheme of implementation conferences in order to collect the necessary information and to bring all the relevant actors on board. These conferences are not only held on a regular basis with the responsible bureaucrats of the *Länder* administrations, but are also held with the representatives of all the relevant German minority language communities. This gives the minorities a good opportunity to articulate their grievances towards the officials and to enter into a constructive dialogue with their counterparts in the administration. In Germany the positive effect of the co-ordination scheme which had to be created to implement the ECRML has been most openly visible, but also in most other member states the contacts between government officials responsible for minority affairs and the organisations and bodies representing minority interests had to be intensified considerably in the course of the reporting procedure.

The positive effects at the procedural level are thus clearly visible. The contacts between minority organisations and administrations are becoming intensified due to the functioning of the monitoring mechanism. The strengthening of the communicative network between both sides leads to a better mutual understanding of the other's perspectives and problems and helps to set up a constructive dialogue. The committee of experts – as a "neutral" participant in the discourse – to a certain degree stabilises the interaction. Conflicts and differences of perspective will inevitably be brought to the attention of the monitoring body. The committee will then take up the conflicting points in its monitoring reports and will express its position in the dispute. Giving a "neutral" standpoint to a disputed question from the perspective of a non-concerned outsider helps to de-emotionalise the issue. The committee of experts thus takes over to a certain degree the role of an intermediary, if not of a mediator. This is not a formal role; the position given by the committee of experts is not binding, does not contain a ruling or an operative proposal for a conflict solution. The "neutral" assessment of a disputed question by a third, "authoritative" body helps the two sides, however, to agree on an adequate solution.

The committee of experts is not an arbitrary tribunal or an arbitrator. Individual cases are not easily catered for in the monitoring process, since they do not fit into the construction of a "political" monitoring mechanism centred upon structural questions. Most points disputed in practice between government organs and minority communities are not easily decided under the charter in clear judgments according to the legal/illegal divide. The ECRML contains clear answers to most issues of "political choice" in dealing with the status of minority languages, but it does not contain standards which are precise enough for individual cases to be solved under these standards. To give an example: in principle, every family in the territory in which the minority language is used has a right to receive instruction in the minority language for its children. But – in order to be practicable – such families must live in a certain concentration; the demands must add up to numbers of requests where the creation of a separate class or learning group is useful. What the ECRML does not answer in detail is the question of precise thresholds – must there be eight, ten, fifteen or twenty demands in order to fulfil the criterion "whose number is considered to be sufficient"? Obviously, the state in question enjoys a certain "margin of appreciation" in deciding upon the required minimum numbers, although the committee of experts exercises a certain control as to whether the minimum numbers set in practice by the state authorities are not excessive.

Accordingly, the monitoring mechanism of the ECRML with the committee of experts as its central organ is well suited to raise the "big", structural questions of language policy, but is not comparably well-equipped to give clear answers to concrete cases which are disputed between the state and the minorities. Here other mechanisms should be used. This is not to say that the ECRML could not be helpful in resolving individual cases. Case disputes are simply not well placed as an issue to be dealt with in the monitoring mechanism. Individual cases belong to the business of courts – and if there is no international court for a certain category of questions, they belong to national courts. At least in continental European legal systems, the ECRML may be invoked before national courts and tribunals. Some of the governments have even come to the conclusion that the ECRML mainly contains obligations of a "self-executing" nature. This would mean that any claimant may invoke the provisions of the charter as a legal yardstick in a case dispute, or even as the source of a subjective right, in a judicial proceeding before national courts. For some provisions, such as the clear and unconditional requirements of Article 8, paragraph 1, this is arguable – although the drafting history clearly demonstrates that the states parties intended not to create "subjective rights", but only "objective standards". Even purely "objective standards", however, are not irrelevant in most legal orders for deciding a case dispute. They bind the executive and the judiciary and may be invoked, for example, as a source of law when controlling the exercise of discretionary powers of an executive organ. An exercise of administrative discretion which ignores a binding obligation of international law and comes to a result that would violate international legal commitments of the state could not be upheld in a proceeding of judicial control. Certain legal standards may even render discretionary powers irrelevant, if there is only one possibility to fulfil the international obligations. This means that the obligations under the ECRML could give a much more prominent role to minority rights in adjudication before national courts, at least in matters such as education, official use before courts and administrations, or in the distribution of cultural subsidies. The persons concerned, and their lawyers and the associations assisting in such lawsuits, must learn about this potential and how it might be exploited in practice. Since precedents in this regard are still lacking, legal scholarship bears a certain burden in demonstrating where the ECRML is really of relevance for the adjudication of case disputes in the national judiciary, and how the provisions of the charter may best be invoked in such cases. The ECRML is still an instrument too new to be widely known to plaintiffs and their lawyers, but also to administrators and judges. Not only governments, which are under an obligation to disseminate knowledge about the international legal obligations of the state, but also associations and bodies involved in minority protection should endeavour to make known the possibilities granted under these instruments. Otherwise, mechanisms like the ECRML with its monitoring scheme will remain of little relevance for everyday patterns of language use.

Concluding remarks

For the current state of affairs the sceptical question remains: are there any positive effects which may be observed as resulting from the ECRML with its monitoring mechanism? After analysing the work over the past five years, one has to admit that the ECRML has had more effect than initially expected. While at the beginning most professional observers were rather sceptical of possible positive improvements in the foreseeable future, it can be said that today there are reasons to be optimistic. One of the major experiences of all the attempts to establish a functioning international framework of minority language protection was the insight that real progress in minority language matters needs a change in the minds of national politicians, bureaucrats and the majority population in a given country. Such a change in mentality is a slow and extremely painful process, a process where the role of international law is rather limited. But international legal instruments may have significant impact – and the ECRML is the one proof of that. The charter has served as a catalyst for an important learning process in most member states. Already the step of preparing a sensible instrument of ratification is this kind of learning process, a cumbersome, but extremely valuable form. I would prefer to say that ratifying the ECRML is not an easy process for a country. One cannot simply compare the existing state of legislation and policy for minority languages with a given arrangement of international legal obligations. States must define this set of obligations first, and it was intended from the beginning that designing such a "menu" would begin with a review of the national policy of minority language protection and the corresponding legislation and administrative practice. This "cooking" up of the "menu" is cumbersome and slow, but is a helpful process.

In order to define the obligations that make sense in a certain institutional and legal environment, governments must gain a clear overview of the existing national legislation and administrative practices. The central state, setting the policy, is not always aware of the concrete administrative practice in peripheral regions, not to mention the real needs of languages spoken by peripheral local communities living in border regions. Thus, before ratification, and before the adoption or changing of minority language policy, it is important that the central authorities consult and collect information permitting them to have a clear overview of the real need of the languages and to evaluate the opportunities that can be provided by the state. Then a series of political decisions have to be taken. In a way, bureaucracies dealing with the preparation of an instrument of ratification for the ECRML must systematise existing bits and pieces of a minority language policy and must put these pieces together in order to form some kind of coherent national minority language policy. The resulting effect of "rationalisation" should not be underestimated. If you act in a decentralised or even federal state, like Germany, this effect is even stronger. The various levels of government have to enter into a constant dialogue on policy formulation, implementation and reporting if the instrument of ratification and the reports are to conform to the standards. Often, the minorities themselves and their organisations are involved in such a process of more or less constant dialogue. The ECRML thus induces the actors within the states to form an institutionalised communicative network, engaging in a permanent discourse about the reform of relevant policies. This means entering into an unknown learning process in most states. If you look at the German experience, already the ratification procedure and the first report have been so enormously fruitful in creating a communicative network, that I would be content in counting this as a serious success. But the process continues, with the committee of experts and the Committee of Ministers entering the field. The dialogue with third parties from outside, set in motion by the reporting requirement, forces national actors to constantly rethink their positions. It is no longer pure power that counts, but political actors have to justify their actions in legal terms. Minorities and the government offices dealing with minority matters have a strong supporting argument in their quarrels with other offices and ministries.

But what about the substance of the obligations? Does the "menu approach" not lead to sets of obligations that remain insignificant, simply mirror the pre-existing state of legislation and administrative practice? Experience under the ECRML tells us that this is not the case. Remember the factor of ignorance at the central level. Usually the state of minority language policy is much worse than central authorities are inclined to assume. The menu is dominated by the self-image of a certain state, not by its real practice. And often states willingly go beyond the existing state of policy, because they want to give a better image or are willing to make public assurances which are consolidated by transforming these assurances into international legal obligations. The role of the committee of experts is thus more to remind states of their proclaimed self-image and of their political promises than to impose externally defined standards from the outside. This is a much better role than deducing standards from an abstract and open text, intended by states to hide their lack of willingness to progress in minority rights issues. The ECRML thus makes the business of the committee of experts easy – and gives associations and bodies struggling for better minority rights a great chance to confront states with their own "Sunday rhetoric". But such rhetoric is no simple question of politics any more – it has been transformed into concrete legal standards. Such legal standards are created to be exploited by the speakers of minority languages and their organisations. The minority associations and bodies should make adequate use of the mechanisms offered under the charter.

*Professor of German and Comparative Public Law and Public International Law; Director of the Institute for International Affairs, University of Hamburg; Member of the Committee of Experts on the European Charter for Regional or Minority Languages.

1. European Charter for Regional or Minority languages, adopted on 5 November 1995, entered into force on 1 March 1998, ETS No. 158.

2. See also Gaetano Pentassuglia, *Minorities in International Law* (Strasbourg, 2002), p. 130.

3. On the enterprise of creating a workable regime of minority protection in Europe see Christian Scherer-Leydecker, *Minderheiten und sonstige ethnische Gruppen. Eine Studie zur kulturellen Identität im Völkerrecht* (Berlin, 1997), pp. 141-167.

4. Ibid., at pp. 146/47; see also the explanatory report to the ECRML, paragraphs 3-8.

5. As to these draft instruments, see Scherer-Leydecker, op.cit., pp. 151-159.

6. See Pentassuglia, op.cit., pp. 130/31.

7 As an example, see ibid., p.131.

8. Concerning the definition of minority languages in Article 1.a of the ECRML, see Scherer-Leydecker, op.cit., pp. 147/48; see also the explanatory report to the ECRML, paragraphs 18-21 and 30-33.

9. Pentassuglia, op.cit., p. 130; see also the explanatory report to the ECRML, paragraph 11.

10. See in that direction the explanatory report to the ECRML, paragraphs 11 and 13.

11. As to the differences between Part II and Part III see ibid., paragraphs 38-41.

12. Ibid., paragraph 39.

13. Some assistance in understanding the meaning of these rather broad principles might be gained from the explanatory report, ibid., paragraphs 58-75.

14. Concerning this situation, see ibid., paragraph 42.

15. As to this commitment, see ibid., paragraphs 59-60.

16. This is the case in Hungary, for example – see the initial periodical report by Hungary presented to the Secretary General of the Council of Europe in accordance with Article 15 of the ECRML, 7 September 1999, Doc. MIN-LANG/PR (1999) 6, 18-20.

17. See Report of the Committee of Experts of 20 September 2001, Application of the Charter in the Netherlands, Doc. ECRML (2001) 1, paragraphs 10, 21, 22.

18. Article 2, paragraph 2 of the ECRML; see also the explanatory report, paragraphs 43-47.

19. Explanatory report, paragraph 22.

20 Ibid.

21. This advantage is overlooked when critics of the charter's approach claim: "The notion that a variety of factual situations can be addressed through a diversity in legal duties rather than the means of implementing a body of common prescriptions appears questionable ..." – Pentassuglia, op.cit., p. 131.

22. See only the explanation in the explanatory report to the charter, paragraphs 44-45.

23. See more in detail Pentassuglia, op.cit., p. 201-2.

24. See also the explanatory report to the charter, paragraph 127.

25. See Article 15, paragraph 2 of the ECRML.

26. See also the explanatory report, paragraph 131.

27. See also the explanatory report, paragraphs 128-29.

29. See Article 17, paragraph 3 of the ECRML.

30. Biennial report by the Secretary General to the Parliamentary Assembly on the Application of the European Charter for Regional or Minority Languages, Doc. 8879 of 18 October 2000, 2; the report may be found under

http://www.coe.int/T/E/Legal_Affairs/Local_and_regional_Democracy/Regional_o
r_Minority_languages/Documentation/4_Secretary_General's_reports

31. As to the role of the "on-the-spot visits", see the biennial report by the Secretary General to the Parliamentary Assembly on the application of the charter, Doc. 9540 of 11 September 2002, 3; cf. also Pentassuglia, op.cit., p. 202.

32. See Pentassuglia, op.cit., p. 202.

33. As to the role of "inspections" in other schemes of compliance control, see Stefan Oeter, "Inspection in International Law. Monitoring Compliance and the Problem of Implementation in International Law", 28 *Netherlands Yearbook of International Law* (1997), pp. 101-169.

34. See Article 16, paragraph 3, second sentence, of the ECRML.

35. For the state of ratification see http://www.coe.int/T/E/Legal_Affairs/Local_and_
regional_Democracy/Regional_or_Minority_languages/Charter/6_States

36. The reports of the committee of experts may be found under http://www.coe.int/T/E/Legal_Affairs/Local_and_regional_Democracy/Regional_or_Mi
nority_languages/Documentation/2_Committee_of_Experts_reports

37. The recommendations of the Committee of Ministers may be found under http://www.coe.int/T/E/ Legal_Affairs/Local_and_regional_Democracy/Regional_or_Mi
nority_languages/Documentation/3_Committee_of_Ministers

38. These reports may be found under http://www.coe.int/T/E/Legal_Affairs/Local_
and_regional_Democracy/Regional_or_Minority_languages/Documentation/4_Secreta
ry_General's_reports

39. See the survey of monitoring activities at http://www.coe.int/T/E/Legal_
Affairs/Local_and_regional_Democracy/Regional_or_Minority_languages/Charter/6_States

40. See the explanatory report to the ECRML, paragraphs 57-58 and 61-64.

41. See only Miklós Kontra et al., "Conceptualising and Implementing Linguistic Human Rights", in Miklós Kontra et al. (eds), *Language: A Right and a Resource. Approaching Linguistic Human Rights* (Budapest, 1999), 1, at p. 13.

42. See Andrea Szalai, "Linguistic Human Rights Problems among Romani and Boyash Speakers in Hungary with Special Attention to Education", in Miklós Kontra et al. (eds), op.cit., pp. 297-315.

43. Biennial report by the Secretary General to the Parliamentary Assembly on the application of the charter, Doc. 9540 of 11 September 2002, 3.

44. Concerning this problem, see also Kontra et al., op.cit., pp. 10-11.

45. See only the committee of experts' report on the application of the charter in Germany, ECRML (2002) 1, paragraphs 142, 181, 219, 297, 328, 359, 400, 438, 480, as well as Finding K at the end of the report.

46. See ibid., paragraphs 180, 481-485.

47. See also the biennial report by the Secretary General to the Parliamentary Assembly on the application of the charter, Doc. 9540 of 11 September 2002, 3.

48. Ibid., 4.

49. Ibid., 4.

50. Ibid.

51. Ibid.

52. See the survey of monitoring activities at http://www.coe.int/minlang

53. See Pentassuglia, op.cit., pp. 203-04.

54.
See http://www.coe.int/T/E/Legal_Affairs/Local_and_regional_Democracy/Regional_
or_Minority_ languages/Documentation/ 2_Committee_of_Experts_reports

CHAPTER 7

IMPLEMENTING MINORITY RIGHTS IN THE FRAMEWORK OF THE CSCE/OSCE

Claus Neukirch*, Katrin Simhandl, Wolfgang Zellner

Introduction

The Conference on Security and Co-operation in Europe (CSCE) was founded in the days of the Cold War. The aim was to contribute to a reduction of tensions between the East and West by providing a channel for communication as well as a platform for co-operation. Following the end of the East-West confrontation, the de facto institutionalisation of the CSCE, which was originally designed as a series of follow-up conferences, led to it being re-named the Organization for Security and Co-operation in Europe (OSCE) in 1994. Built upon the principle of consensus, the OSCE documents are not legally binding, but entail strong political commitment. During the Cold War period, minority topics played only a minor role; the main focus was on hard security policy, such as arms control. Although the minority issue was mentioned comparably early, concrete formulations of standards had to be developed in the following decades. Based on the principles of the Helsinki Final Act (1975), the CSCE/OSCE developed different political mechanisms relevant for minority protection. Moreover, it established two particular instruments, the High Commissioner on National Minorities and the long-term missions active in this field.

The CSCE/OSCE mechanism regarding minorities

Political commitments and mechanisms in the human dimension

The consultations on what became later known as the "Helsinki Process" started in 1973. The concluding document of this first conference, the Helsinki Final Act (1975),[1] laid down ten basic principles ("Decalogue") regarding relations among the participating states, on the one hand, and between governments and citizens, on the other. "Questions relating to Security in Europe" are found in the first section (Basket I), minority issues are mentioned in Principle VII, "Respect for human rights and fundamental freedoms, including the freedom of thought, conscience, religion or belief":

> The participating States on whose territory national minorities exist will respect the right of persons belonging to such minorities to equality before the law, will afford them the full opportunity for the actual enjoyment of human rights and fundamental freedoms and will, in this manner, protect their legitimate interests in this sphere (Principle VII, paragraph 4).

With the formulation of "on whose territory national minorities exist", it is left up to the states to define whether national minorities exist on their territory or not. This could of course prevent talks on national minority issues from the very start.

A follow-up meeting of the Helsinki conference was held in Madrid 1980-83. Its concluding document did not provide any new provisions on minority issues. What had been agreed on in Helsinki was merely reaffirmed but not enhanced (Chapter I, paragraph 16). Against the background of "perestroika" and "glasnost", the Vienna follow-up meeting (1986-89) addressed minority questions within these increasingly co-operative surroundings more prominently. In addition to reaffirming the principle of non-discrimination (paragraph 18), the concluding document also calls for the protection or creation of conditions for the promotion of the identity of national minorities (paragraph 19).

The Concluding Document of the Copenhagen Meeting of the Conference on the Human Dimension of the CSCE held in November 1990 (Copenhagen Document) expressed a new consensus on minority issues. While the Charter of Paris for A New Europe – adopted at the very same time at the summit meeting of the CSCE – was mainly driven by euphoria at the end of the Cold War, the Copenhagen Document is widely regarded as a key success for the development of minority rights. Its provisions inspired the formulation of other documents and their being incorporated into bilateral treaties. Thus, these provisions also became legally binding.

A whole chapter of the Copenhagen Document is dedicated to detailed provisions regarding the treatment of minorities (Chapter IV, paragraphs 30-40). Apart from the more general obligation to create conditions for the promotion of the identity of national minorities (paragraph 33), the document includes provisions such as a minority-specific ban on discrimination (paragraph 31), the right of minorities to use their mother tongue (paragraph 32.1), the right to profess and practise their religion freely (paragraph 32.3), the freedom of assembly including cross-border contacts (paragraph 32.6), the right to establish and maintain their own educational, cultural and religious institutions (paragraph 32.2), and to participate effectively in public affairs (paragraph 35). Finally, the participating states have committed themselves to the endeavour of ensuring that persons belonging to national minorities have adequate opportunities for instruction of, or in, their mother tongue (paragraph 34). More generally, the importance of a democratic framework for the respect of minority rights, as well as the impact of these rights on peace and stability in the respective states are underlined (paragraph 30); furthermore, xenophobia and discrimination are condemned. With regard to the latter, "the particular problems of Roma/Gypsies" are mentioned (paragraph 40). This is the only minority specifically mentioned in the document.

But most importantly, according to the Copenhagen Document, it is no longer up to the state to define which minorities live on its territory and which individuals belong to it. Rather, it lies with the individual to declare whether he or she belongs to a minority or not: "To belong to a national minority is a matter of a person's individual choice and no disadvantage may arise from the exercise of such choice" (paragraph 32).

In the following year (1991), an expert meeting on national minority issues was held in Geneva. It aimed to develop regulations to prevent violent outbreaks of ethnic conflict. After the encouraging results of the Copenhagen Document, this meeting might be regarded as a setback compared to what had already been achieved. And it is especially one remark that calls the former achievements into question: "not all ethnic, cultural, linguistic or religious differences necessarily lead to the creation of national minorities" (Chapter II, paragraph 4). As this formulation might be interpreted in such a way that it would be again up to the state to decide what group represents a national minority and what group does not, several states have filed a caveat against this provision. Quite encouragingly, however, is the following formulation of the Geneva document:

> Issues concerning national minorities, as well as compliance with international obligations and commitments concerning the rights of persons belonging to them, are matters of legitimate international concern and consequently do not constitute exclusively an internal affair of the respective State (Chapter II, paragraph 3).

By this statement the principle of non-intervention in internal affairs was softened. This principle had been one of the OSCE rules since its incorporation into the Decalogue of the Final Act in 1975.

The Moscow meeting of the Conference on the Human Dimension of the CSCE in 1991 did not provide any new minority standards. However, an already existing monitoring instrument, the so-called Vienna Mechanism, was enhanced. The Vienna Mechanism had been introduced at the Vienna follow-up meeting in 1989 in order to monitor compliance with CSCE/OSCE commitments relating to the human dimension more closely.

The Vienna Mechanism is a political mechanism, which is separated into four different phases. In the first phase, participating states are obliged to respond to requests for information made to them by other participating states on questions related to the human dimension of the OSCE. In the second phase, countries are obliged to hold bilateral meetings if so requested by another participating state, with the aim to resolve specific problems regarding the human dimension. In the third phase, such issues can also be brought to the attention of other participating states and the last phase foresees the possibility to discuss them in the framework of review conferences, human dimension implementation meetings or meetings of the Permanent Council (Section "Human Dimension of the CSCE", paragraphs 1-4).

The 1991 Document of the Moscow Meeting of the Conference on the Human Dimension of the CSCE further elaborated this mechanism which was already quite strong with regard to the OSCE's otherwise consensual culture, as the agreement of the state concerned is not required. Firstly, participating states enhanced the effectiveness of the existing provisions by introducing clear time frames for the first and second phase of the human dimension mechanism. Under the Moscow Mechanism, participating states were now obliged to respond within ten days to requests for information and to representations; bilateral meetings were to take place as soon as possible, as a rule within one week of the date of the request (paragraph 2). Moreover, a resource list of human dimension experts was compiled and provisions were introduced allowing for the establishment of missions of experts or rapporteurs. This procedure represented a considerable improvement, for one of the limitations of the Vienna Mechanism had been that there was no provision for fact-finding or independent examination of situations disputed between the states involved.

The Moscow Mechanism consists of four different procedures to establish missions of experts or rapporteurs. According to the first procedure, a participating state may invite, on his own initiative, an expert mission, consisting of up to three experts, to address or contribute to the resolution of questions within its territory relating to the human dimension. In the second procedure, one or more participating states, having put into effect the first or second phase of the human dimension mechanism, may request the Office for Democratic Institutions and Human Rights (ODIHR) of the OSCE to "inquire of another participating State whether it would agree to invite a mission of experts to address a particular, clearly defined question on its territory relating to the human dimension of the CSCE" (Chapter I, paragraph 8).

Apart from the possibility that a state can invite a mission of experts, states can also initiate obligatory missions of rapporteurs to another state. In case a participating state has not established a mission of experts within a period of ten days after such an enquiry has been made, or in case the requesting state judges that the issue in question has not been resolved, the requesting state may, with the support of at least five other participating states, initiate the establishment of a mission of up to three rapporteurs (paragraph 9).

Finally, as a fourth procedure, a participating state, with the support of at least nine other participating states, might invoke a mission of rapporteurs if it considers that a particularly serious threat to the fulfilment of the provisions of the human dimension has arisen in another participating state. Alternatively, the Permanent Council, upon the request of any participating state, may decide to establish a mission of experts or rapporteurs.

Missions of experts under the Moscow Mechanism are more powerful than missions of rapporteurs, which can also be established against the consent of the host state. Expert missions are not only entitled to gather information necessary for carrying out their tasks, they may also, as appropriate, use their "good offices and mediation services to promote dialogue and co-operation among interested parties" (paragraph 5). In contrast, missions of rapporteurs are confined to a fact-finding and advising function.[2] At the same time, the host state has less influence on missions of rapporteurs than on missions of experts, thereby balancing the greater strengths of the latter. Whereas, according to the procedures for establishing missions of experts, the inviting state shall select the experts from the resource list (paragraph 4), the requesting and the requested state are entitled to choose each one of the rapporteurs from the list of experts. Moreover, a mission of experts shall submit its observations only to the inviting state within three weeks after the mission has been established, whereas the report of the rapporteurs shall be submitted to all participating states concerned and to the ODIHR within three weeks after the appointment of the last rapporteur. In the first case, the inviting state shall then transmit the report of the mission of experts within the next three weeks, together with a description of actions it has taken or intends to take upon it, to the other participating states (paragraph 7). In the second case, the requested state shall submit its observations on the report of the rapporteurs to the ODIHR within the following three weeks and the ODIHR shall then circulate the report to all participating states without delay. In both cases, the reports may be discussed in the Permanent Council, which may decide on any possible follow-up action.

As mentioned above, the human dimension mechanisms of the OSCE are political mechanisms. They are state-centred and can be activated only by governments. Individuals or non-governmental organisations (NGOs) cannot directly activate the mechanisms but they can be involved in the procedures at different stages. First of all, they can press governments to activate the mechanism. Moreover, missions of experts and rapporteurs can turn to individuals and NGOs within the framework of their fact-finding and mediating activities.

In 1992, the follow-up conference in Helsinki adopted the mandate of the High Commissioner on National Minorities (HCNM) and introduced provisions which were later used for the establishment of long-term missions. Both instruments proved to be a great success (see below); however, as far as the protection of minorities is concerned, the HCNM has certainly to be regarded as more important.

With the 1992 Helsinki Document, the CSCE/OSCE standard-setting process, with regard to national minorities questions, was largely concluded. Neither the concluding document of the Lisbon summit (1996), nor the documents adopted at the Istanbul summit of 1999, provided new minority provisions. Instead they reaffirmed the existing ones. From then on, the implementation of the agreed principles would become increasingly important.

The High Commissioner on National Minorities (HCNM)

If one compares the HCNM's mandate and the instruments he actually employs, one will quickly realise that the mandate provides only a flexible basis, and that nearly everything that represents the institution of the High Commissioner today was developed by its first incumbent Max van der Stoel who served as HCNM from 1993 to 2001. Therefore, we will first outline the main stipulations of the mandate of the HCNM, and then introduce its self-made working instruments.

a. The mandate of the High Commissioner on National Minorities

The following paragraph makes clear that the HCNM's primary task is lowering tensions and solving conflicts and that, although ensuring compliance with minority rights is, in and of itself, a high-ranking aim, it is subordinate to two superior objectives. This is highlighted in the following key sentence in the High Commissioner's mandate, comprised in the 1992 Helsinki Document, which reads:

The High Commissioner will provide "early warning" and, as appropriate, "early action", at the earliest possible stage in regard to tensions involving national minority issues which have not yet developed beyond an early warning stage, but in the judgment of the High Commissioner, have the potential to develop into a conflict within the CSCE area, affecting peace, stability or relations between participating States, requiring the attention of and action by the Council or the CSO [Committee of Senior Officials] (Section II, paragraph 3).

Therefore, Alfredsson and Türk rightly state that the whole concept of the High Commissioner represents a "security-oriented approach to minority rights".[3] This is also underlined by three basic principles stressed in the mandate: impartiality, confidentiality and co-operation (paragraphs 4 and 8). While the principle of impartiality seems to be self-evident at first glance, a close look shows that it is not. From this principle follows that the High Commissioner is not "an instrument for the protection of minorities or a sort of international ombudsman who acts on their behalf. This is reflected in the title: OSCE High Commissioner *on* National Minorities and not *for* National Minorities."[4] Van der Stoel himself added that the HCNM "has not been defined as an instrument of the human dimension",[5] but rather its mandate defines it as an instrument for dealing with "*tensions* involving national minority issues" (mandate, paragraph 3, emphasis added). This is also underlined by the stipulation of the mandate that the High Commissioner shall not deal with individual cases (paragraph 5.c). The main function of the principle of confidentiality is to provide a low profile to the HCNM's activities in order to prevent actors from exploiting international attention through raising the level of escalation. The principle of co-operation is not explicitly mentioned in the mandate, but it can be derived from the inherent logic of the institution of the High Commissioner and of the whole OSCE as a non-coercive international organisation. Consequently, the HCNM's recommendations (see below) are neither legally nor politically binding, their impact is solely based on the institutional and personal authority of the High Commissioner and on the support they enjoy by the participating states and other international organisations.

The mandate is very brief in outlining specific working instruments for the HCNM. Its paragraph 11.a stipulates that the High Commissioner shall "collect and receive information regarding national minority issues" from a series of sources including the parties directly concerned, the media and NGOs. Paragraph 25 stresses that the "High Commissioner will not communicate with and will not acknowledge communications from any person or organisation which practises or publicly condones terrorism or violence". Paragraph 11.c stipulates that the High Commissioner shall "be able to pay a visit" to "any participating State" and communicate "with parties directly concerned" in order to collect information and assess the situation. During these visits, the High Commissioner may also "discuss the questions with the parties, and where appropriate promote dialogue, confidence and co-operation between them" (paragraph 12). It should be pointed out that both the instruments of paying visits and of having discussions are derived from the main function of collecting information under the headline of early warning. This clearly underscores that the spirit of the mandate was mainly guided by the task of early warning and not, as it was developed by the High Commissioner later on, by early action. Paragraphs 31 to 36 provide the High Commissioner with the possibility to involve experts, and it is only in this context that the term "recommendations", in the sense of recommendations made by these experts, is mentioned (paragraph 34).

b. Working instruments developed by the High Commissioner

The scarcity of concrete working instruments provided by the mandate reflects the inability or unwillingness of many participating states to conceive the High Commissioner as the highly operational institution into which it soon developed. On the other hand, this *tabula rasa* situation in combination with a highly flexible mandate and the broad support Van der Stoel enjoyed – both from nearly all participating states and important international organisations, namely the EU – enabled him to introduce a whole series of working instruments.

Specific recommendations to governments: As provided by the mandate, Van der Stoel held thousands of discussions with primary actors. On this basis, he developed the instrument of specific recommendations to governments, mostly in the form of a letter to the respective foreign ministers. Originally, the High Commissioner wanted "to repeat in concise form what I had tried to convey" and "to complete this by suggesting specific steps."[6] But soon Van der Stoel found out that presenting these letters to the Permanent Council would substantively raise their authority by mobilising the support of many participating states. This soon became standard procedure and, after some time, some but not all recommendations were also released to the general public and published on the HCNM's website.[7]

General recommendations: International minority norms are frequently too abstract to be applied to concrete problems. This concerns especially the issue areas of education, language use and participation in public life of national minorities. Van der Stoel therefore asked the Foundation on Inter-Ethnic Relations, an NGO he founded to support his work, to convene with panels of experts to work out three sets of general recommendations: the Hague Recommendations regarding the Education Rights of National Minorities; the Oslo Recommendations regarding the Linguistic Rights of National Minorities; and the Lund Recommendations on the Effective Participation of National Minorities in Public Life.[8] Although neither the High Commissioner nor the groups of experts had any mandate to set new OSCE norms, the three sets of recommendations had a certain impact just by their mere existence and because they targeted the three fields where there was an urgent need for practicable concepts. However, the attempt to include the Lund recommendations in the document of the 1999 Istanbul summit, and thus make them politically binding, failed.[9]

Statements: The High Commissioner is, in general, very restricted concerning media contacts and public statements. In selected cases, however, he did issue statements, which did not contradict the principle of confidentiality. Such statements followed discussions and consultations by the High Commissioner with the actors concerned and had the function of reassuring some groups of actors and of increasing the commitment of others by making it public. In very rare cases, the High Commissioner also issued statements without prior consultations, especially when he was concerned by rising tensions.

Problem-solving workshops and projects: In situations of either an imminent crisis or of an apparent need of new concepts for strategic problems, the High Commissioner invited majority and minority actors to so-called problem-solving workshops. In addition, in order to support his preventive diplomacy, the High Commissioner organised a series of projects, mainly with the help of the Foundation on Inter-Ethnic Relations. Examples include "projects in the educational field ... for the improvement of minority education, including the training of teachers and the publication of school books ..., *inter alia,* in Albania, ..., Macedonia, Kyrgyzstan and Ukraine."[10] In Estonia and Latvia, information brochures on citizenship questions were published. In Ukraine, the High Commissioner took over the chair of an international donors' conference for the Crimean Tatars. These few examples show that the classical means of preventive diplomacy have to be supported by more practical efforts in order to become effective.

The High Commissioner's office at The Hague: Finally, the development of the High Commissioner's office has to be mentioned. In 1993, Van der Stoel started with two staff members, today the office roughly comprises a 15-person staff covering all relevant countries in which the HCNM is active.

To sum up, the first incumbent High Commissioner invented and established a whole range of working instruments, which, though fully covered by the spirit of the mandate, go far beyond its letter. Thus, Van der Stoel succeeded in translating an innovative idea for the regulation of interethnic conflicts into a workable institution.

Field activities

Apart from the missions of experts and rapporteurs, established in the framework of the human dimension mechanisms, the OSCE can also establish long-term missions in participating states, which might be mandated to engage in the human dimension and especially in the field of minority protection. As a rule, each OSCE field activity is provided with a specific mandate describing the goals and tasks of the particular mission. Mandates are normally restricted to a period of six months, but are regularly extended. Missions are established, mandated and provided with a budget by the Permanent Council. As the Permanent Council decides only by consensus, the mandate as well as the budget of each mission is a result of political negotiations aimed at bringing together differing views and interests. Consequently, mission mandates are mostly broad and vague and rarely give clear guidance on what to do and not to do. It is within the competence of the Permanent Council and the Chairman-in-Office to provide missions with additional guidance, but, as a rule, heads of missions have a relatively broad autonomy in deciding in which issues and how a mission should become engaged. Thus, OSCE field activities might become active in the field of minority protection even if this task is not clearly written down in their official mandates. According to the Charter for European Security (paragraph 38), adopted by the OSCE Istanbul summit of 1999, mandates of long-term missions may, *inter alia*, include the following:

- providing assistance and advice or formulating recommendations in areas agreed by the OSCE and the host country;
- observing compliance with OSCE commitments and providing advice or recommendations for improved compliance;
- assisting in the organisation and monitoring of elections;
- providing support for the primacy of law and democratic institutions and for the maintenance and restoration of law and order;
- helping to create conditions for negotiation or other measures that could facilitate the peaceful settlement of conflicts;
- verifying and/or assisting in fulfilling agreements on the peaceful settlement of conflicts;
- providing support in the rehabilitation and reconstruction of various aspects of society.

The task of observing compliance with OSCE commitments and providing advice or recommendations for improved compliance, which is inherent, at least indirectly, in every mission mandate, strongly links the work of the missions to the Copenhagen Document and other provisions mentioned above. Also, the recommendations of the HCNM might be a starting point for a mission to take action. However, missions can also take the initiative to deal with minority issues on their own. The way missions act in such cases will be discussed later in the next section of this chapter.

Main results in the field of minority rights

The human dimension mechanism in practice

The Vienna Mechanism was used at least 103 times between 1989 and April 1990, but predominantly in the context of East-West relations and hardly with regard to minority issues, as single human rights cases had dominated the CSCE during that time. With respect to national minorities, the Vienna Mechanism was applied for the first time by Hungary in 1990 against Romania in connection with the riots in Transylvania. In 1992, Austria invoked the mechanism in relation to the Kurdish minority in Turkey, and Russia requested the exchange of information under the provisions of the mechanism in that same year from Estonia. Russia did this with regard to the new Estonian citizenship legislation, which effectively prevented Russians and other non-Estonians, who settled in Estonia after 1940, from receiving Estonian citizenship.

The Moscow Mechanism was only activated a few times, but when it was invoked it mostly involved questions regarding minority protection. The most prominent examples are the expert missions to Moldova and Estonia.

On the request of the Moldovan government, the ODIHR sent an expert mission under the Moscow Mechanism to Moldova between 30 January and 4 February 1993 to conduct an investigation on the current legislation and implementation of minority rights and interethnic relations in the country.

The mission had meetings with representatives of political parties, national minorities and various officials, including representatives of the self-proclaimed republics of Transnistria and Gagauzia. In its report, the expert mission came up with a series of recommendations on how to further improve interethnic relations in Moldova.[12] Given the fact that a long-term mission was established in Moldova around the same time, and that a Personal Representative of the OSCE Chairman-in-Office had, already in September 1992, reported extensively to the Committee of Senior Officials on the situation in the Transnistrian region, the full impact of the expert mission can hardly be estimated. During the following years the OSCE mission to Moldova and the HCNM were the main political instruments for the OSCE in the field of minority protection in Moldova.

Also, the expert mission invited by the Estonian government, under the Moscow Mechanism, to study Estonian legislation and to compare it with universally accepted human rights norms was later followed up by a long-term mission. The expert mission visited Estonia from 2 to 5 December 1992 and met with representatives of the Estonian Government, NGOs and the local administration of the cities in north-eastern Estonia, which were mainly inhabited by Russian-speakers. The "mission found no evidence of deliberate discrimination among individuals on the basis of membership in ethnic, religious or language groups",[13] but issued several recommendations aimed at improving the situation of the non-Estonian population. The expert mission paid particular attention to the question of citizenship, immigration and language legislation, and so did the HCNM and the long-term mission, which was active in Estonia from 1993 to 2001. It was rather the long-term involvement of the OSCE through these instruments – which were backed by the continued efforts of other international organisations such as the Council of Europe and the European Union – that helped to improve the situation of the non-Estonian population in Estonia over the years, than the expert mission under the Moscow Mechanism. The substantive recommendations of this mission represented a starting point for the long-term mission, which was headed, in its first months, by one former member of the expert mission. The notion that it should be in the interest of Estonia to facilitate the integration of the Russian-speaking population and to provide them with equal rights, including citizenship, had been a valid presumption of OSCE activities, not only in Estonia but also in neighbouring Latvia.

Nevertheless, one has to concede that the Moscow Mechanism has not produced any substantive results or achievements in the field of minority rights and that its importance was minor in comparison to the HCNM and the long-term missions through which the OSCE was and still is active in a series of countries.

The High Commissioner on National Minorities in action

A detailed description of the activities of the High Commissioner on National Minorities (HCNM) or even an analysis of his effectiveness[14] are far beyond the scope of this article. What can be provided here is a brief overview of the main activities of the HCNM in the countries where he has been active as well as some tentative remarks on his effectiveness in contributing to the solution of interethnic conflicts.

Until 2003, the High Commissioner has worked in or on the following countries: Albania, Croatia, Estonia, the Federal Republic of Yugoslavia including Kosovo, Georgia, Greece, Hungary, Kazakhstan, Kyrgyzstan, Latvia, Lithuania, "the former Yugoslav Republic of Macedonia", Moldova, Romania, the Russian Federation, Slovakia, Tajikistan, Turkey, Ukraine, and Uzbekistan. With the exception of two, these are all post-communist states. In addition, the High Commissioner has issued two reports on the situation of the Roma/Gypsies. However, at the same time he stressed that it would be better for the ODIHR to address this issue within the human dimension, because it lacked the triangular relationship between majority, minority and kin-state typical for the HCNM's mandate.[15]

a. The Baltic countries

The HCNM paid only one visit to Lithuania in 1993 with hardly any follow-up activities.[16] Estonia[17] and Latvia,[18] however, represent one of the High Commissioner's main focal points from 1993 onwards. Contrary to Lithuania, which followed the so-called zero option granting citizenship to each permanent resident of the country, Estonia and Latvia have adopted new citizenship laws which only gave citizenship to the citizens of the pre-war republics and their descendants. This consequential decision has placed large numbers of Russian-speaking migrants from the Soviet period, roughly one third of the populations, under the status of "alien" or even stateless persons. When assessing the security risks of this situation, one has to remember that the Russian Federation, which increasingly made the protection of the rights of its ethnic kin living abroad a part of its foreign policy programme, still had armed forces stationed in both countries until 1994. In the early 1990s, governments and majorities both in Estonia and in Latvia followed a clearly exclusionist approach hoping that most of the Russian speakers would leave these countries in order to facilitate integrating the rest. Although the High Commissioner had to accept the basic construction of citizenship legislation in Estonia and Latvia – as these laws were already in place when he started his activities there in 1993 – he continually tried to liberalise them and at the same time to replace the exclusionist policies in both countries by a more integrative approach. Consequently, he had to deal with a broad range of highly detailed questions on the naturalisation process, including the eligibility of different minority groups for naturalisation, the (interim) status of alien and stateless persons, the treatment of otherwise stateless children as well as the level of difficulty, the organisation and the fees of language and other examinations conditional for naturalisation. In addition, in both countries, he had to address the topic of legislation to protect the state languages which restricted the use of minority languages, namely Russian, even in the private sphere.

Taken together, the activities of the High Commissioner in Estonia and Latvia represent a clear success story. Of course, not all the problems in the implementation of the norms of minority protection have been solved up to now, particularly not in Latvia. However, in view of his mandate, the High Commissioner has been completely successful, as majority-minority relations in Estonia and Latvia no longer represent a threat to stability and security in Europe. This has been achieved by a substantial liberalisation of the naturalisation process combined with a gradual transition to more integrative policies by the majority governments. In addition to other international organisations, the HCNM co-operated closely with the OSCE missions in the two countries. The main reason for his success, however, was the desire of Estonia and Latvia to join the European Union, the readiness of the majority elite in both countries to change their minority policies in order to reach this aim and the policy of the European Commission which strongly backed the recommendations of the High Commissioner and, in fact, made them part of the 1993 Copenhagen accession criteria. Thus, the success of the HCNM is inseparably linked to that of the EU. It must be stressed, however, that it was the High Commissioner who was the focal point of all minority-related activities in Estonia and Latvia. An interesting question will be whether the HCNM will be able to continue to address minority-related questions in these two countries once Estonia and Latvia have joined the European Union.

b. Hungarian minorities and Hungary proper

In the early 1990s, renowned experts assessed the conflicts related to Hungarian minorities as being the most inflammatory after those in the former Yugoslavia and there was concern that these two originally separated conflicts would become amalgamated through the Hungarian minority in Vojvodina.[19] Therefore, it is no surprise that the High Commissioner started to deal with Romania and Slovakia from his very first year in office.[20]

In Romania, minority education and language use were the most prominent issues the HCNM had to address. In the first half of the 1990s, the situation was aggravated by the fact that a post-communist government was co-operating with extremist nationalist parties, while the Democratic Alliance of Hungarians in Romania (RMDSZ) was flirting with concepts of (territorial) autonomy. In 1995, the adoption of the highly contested Law on Education threatened a substantially higher level of escalation. In this situation, the High Commissioner succeeded in reducing tensions by issuing a public statement which stressed the flexibility of the implementation of this law. In 1996, he facilitated the signing of the Hungarian-Romanian Treaty on Friendship and Co-operation. When in late 1996 a broad centrist coalition including the Hungarian Alliance had entered government, the minority-related agenda changed. While questions of secondary education and minority language use in local administration were gradually solved, the centre of discussion shifted to minority-language university education. The RMDSZ demanded a Hungarian-language university, which would have led to the *status quo ante* of the 1950s before the Romanian Babes University and the Hungarian Bolyai University were forcibly merged. In contrast, majority representatives backed by the High Commissioner supported the concept of multiculturalism developed at the Babes-Bolyai University in Cluj, since the early 1990's. While this issue has still not been solved definitively, it has lost much of its explosiveness – and it is virtually the only question which is still debated upon between majority and minority. Today, on the basis of protocols renewed yearly, the RMDSZ supports a minority government formed by the meanwhile social democratic and formerly post-communist party, which only a couple of years ago, the Hungarian Alliance saw as its arch enemy. Thus, Romania represents an example of a successful conflict transformation to which the High Commissioner has contributed substantially. And while the general political aim in Romania – to join the EU – is the same as in the Baltic states, it must be noted that the EU has not dealt very intensively with the issue of the Hungarian minority in Romania but focused much more on the plight of the Roma/Gypsies.

In Slovakia, the High Commissioner also dealt with questions of minority education and language use as well as with the minority-related consequences of administrative reforms. In 1993, he succeeded in guiding the Slovak and the Hungarian governments into reaching consensus on the establishment of an international team of experts to study the situation of the Hungarian minority in Slovakia and the Slovak minority in Hungary. This confidence-building measure was implemented between 1993 and 1996 over a period of ongoing conflicts between the Slovak and the Hungarian governments peaking with the adoption of the highly contentious Law on State Language in November 1995 as well as discussions on territorial autonomy in 1995 and 1996. On the latter issue, the HCNM wrote in a letter to the Slovak foreign minister in February 1996 that there was no legal obligation to introduce territorial autonomy on an ethnic basis.[21] After the September 1998 elections, the Meciar era came to an end and a new coalition including Hungarian minority representatives entered government. Debates were soon focused on the Law on Use of National Minority Languages, which, after several meetings between the HCNM, government officials as well as representatives of the European Commission and the Council of Europe, was finally adopted in July 1999. After the 2002 elections, the Hungarian party remained in the government. As in Romania, the High Commissioner helped in Slovakia to keep governments composed of interethnic groups together by assisting in the solution of concrete problems. In this way, the HCNM also contributed substantially to the accession of Slovakia to the EU and, in more general terms, to a process of successful conflict transformation.

As Hungary hosts only small groups of national minorities but as a kin-state gives strong support to the Hungarians living abroad, the High Commissioner's activities there were different from those in Romania and Slovakia. Although the HCNM dealt in Hungary with the implementation of the Act on the Rights of National and Ethnic Minorities and related issues, thereby introducing an element of reciprocity, his main task was to discuss questions on external Hungarian minorities, the related policies of the Hungarian Government as well as the bilateral treaties between Hungary and Romania and/or Slovakia.

c. The Balkan countries

In the Balkans, the High Commissioner was active in Albania, Croatia, "the former Yugoslav Republic of Macedonia", and in the Federal Republic of Yugoslavia including Kosovo. In Albania, he was mainly engaged in 1993 and 1994 in addressing issues surrounding the minority-language education of the Greek minority. Disputes on this question had reached a level that threatened interstate relations. After the Law on the Pre-University Education System was adopted in June 1995, the interethnic situation improved.[22] With the breakdown of state structures during the 1997 crisis, the focus of the conflict shifted away from interethnic issues and efforts to regulate the conflict were assumed by the OSCE presence in Albania.

In Croatia, the HCNM got involved immediately after the conclusion of the 1995 Dayton Accords. His main concern was the two-way return of refugees and internally displaced persons, of Croats to eastern Slavonia and Serbs to Krajina and western Slavonia. Although the High Commissioner, together with the OSCE Mission to Croatia and other international organisations, put constant pressure on the Croatian Government to live up to its obligations, progress was very limited until the death of President Tudjman. After the elections in January and February 2000, the political climate improved greatly, but strong resistance to refugee returns remained at the level of the local authorities.[23]

"The former Yugoslav Republic of Macedonia" has been the prime focus of the High Commissioner in the Balkans. Since 1993, he has paid more than 50 visits to this small country which, deeply split between the Macedonian majority and a nearly 23% Albanian minority, had to fight heavily to safeguard its statehood. The HCNM focused mainly on issues related to the Albanian minority, namely the national census, Albanian-language education, especially higher education, employment of ethnic Albanians in the public sector, especially in the army and the police, local self-government, and the use of the minority, that is, the Albanian, flag. The members of the Albanian community felt that they were being treated as "second-class citizens". On the other hand, ethnic Macedonians were concerned that the rising demands by ethnic Albanians would lead to the break-up of this in any case weak country. As early as 1993, the High Commissioner recommended the establishment of a pedagogical faculty for Albanian-language teachers. However, the reaction of the Macedonian authorities was slow, and in 1995, radical ethnic Albanians, supported, however, by all Albanian parties in "the former Yugoslav Republic of Macedonia", founded the unofficial University of Tetovo which was reminiscent of parallel structures in Kosovo. In riots following the foundation of the university, one person was killed and several others injured. The High Commissioner set off for "the former Yugoslav Republic of Macedonia" immediately to try to reduce tensions. During the following years, he focused increasingly on the issue of Albanian-language university education. In 1995, he proposed the establishment of a Higher Education Centre for Public Administration and Business, and in 1998, he suggested the foundation of an Albanian-language State University College for teacher training. In the meantime, the country was burdened by the huge wave of refugees from Kosovo in April and May 1999, which led the High Commissioner to issue his first formal early warning statement before the OSCE Permanent Council on 12 May 1999. In April 2000, the HCNM presented detailed recommendations for a private institution for Albanian-language higher education, and in July of the same year, the Law on Education was changed so that, for the first time, it authorised private institutions of higher education in minority languages. In October 2000, the High Commissioner presented a business plan for the South East European University at Tetovo, which finally started its activities in autumn 2001.

The activities of the High Commissioner as well as those of many other international organisations could not prevent the outbreak of the crisis in the spring and summer of 2001, which led the country to the brink of a full-scale civil war. However, the then incumbent HCNM Max van der Stoel was one of the very few actors who had not only not subscribed to the widely-shared illusion of "the former Yugoslav Republic of Macedonia" as a paradise of interethnic accord in the Balkans, but had even warned of the possibility of violence. In addition, the South East European University at Tetovo is a key contribution to the post-conflict peace-building process. [24]

d. Federal Republic of Yugoslavia (FRY) including Kosovo

Access to the Federal Republic of Yugoslavia and Kosovo was difficult for the High Commissioner as long as Milošević was in power. However, there was another factor specific to Kosovo which made this problematical: when Van der Stoel was appointed as Personal Representative for Kosovo of the OSCE Chairman-in-Office in 1997, the Albanian Kosovans refused to accept him because of his parallel capacity as High Commissioner on National Minorities, stating that they were not a minority in Kosovo. In addition, the Serb authorities refused to give him a visa. When Van der Stoel was finally able to visit Kosovo in a private capacity in early 1998, it was already too late. Only a few days after his urgent warning before the OSCE Permanent Council, immediately following his trip to Kosovo, violence broke out.[25]

e. Ukraine and Moldova

The High Commissioner has been active in the Ukraine since 1994 and has dealt with three key issues there: the (autonomy) status of the Republic of Crimea; the improvement of the Crimean Tatars' social situation, citizenship, legal status, representation and language rights; and the protection of the language rights of Russian speakers in the Ukraine. The HCNM's task was seriously complicated by the fact that the issues of Crimean autonomy and Crimean Tatars were so closely linked that solutions favoured by one group were disputed by the other. In addition, two of the three issues were directly linked to Russian interests.

At the end of the day, the solution to the problem of Crimean autonomy was relatively close to that recommended by the HCNM. It is, however, not completely clear to what degree the High Commissioner – or other actors – had an effect on this outcome.[26] However, it can be said that the HCNM, especially in two essential crisis situations, maintained a long-lasting negotiation process which finally led to a solution. In the case of the Crimean Tatars, the HCNM succeeded in raising international awareness and in relieving the Tatars' social plight. However, success in solving the other questions mentioned above was very limited. Finally, the High Commissioner was instrumental in appeasing the Russian Federation which had asked him to look into the issue of the linguistic rights of Russian speakers in Ukraine. As a whole, there has been a great deal of success in substantially diffusing the domestic and international conflict potential even though problems in implementing minority norms remain.[27]

In Moldova, the High Commissioner dealt in 1994 with the request of the Gagauz population to receive autonomy in southern Moldova and with the linguistic rights of Moldovans in Transnistria who were prohibited from using the Moldovan (Romanian) language in Latin script. Both issues had been already taken up by the long-term mission established in Moldova in April 1993 and were also later followed up by this mission. In 1999, in close co-operation with the mission, the HCNM worked on a Moldovan draft law on commercial advertising aimed at making the use of the Moldovan state language obligatory, thereby interfering in the private sphere. In 2000, the Office of the High Commissioner set up a project on language teacher training in Moldova. This project aims at promoting the use of Moldovan (Romanian) as a tool of social integration for minority students.[28]

f. Central Asia and the Transcaucasus

Compared to central and south-eastern Europe the engagement of the High Commissioner in central Asia and the Transcaucasus has been much more limited.

The HCNM paid visits in 1997 and 1998 to Georgia in order to familiarise himself with the Abkhazia problem, but then decided to leave it to the responsibility of the OSCE Mission. With regard to the Meskhetian Turks, he took on a more active role organising a conference in September 1998 as well as follow-up activities. In 2000, he also initiated the establishment of a monitoring network in south-west Georgia.[29]

In central Asia, the High Commissioner, between 1998 and 2000, paid visits to both Uzbekistan and Tajikistan, mainly to study the relationship between Islamic extremism and interethnic relations.

The High Commissioner visited Kazakhstan for the first time in April 1994. At that time, Russians in Kazakhstan were afraid of a possible "Kazakhisation"[30] of the country, a concern which was convincingly addressed by the Kazakh authorities. The High Commissioner showed special interest in the work of the Assembly of the Peoples of Kazakhstan and suggested adding a research and information centre to this institution. The Kazakh Government followed this recommendation and a network of monitors was also added. Continuous co-operation developed between the assembly and the Office of the HCNM and led to a series of seminars including one on religious extremism.[31]

174

When the High Commissioner visited Kyrgyzstan in April 1994 for the first time, he was especially concerned about the situation in the southern region of Osh, where a sizeable Uzbek minority lives. On several occasions, the HCNM questioned the Kyrgyz authorities including President Akaev about this matter. Since 1996, a monitoring network has been observing interethnic developments in southern Kyrgyzstan. Although the Kyrgyz authorities were far more responsive to the High Commissioner's recommendations than, for example, the Uzbek ones, violent riots occurred in the south Kyrgyz district of Aksy in 2002, which showed that the HCNM's apprehensions were more than justified.[32]

g. Greece and Turkey

The communications between the High Commissioner and these two states indicate that some states in the West and/or those states striving to be integrated into the West have considerable problems in coping with the very concept of "national minorities" contained in the politically binding CSCE/OSCE documents to which they have agreed.

The HCNM addressed several issues in Greece: first, Greece in its function as the kin-state of the Greek minority in Albania (see above); second, Greece's bilateral relations with Albania and "the former Yugoslav Republic of Macedonia" and third, the most delicate issue, the national minorities in Greece proper. With regard to the second question, the High Commissioner contributed to softening the Greek position on "the former Yugoslav Republic of Macedonia's" admission to the CSCE/OSCE which Greece had originally rejected. Upon the request of the Albanian president, the HCNM tried to address the issue of the Albanian and other minorities in Greece. However, according to the 1923 Treaty of Lausanne, the Greek authorities do not recognise minorities in Greece other than "Muslim" ones. It was only in 1998 that the High Commissioner found a more open counterpart in Foreign Minister Papandreou. Although this did not lead to substantial policy changes, it did lead, through an interview given by the foreign minister and subsequent comments by the High Commissioner, to a public debate which gave him the opportunity to introduce the basic idea of the 1991 CSCE Copenhagen Document affirming that it is not up to states to identify (and recognise) minorities but only to the persons belonging to these minorities themselves.[33]

Turkey represents a rather comparable case. Although he was frequently questioned about the Kurdish issue, the High Commissioner had always refused to deal with this problem because of the existence of organised acts of terrorism. Nevertheless, he realised it was necessary to discuss the Turkish definition of minorities which, according to the 1923 Treaty of Lausanne, only recognises "non-Muslim" minorities. In June 2000, the High Commissioner asked the Turkish foreign minister as well as one other minister to meet with him to address this basic question at the same time assuring them that he had no intention of broaching the Kurdish question. This request was bluntly dismissed and for the first time the High Commissioner was denied access to an OSCE participating state. After a letter had been sent to the Chairperson-in-Office, the issue was debated in the OSCE Permanent Council on 12 October 2000 where the High Commissioner got the support of many important states including the US and the European Union. It was agreed that the he would meet the Turkish foreign minister on the sidelines of the Vienna ministerial conference in 2000. Thus, as was comparable in Greece, a small but important starting point for further discussion was reached.[34]

Against the background of this brief overview on the activities of the High Commissioner on National Minorities, his political functions and achievements can be summarised as follows:

First, the HCNM has provided political early warning through his strictly confidential reports to the Chairman-in-Office, his regular reports to the OSCE Permanent Council, his recommendations and statements as well as hitherto, in one case, a formal early warning statement. It is of essential importance that this steady flow of early-warning information comes from a recognised international personality who enjoys the trust and support of states and international organisations. Thus, the HCNM functions as an agenda setter for interethnic relations and conflicts.

Second, the High Commissioner serves as a mandated institution to translate relatively abstract minority-protection norms into concrete solutions also for those (potential) minority-related conflicts which do not enjoy wider attention. The most important aspect of this political function is not to present immediate solutions, but to provide an institution with the legitimate right to offer proposals for solutions which can then be discussed by the primary actors as well as by the international community.

Third, the High Commissioner facilitated in indirect ways processes which finally led to solutions framed by the primary actors themselves. The HCNM's tools for this function include thousands of discussions, workshops and conferences and a range of supporting projects.

Fourth, in a series of cases, the High Commissioner was able to assume a more proactive role which led to solutions worked out in conjunction with primary actors. Frequently, but not always, this happened in countries seeking accession to the European Union. A part of these successes can be traced back to the political leverage the High Commissioner was able to mobilise from more powerful actors. The other part, however, can be attributed to the political weight of the institution of the High Commissioner itself as well as to the political reputation of its incumbents.

Missions in action

Since 1992, the OSCE has established 25 field operations in 21 countries of the post-communist space, 18 of which still operate in 2003. As mentioned earlier, in principle all OSCE field operations are engaged to a higher or lesser extent in minority questions. Like the HCNM, OSCE field operations do not restrict their activities to minorities recognised as such by the host state, but use their respective mandate and the OSCE commitments in the human dimension as a starting point for a broader approach. Most prominently, the

OSCE missions to Estonia and Latvia (1993-2001) focused their activities on the rights of the Russian-speaking population in these countries who did not have Estonian, or respectively Latvian citizenship, and therefore were not classified as national minorities under the national legislation. The OSCE mission to Moldova deals, *inter alia*, with the question of Romanian language schools in the Transnistrian region. Being the titular nation of the Republic of Moldova and even a relative majority in the Transnistrian region, Moldovans in Transnistria are in a typical minority situation, especially in the field of education. Therefore, the OSCE mission to Moldova considered the minority-related stipulations of the International Covenant on Civil and Political Rights, the UN Convention on the Rights of the Child as well as the principles laid down in the Copenhagen Document as applicable in this case. The OSCE mission to Moldova also deals with the rights of the Roma/Gypsy community and has a particular interest in the rights of the Gagauz, a Christian-orthodox Turk people in the southern part of Moldova.

Currently, the missions most prominently involved in the protection of classical minorities are the missions to Croatia, Kosovo, "the former Yugoslav Republic of Macedonia" as well as Serbia and Montenegro. In Bosnia and Herzegovina, to refer to another example mirroring the complexity of minority protection in the framework of the OSCE, the sustainable return of refugees and internally displaced persons is one of the central tasks of the mission's Human Rights Section. Together with the missions to Bosnia and Herzegovina, the missions to Croatia and to Serbia and Montenegro have also developed a joint action plan in order to facilitate the cross-border return of refugees. However, as far as Bosnia and Herzegovina is concerned, Bosnians, Croats and Serbs are equally considered the constituent peoples of that state, and thus even the so-called minority returnees are, in most cases, not considered members of a national minority, but are only the minority in the area to which they return. The OSCE mission to Bosnia and Herzegovina, however, also conducts projects in the field of classical minority rights, in particular, with regard to the Roma/Gypsy community.

The OSCE mission to Croatia concentrates its efforts on the return of refugees and on safeguarding the rights of the Serb minority. With this aim in mind, the mission uses part of its mandate – whose task it is to "assist with and to monitor the implementation of Croatian legislation [and] to make specific recommendations to the Croatian authorities"[35] – to bring forward changes in the legislative framework related to minorities and the situation of refugees. Moreover, the mission works to ensure that programmes for refugee return are carried out in practice and that the respective legislation is applied correctly. The mission sets guidelines and benchmarks for the Croatian Government and develops expertise on legislation and legal practice. The wide field presence of the mission enables it to also keep in touch with local and regional problems and to intervene diplomatically in order to speed up bureaucratic processes or to solve practical problems. However, the mission to Croatia as well as other OSCE missions are neither mandated nor equipped to act as an ombudsman, which would require following up individual complaints in a systematic manner. In the event that missions refer to individual cases, they should use them to point out structural problems. Therefore, specific cases are most likely to be followed up by a mission when they represent a typical case of non-compliance by state authorities. Moreover, the mission to Croatia, like other missions, keeps contact with and supports ombudsman institutions as well as NGOs and local roundtables through seminars, training, literature and other capacity-building projects.

Capacity-building and training is also one of the main activity areas of the OSCE mission to Kosovo with regard to minority questions. They are within the competence of the Human Rights Division, which runs a range of programmes in areas such as human rights education, NGO human rights programming, and women's participation in society. Human rights officers are also active in improving access to education for minority children, particularly those from the Roma/Gypsies, Ashkali and Egyptian communities. Another priority has been the development of the media for Kosovo's minority communities. The mission has carried out several projects to help minorities develop their own media and distribute independent newspapers.

In "the former Yugoslav Republic of Macedonia", the OSCE mission is mainly involved in confidence-building activities. After the 2001 conflict, it has worked with so-called confidence-building monitors and police advisers in Albanian-populated villages in order to facilitate the return of the police to the region and to prevent renewed frictions between ethnic Albanians and Macedonians. In a second step, the OSCE mission trained multi-ethnic police forces and advised the Macedonian authorities to revise their policing concept. The mission also conducts a number of projects aimed at fostering co-operation between municipalities and further strengthening radio, television and print media as well as multi-ethnic media, especially in the Albanian language. It also monitors the return of refugees and internally displaced persons.

In Serbia, the OSCE mission also directed its activities towards confidence-building in the mainly Albanian-populated regions of southern Serbia. As in "the former Yugoslav Republic of Macedonia" and Kosovo, the mission devised and implemented a plan to train a new multi-ethnic police force in this area in order to rebalance the ethnic Albanian component within the police. Moreover, it facilitated local elections in the region.

The OSCE mission to Georgia is mainly active in the field of conflict regulation and mediation between the Georgian government and the Abkhaz, or respectively the Ossetian authorities. Activities related to the protection of national minorities living in areas controlled by the Georgian Government also take place, but are rather limited. Also, the mission to Ukraine (1994-1999) acted mainly as a mediator between the Ukrainian Government and the Russian-dominated Republic of Crimea. However, the mission also pressed for the naturalisation of the Crimean Tatars, deported under Stalin and now returning to their original homeland, as well as for their adequate political representation and their cultural and educational rights. OSCE field activities in Albania, Armenia, Azerbaijan, Belarus and central Asia hardly deal with minority issues, as they concentrate their efforts on institution building, democratisation and human rights in general. However, in covering the human dimension in general and the area of accepting complaints by individuals, groups and organisations, all missions are in principle prepared to follow minority issues.

To sum up, one can conclude that OSCE field activities, by the virtue of their flexibility, have been able to address minority issues in their host country in a broad manner, as they are not restricted to narrow definitions of national minorities. At the same time, OSCE field activities are instruments, which are not primarily designed for the protection of minorities. Rather, they are instruments to promote peace and stability in the OSCE region through democratisation, institution building, mediation and conflict regulation. Although OSCE missions might get involved in individual cases, they concentrate more on structural aspects. The missions in Estonia, Latvia, Croatia and Moldova, in co-operation with the HCNM and other international actors such as the EU, certainly contributed to improvements made in the field of minority rights in those countries, although in each of these cases further concerns remain. It is therefore difficult to identify clear success stories, but the mixture of political-diplomatic involvement and NGO-type field work, which is a specific feature of OSCE missions, is also successfully applicable in the field of minority rights.

Recommendations for minority rights practitioners

The OSCE is a highly political international organisation. This has two basic consequences: first, OSCE commitments are politically and not legally binding. There is no national or international court where persons or institutions concerned can take legal action. Second, OSCE commitments basically refer to interstate behaviour even if they comprise the rights of individuals, that is, persons belonging to national minorities. This means that these commitments are not constructed primarily for individuals or private institutions, but represent a reference for state actors. In a nutshell, OSCE commitments are state-oriented. This does not mean, however, that sub-state actors, whether these are individuals, private institutions or NGOs, could not use OSCE commitments fruitfully to influence the political process. To do this, these actors should be aware, first, of the status of the various OSCE documents, and second, of how to use these documents in the political process.

Status of the various OSCE documents

Although all OSCE documents are binding only politically, certain differentiations can be made concerning their relative strengths. OSCE commitments adopted by all participating states are politically binding with the most important set of minority-related commitments included in the 1991 Copenhagen Document. Only this category of documents can be said to contain true OSCE commitments. Recommendations to governments by the HCNM or by OSCE missions or by experts mandated by the OSCE are weaker than OSCE commitments as the host state has not agreed to them. Although they are based on OSCE commitments, they represent an interpretation of these commitments possibly not shared by the host state or other states. The same holds true for the High Commissioner's general recommendations, the Hague, Oslo and Lund recommendations. Although these three sets of recommendations represent three highly important approaches to soft norm-setting in a substantial manner, it cannot be claimed that they have any politically binding quality. That means that the High Commissioner's recommendations basically do not represent more than a piece of political advice, albeit from a highly legitimate institution. This qualification can also be applied to ODIHR election reports, which may contain minority-related topics. However, there is one exception to this rule: some OSCE commitments have been included in legally binding international treaties. In this case, they also become legally binding. In point of fact, many bilateral treaties on friendship and good neighbourliness contain such paragraphs.

Thus, a word of advice to the practitioner: first, check the existing OSCE commitments as well as general and country-specific recommendations. Second, check whether commitments have been included in legally binding international treaties.

How to use OSCE documents in the political process

There is one basic difference between a legally binding and a politically binding document. A legally binding document is as powerful as the norms and implementation mechanisms it contains. A politically binding document is as strong as the political support it enjoys from states and/or international organisations at a certain moment. This can imply that a specific recommendation by the High Commissioner can have more impact on a state than politically binding OSCE commitments, if and when it is backed by powerful international actors providing meaningful sticks and carrots. The prime example of this is the HCNM's recommendations which the European Commission has taken on as accession criteria. It is important to note that relationships of this kind occur within political processes, thus the impact on a situation in one phase of a political process may not be reproducible in another. It should also be stressed that this kind of power-based norm implementation does not have the same quality as pure power politics in a realist sense. The most important difference is the high legitimacy of OSCE commitments based on their adoption by all participating states.

Thus, the following advice to the practitioner: check the political process and the positions taken by key players. In addition, be aware of changes in the political process which might devalue certain documents.

*Claus Neukirch contributed to this article while working as researcher at the Centre for OSCE Research, Hamburg, Germany; he is currently Spokesperson of the OSCE Mission to Moldova.

1. CSCE/OSCE documents can be found at the OSCE website: www.osce.org.

2. Cf. Cohen 1998, p. 20.

3. Alfredsson/Türk 1993, p. 175.

4. FIER 1997, p. 22.

5. Van der Stoel, 28 October 1994, in: Van der Stoel 1999, p. 51.

6. Van der Stoel, interview with Zellner, 28 May 1999, in: Van der Stoel 1999, p. 17.

7. See www.osce.org/hcnm.

8. Cf. FIER 1996, 1998 and 1999.

9. Cf. Oberschmidt/Zellner 2001, p. 10-11.

10. Van der Stoel, 4 November 1996, in: Van der Stoel 1999, p. 130.

11. See Cohen 1998, p. 12.

12. CSCE, Report of the CSCE Human Dimension Mission to The Republic of Moldova, January 30-February 4, 1993.

13. CSCE, Report of the CSCE ODIHR Mission on the Study of Estonian Legislation, December 1992, by Christian Tomuschat, Klaus Törnudd, et al. on behalf of the CSCE Office for Democratic Institutions and Human Rights, paragraph 8.

14. For a country-by-country description of the activities of the HCNM until 2000/2001, cf. Kemp (ed.) 2001 pp. 141-285. For in-depth studies on the effectiveness of the HCNM in Estonia cf. Sarv 2002, in Latvia cf. Dorodnova 2003, in the Ukraine cf. Kulyk 2002, in Romania cf. Horváth 2002, and in "the former Yugoslav Republic of Macedonia" cf. Arifi 2003 (unabridged versions are available at the website of the Centre for OSCE Research (CORE): www.core-hamburg.de). These studies were implemented within the framework of a research project on the effectiveness of the HCNM (cf. Zellner 1999).

15. Indeed, ODIHR does have a Contact Point for Roma/Gypsies and Sinti Issues. Although the Crimean Tatars also lack a kin-state, the High Commissioner dealt extensively with this issue.

16. Cf. Kemp (ed.) 2001, pp. 167-168.

17. Ibid., pp. 141-152, Sarv 2002.

18. Cf. Kemp (ed.) 2001, pp. 153-165, Dorodnova 2003.

19. Cf. Schöpflin 1993, p. 1, Brown 1993, p. 404.

20. Cf. Kemp (ed.) 2001, pp. 237-243, and Horváth 2002 for Romania and on Slovakia cf. Kemp (ed.) 2001, pp. 251-260.

21. Cf. Kemp (ed.) 2001, pp. 253-254.

22. Ibid., pp. 177-181.

23. Ibid., pp. 169-175.

24. Ibid., pp. 183-196, Arifi 2003.

25. Cf. Kemp (ed.) 2001, pp. 197-204.

26. Cf. Kulyk 2002, pp. 128-130.

27. Cf. Kemp (ed.) 2001, pp. 217-229, Kulyk 2002.

28. Cf. Kemp (ed.) 2001, pp. 231-236, Neukirch 2003, interview with OSCE officials.

29. Cf. Kemp (ed.) 2001, pp. 269-272.

30. Ibid. p. 273.

31. Ibid., pp. 273-278.

32. Ibid., pp. 279-282.

33. Ibid., pp. 205-209.

34. Ibid., pp. 211-216.

35. OSCE PC Decision No. 176, 26 June 1997.

CHAPTER 8

EUROPEAN UNION STANDARDS AND MECHANISMS FOR THE PROTECTION OF MINORITIES AND THE PREVENTION OF DISCRIMINATION

Kyriaki Topidi*

Introduction: from market integration to human rights and non-discrimination

Human rights, in the broadest sense, are hardly mentioned in the Treaty establishing the European Coal and Steel Community (Treaty of Paris) of 18 April 1951. The most common explanation for this is probably the economic character of the new European organisation, thus leaving very little scope for political integration.

The Treaty of Rome establishing the European Economic Community (EEC), signed on 25 March 1957 advances the cause of human rights by including two fundamental rights, in direct relation with the objectives of the Community: the freedom of movement for workers and self-employed persons (Articles 48 to 58 of the Treaty of Rome) and the prohibition of any discrimination on grounds of nationality (Articles 7, 48, 220 of the Treaty of Rome) or sex (Article 119 of the Treaty of Rome).[1]

The Single European Act (SEA), in force since 29 June 1987, was the first legal text to clearly mention human rights in the preamble of the Act, in relation to their protection within the Community by reference to the constitutions of the member states and the European Convention on Human Rights (ECHR) and also in relation to third countries by reference to the United Nations Charter. Two intergovernmental agreements on asylum (signed in Dublin in June 1990) and on the free movement of persons in a frontier-free area (signed in Schengen in June 1990) contributed indirectly to the establishment of a protection regime for selected fundamental rights.

The Treaty of Maastricht on European Union (TEU) signed on 7 February 1992, also does not include any reference to minorities.[2] As such, this is also indicative of the "embryonic" status of minority protection in the EU. Slight progress was made in the Treaty of Amsterdam, where member states in Article 6 declare respect for human rights (paragraph 1) and respect of the national identities of its member states (paragraph 3). The latter provision actually dates since the TEU.[3] Still, no coherent policy with regard to minority protection within the EU has been adopted so far, especially since coalitions between states keep shifting on the various policies. The most encouraging political sign was the one concerning "serious and persistent" violations of human rights as expressed in Article 7 of the TEU. Member states engaging in such behaviour run the risk of seeing certain of their rights within the Union suspended.[4]

Finally, according to the Treaty of Nice, which came into force on 1 February 2003, provisions have been included to allow for the adoption of incentive measures countering discrimination to be adopted by the Council of the European Union by qualified majority voting.

Given this background and reflecting the specificity of the EU case where there is no fully-fledged minority protection system, this chapter will concentrate first on the functioning of the EU institutional actors in the making of EU law on minority rights and second on the results of this process in terms of law and policy. The final section will conclude with an evaluation of the current framework, while providing some advice for those wishing to put into practice the nascent EU mechanism in the future.

Description of the mechanisms: the EU contribution to the development of standards and mechanisms for the protection of minorities

Unlike other international organisations, partly due to the nature of its legal system, the European Union does not dispose of a separate implementation body on minority rights. Furthermore, it has only recently started developing anti-discrimination legislation and this has not been fully implemented yet in its member states. There has been nevertheless a steady evolution reflected in the work of the European Court of Justice and the European Commission that is worthy of analysis and consideration as it demonstrates a strong tendency towards more comprehensive policy and legislation on the matter. It is however too early to provide an assessment of the mechanism, as it is still under development at both the political and the legal level.

The role played by institutional actors is indicative in this context of the trends in standard setting for non-discrimination and the protection of minorities within the Union. Each organ in the EU has contributed to various levels and extents for the emergence of human rights in the legal and political landscape of the European edifice.

The European Court of Justice (ECJ)

It is the responsibility of the European Court of Justice, that sits in Luxembourg, to ensure that the law is observed in the interpretation and application of the treaties establishing the European Community and of the provisions laid down by the competent Community institutions. To enable it to carry out that task, the ECJ has wide jurisdiction to hear various types of actions and to give preliminary rulings.

Preliminary rulings are designed to guarantee a uniform interpretation of Community legislation between the various national courts of member states. More specifically, if national courts are in doubt about the interpretation or the validity of Community law, they may, under particular conditions, ask the ECJ for advice. Other types of actions include proceedings for failure of a member state to fulfil an obligation, proceedings aiming at the annulment of a Community provision, which private individuals may also request provided that they can demonstrate that they are affected directly and individually, and finally provisions for failure of the European Parliament, the Council or the Commission to act.

In its early case-law, the ECJ, in mainly Italian and German cases, adopted the position that human rights were not included in the treaty and as such, the ECJ could only apply and interpret what at the time constituted Community law. Interpretation and application of national law was therefore excluded. Under such conditions, it became literally impossible for individuals to challenge any violations of their rights by national law before the ECJ. Strauder v. City of Ulm[5] was a decisive case in so far as the court recognised "... the existence of fundamental rights enshrined in the general principles of Community law and protected by the Court".[6] The ECJ chose an original formula and attempted the recognition of human rights through unwritten Community law.[7]

Later on, the ECJ started referring to international human rights treaties to which member states are signatories[8] and specific reference to articles of the Council of Europe's European Convention on Human Rights (ECHR) was made as a guideline for human rights protection in the Community legal order.[9] Still, although the ECJ has used the ECHR as a source of human rights protection in many instances, it has not stated that certain provisions form part of Community law.[10]

The ECJ has also recognised rights deriving from the International Labour Organisation treaties, the Council of Europe's European Social Charter,[11] as well as the International Covenant on Civil and Political Rights and the International Covenant on Economic, Social and Cultural Rights.[12]

It is clear today that the ECJ has opted for a "case-by-case" recognition of fundamental rights. When discussing the rights already singled out by the ECJ, there are two kinds of limitations. First, the degree of protection afforded is limited to the cases where a particular right is relevant to the proceedings and does not harm an important Community goal with respect to the Single Market.[13] In such cases, the ECJ simply tends to recommend a limited interpretation of the right in question so as to protect the functioning of the EU.[14]

The second limitation occurs within the context of the effect of EU law on member states. Again, whilst there is no direct reference to minority rights, the ECJ chose to refuse initially to examine the conformity of national legislation with human rights principles, when the legislation in question was within the jurisdiction of national authorities.[15] Yet, some years later, the ECJ stated that national authorities, when implementing Community rules are bound by human rights as general principles of Community law.[16]

The ECJ went further in Elliniki Radiofonia Tileorassi Anonimi Etairia v. Dimotiki Etairia Pliroforissis and Sotirios Kouvelas[17] and ruled that once national legislation is within the Community framework, the ECJ must provide elements for the interpretation in order to determine whether the legislation in question is in conformity with the human rights recognised by the ECJ.[18] In sum, a fundamental right and by analogy a minority right seems enforceable before the ECJ only if it is relevant to the proceedings, does not substantially harm the functioning of the EU and is within the EU legal frame-work, when referring to national implementing measures of EU legislation.

More recently the ECJ in Bickel and Franz[19] in relation to a linguistic right conferred to German speakers in Italy concluded that the protection of a minority may constitute a legitimate aim that would not be undermined if the rules protecting a minority were extended to cover other EU nationals in a similar situation exercising their freedom of movement. Similarly in Angonese[20] the ECJ held that the principle of non-discrimination precluded any requirement that linguistic knowledge required for an employment posi-tion must have been acquired within the national territory.

The general conclusion that may be drawn is that it seems that the domes-tic legislation enacted with the aim of protecting the identity and rights of ethnic minorities must be proportional and compatible with Community law. The ECJ has nevertheless addressed so far only the aspect of minority-majority relations relating to non-discrimination.

Minority rights have obviously a long way to go before being formally and directly recognised before the ECJ.[21]

The attitude of the main European Union institutions on non-discrimination and the protection of minorities

The European institutions and in particular the European Parliament (EP), have recognised at a relatively early stage the importance of combating dis-crimination. In 1986, the first Joint Declaration against racism and xenopho-bia was signed by the EP, the Council, the representatives of the member states meeting within the Council and the Commission. Follow-up to that declaration never materialised.

The EP has been in fact the only institutional organ which has focused on minority protection in the long term, in particular in its Committee on Foreign Affairs, Sub-committees on Human Rights and on Security and Defence, and the Committee on Civil Liberties, Justice and Home Affairs. This is largely due to its specific role representing "the peoples of the states brought together in the European Community" as elected by direct univer-sal suffrage, as well as to its strong traditional interest in human rights. Over the years, the EP as it gradually increased its power, has become an impor-tant forum for discussion on human rights and maintains regular contact with human rights organisations and human rights defenders.

It is needless to say that a specific official concept of "minority" has not yet been established in the Union, although there has been an attempt by the Legal Affairs and Civil Liberties committees to draw up a report in 1989 on a charter of rights of ethnic groups. The failure of the latter initiative to pro-vide a general framework of minority protection within the Union was due to lack of political will. The EP opted for a narrower approach: on 9 February 1994, a resolution "on linguistic and cultural minorities in the European Community" was adopted.[22] This resolution re-emphasised the importance for member states to recognise their linguistic minorities and protect them.

However, while there was a clear avoidance of recognising specific rights for minorities,[23] the resolution supported and tried to build upon the provisions of the European Charter for Regional or Minority Languages adopted within the framework of the Council of Europe.[24] The European Bureau for Lesser Used Languages (EBLUL) constitutes part of this effort. As an independent NGO, supported by the EP for a long time, EBLUL aims to promote active EU policy making in favour of regional or minority languages and represent regional or minority languages in dealings with EU institutions.[25]

As the Community's co-legislator and the body responsible for the conclusion of international agreements among its other functions,[26] the Council of the EU has been less active than the EP. At the level of external relations exclusively, it adopted a declaration on 29 June 1991 according to which respect and promotion of human rights were essential for the co-operation and relations between the EC and third countries. Emphasis was put on the protection of minorities and other vulnerable groups such as women, children, old people, migrants and refugees.

The Council's commitment for the protection of human and minority rights seems a lot clearer and more determined when it comes to external relations. There seems to be some vision and well-established principles in that respect, a phenomenon that appears paradoxical. On 28 November 1991, the Council and the member states adopted another resolution on human rights, democracy and development, within the framework of bilateral aid policies to developing countries. Performance in the field of democracy and respect of the rights of the individual became a fundamental criterion for distribution of aid to third countries.[27]

The inclusion of Article 13 in the Treaty of Amsterdam reactivated the Council's interest on the matter. In its meeting in Tampere, on 15 and 16 October 1999, it invited the European Commission to come forward with proposals implementing Article 13 of the EC Treaty, putting the accent on the fight against racism and xenophobia.[28] In addition, the European Council in Helsinki, on 10 and 11 December 1999, required that "attention should be paid to the improvement of the situation of those groups which do not form a majority in any state, including the Roma/Gypsies".[29]

As a result,[30] in November 1999, the European Commission presented a package of proposals under Article 13 composed of three elements that today form part of EU law on anti-discrimination: Council Directive 2000/43 of 29 June 2000 implementing the principle of equal treatment between persons irrespective of racial or ethnic origin,[31] Council Directive 2000/78 of 27 November 2000 establishing a general framework for equal treatment in employment and occupation[32] and Council Decision of 27 November 2000 establishing a Community action programme to combat discrimination for 2001 to 2006.[33]

Within this framework, the Commission undertook two major tasks involving non-discrimination and minority rights separately. First it acted as "mediator" between the conservative vision of the European Council on non-discrimination and the more progressive views of the EP in its proposals for the anti-discrimination package finally adopted in 2000. At the same time, the Commission took on the responsibility of negotiating and monitoring the progress of candidate states in' view of enlargement, which involved minority rights protection conditionality as set in the Copenhagen criteria.

The European Monitoring Centre on Racism and Xenophobia (EUMC)

The EUMC, based in Vienna and established by Council Regulation 1035/97 EC of 2 June 1997[34] commenced its activities in 1998. This institution was the fruit of efforts to combat racism and xenophobia as expressions of intolerance at local, regional, national and European level, thus implementing the principle of non-discrimination within the Community.

The primary task of the EUMC involves providing the Community and its member states with objective, reliable and comparable information and data on racism and xenophobia in the different forms that they may present themselves in EU member states. The aim of this type of research is to help the Community and the member states to take measures to combat these phenomena within their respective spheres of competence. The main instrument employed to fulfil this task is the European Information Network on Racism and Xenophobia (RAXEN), as accomplished via National Focal Points (NFPs) for every member state contracted by the EUMC to collect the relevant data on its behalf. The NFPs are recognised partners at the national level as they are in charge of organising a network between governmental institutions, NGOs, research bodies and specialised bodies or social partners thus co-ordinating the effort to report back to the EUMC in the most accurate and complete way.

The EUMC also initiates and finances a limited number of projects that study and analyse the phenomenon of racism and discrimination. These projects are subject to calls for tender, published in the Official Journal of the European Communities and on the EUMC website.

In addition, the EUMC is charged with the mission to analyse the information gathered and to distribute it as widely as possible. It is worth noting that the Community has entered into an agreement on behalf of the centre with the Council of Europe in order to establish close co-operation between the two organisations in an attempt to make their work programmes complementary.[35]

Institutionally, the EUMC can be described as the most appropriate organ to deal with non-discrimination, due to its mission. Yet, the restrictions in its powers that prevent it from proposing legislation render it less dynamic in the design and implementation standards of non-discrimination and minority rights. A recent Council regulation widening the scope of the EUMC's activities could improve the situation in this respect.

in results: legal and political apparatus of the EU on non-discrimination and minority rights

The EU is a body that produces both legislation and policies. As such, its tools for the protection of minority rights can be studied at two levels. The first level is the "internal" one and is relevant for minorities residing within EU territory. The second level is the "external" one and relates to all the activities of the Union undertaken with third countries. The main issue in this respect concerns the extent to which the EU has influenced and guaranteed minority rights protection in the countries in question.

"Internal" legislation

EU legislation relevant for minority rights concentrates on non-discrimination. It avoids any reference to special rights for ethnic/national minorities. It also targets individuals belonging to such groups and does not confer any rights to groups.

a. Article 13 of the EC Treaty and secondary legislation

The insertion of Article 13 into the Treaty of Amsterdam, which became effective on 1 May 1999, empowered the European Community to adopt measures aimed at combating discrimination based on sex, race or ethnic origin, religion or beliefs, disability, age or sexual orientation.[36]

In fact, Article 13 constituted one of the novelties of the Treaty of Amsterdam in the area of competence of the European Community edifice. Such augmentation of powers was the result of the combined effort of a diverse group of NGOs and of the European Parliament.[37]

The trilogy of anti-discrimination legislation constitutes at present the backbone of EU legislation with regard to the rights of ethnic or national minorities and as such merits more detailed analysis, in particular to the extent that these texts bring about new elements in the area of non-discrimination based on racial or ethnic origin.

i. Council Directive 2000/43

The directive in question, also referred to as the "Race Directive", principally prohibits racial discrimination in employment, social protection, education, access to goods and services as well as cultural activities. It came into force on 19 July 2000 and member states have until 19 July 2003 to bring their national laws, regulations and administrative provisions into line with the directive. Among the three elements of the anti-discrimination package, this is likely to have the largest impact on the protection of the rights of minorities when implemented.

Prohibited activities

The directive prohibits four activities:

— direct discrimination, defined as taking place when a person "is treated less favourably than another is, has been or would be treated in a comparable situation on grounds of racial or ethnic origin" (Article 2, paragraph 2.a, of the directive). The act of discrimination may be contemporary, historic or potential, as long as the element of comparison is present in cases of treatment of same situations differently or of different situation alike;

- indirect discrimination, defined as taking place when "an apparently neutral provision, criterion or practice would put persons of a racial or ethnic origin to a particular disadvantage compared with other persons, unless that provision, criterion or practice is objectively justified by a legitimate aim and the means of achieving that aim are appropriate and necessary" (Article 2, paragraph 2.b, of the directive). The Commission in its explanatory memorandum stressed that no statistical evidence is required as proof that other persons from racial or ethnic minorities have been discriminated by a certain practice, provision or criterion;

- harassment, defined as "unwanted conduct related to racial or ethnic origin ... with the purpose or effect of violating the dignity of a person and of creating an intimidating, hostile, degrading, humiliating or offensive environment" (Article 2, paragraph 3, of the directive) is also considered as discrimination. Again, in the case of harassment, the comparative approach is not required as in the case of indirect discrimination. The effect on the victim is sufficient to qualify an action as discriminatory;

- victimisation, as set out in Article 9 of the directive, may be considered as a fourth type of prohibited activity, as member states are under the obligation to "protect individuals from any adverse treatment or adverse consequence as a reaction to a complaint or to proceedings aimed at enforcing compliance with the principle of equal treatment".

Scope of the directive

The scope of the directive is two-fold. Its personal scope covers "all persons, as regards both the public and private sectors, including public bodies" (Article 3, paragraph 1, of the directive) which includes third-country nationals residing in the EU, with the exception of any difference of treatment based on nationality relating to the status and the conditions of entry and residence of third-country nationals and stateless persons on the territory of member states (Article 3, paragraph 2, of the directive). Its material scope extends beyond employment also to social protection, social security, healthcare, education, social advantages and access to and supply of goods and services (Article 3, paragraph 1, of the directive).

Extension of locus standi

Among the most interesting new elements of this directive is the extension of legal standing to associations, organisations and other legal entities with legitimate interest on behalf or in support of a complainant (Article 7, paragraph 2, of the directive).

Bodies for the promotion of equal treatment

Equally as interesting is the additional obligation on member states to establish independent bodies for the promotion of equal treatment without discrimination on the grounds of racial or ethnic origin (Article 13, paragraph 1, of the directive). The mission of such bodies would be to provide independent assistance to victims of discrimination, to conduct independent surveys on the phenomenon of discrimination and to publish independent reports with rec-ommendations on any issues related (Article 13, paragraph 2, of the directive).

Burden of proof

According to Article 8 of the directive, when alleged victims of discrimina-tion on ethnic and racial grounds establish before a national court facts that allow a presumption that there has been direct or indirect discrimination, it is for the respondent to prove that there has been no breach of the principle of equal treatment. The reversal of proof does not apply however to criminal proceedings (Article 8, paragraph 3, of the directive) and in proceedings in which the court is charged with the investigation of the facts of the case (Article 8, paragraph 5, of the directive).

Sanctions

Along with Article 6 of the directive that stresses that the provisions laid down in the directive constitute minimum standards, member states have to ensure that the standards in question are guaranteed by sanctions applica-ble to relevant infringements. Moreover, the sanctions must be effective, pro-portional and dissuasive (Article 15 of the directive).

ii. Council Directive 2000/78

To a large extent, this directive reflects a similar *état d'esprit* to the previous directive analysed. It seeks to establish a general framework for equal treat-ment in employment and occupation while extending the existing protection in EU law against sex and nationality discrimination. The so-called "equal treatment" directive is nevertheless less relevant for the purposes of the pro-tection of minority rights. This is so because its material scope is limited to employment and occupation and is mainly concerned with combating dis-crimination on the grounds of religion, belief, age or sexual orientation (Article 1 of the directive).

Employment is defined widely (Article 3, paragraph 1, of the directive). The prohibited activities are similar to those contained in the Race Directive (Article 2, paragraph 2, of directive 2000/78). There is also provision for the shift in the burden of proof in actions to enforce the equal treatment princi-ple (Article 10) and member states are under an obligation to establish effec-tive, proportionate and dissuasive sanctions for a breach of the directive (Article 17 of the directive). Very similarly again, *locus standi* is given to asso-ciations, organisations or other legal entities (Article 9, paragraph 2, of the directive) in defence of a victim of unequal treatment.

The deadline for implementation by member states of this directive is 2 December 2003 but, if necessary, member states dispose of an additional period of three years from 2 December 2003 in order to "take account of par-ticular conditions" (Article 18 of the directive).

iii. Action programme to combat discrimination (2001 to 2006)

The Council Decision of 27 November established a Community action pro-gramme to combat discrimination from 2001 to 2006. The programme, the third part of the anti-discrimination trilogy, is intended to foster the exchange of good practices in the member states and to develop new ones along with policy in order to combat discrimination.

It has three main objectives around which community actions are organised (Article 3 of the decision):

- to improve the understanding of issues related to discrimination: analysis and evaluation involve a report on the activities of the EUMC, the establishment of groups of independent experts on racial and ethnic origin, data collection, as well as studies on equality and anti-discrimination;
- to develop the capacity to tackle discrimination effectively: a programme to develop capacity building supports 27 transnational partnerships that exchange good practices in the fight against discrimination, involving local authorities, social partners and non-governmental organisations;
- to promote the values underlying the fight against discrimination: awareness-raising revolves around the organisation of conferences, seminars for judges and legal practitioners and special events and information campaigns.

The Commission, according to Article 4 of the decision must ensure the implementation of Community actions but must also have regular exchanges with representatives of non-governmental organisations (NGOs). It must also promote the involvement of NGOs in the programme per se (Article 4, paragraph 2.a. of the decision), promote the dialogue between those involved in the programme (Article 4, paragraph 2.b, of the decision) and ensure the dissemination of the actions undertaken within the framework of the programme (Article 4, paragraph 2.c, of the decision). Finally, it must provide information, publicity and follow-up with regard to actions included within the programme (Article 4, paragraph 2.d, of the decision).[38]

b. Articles 20-22 of the Charter of Fundamental Rights

The Charter of Fundamental Rights, as proclaimed in December 2000 in Nice, contains three articles relevant to the protection of the rights of minorities and non-discrimination. Article 20 on equality before the law contains a general equality clause that stipulates that "[e]veryone is equal before the law". It corresponds to a principle included in all European member states' constitutions and has previously been recognised by the ECJ as a basic principle of Community law.[39]

More specific to ethnic and national minorities is Article 21, paragraph 1, of the charter that prohibits "any discrimination based on any ground such as sex, race, colour, ethnic or social origin, genetic features, language, religion or belief, political or any other opinion, membership of a national minority, …". Clearly paragraph 1 of Article 21 of the charter draws on Article 13 of the EC Treaty and Article 14 of the ECHR. Yet, contrary to Article 14 of the ECHR, the right to non-discrimination here applies within the whole framework of the treaties and is not confined to the provisions of the charter.

As for Article 22 of the charter, it concerns the respect within the Union of cultural, religious and linguistic diversity. The inspiration for this article is drawn from Article 6 of the TEU and Article 151, paragraphs 1 and 4 of the

EC Treaty concerning culture. The right enshrined in Article 22, however, comes into contradiction with the state of ratification of the Framework Convention for the Protection of National Minorities (FCNM) and of the European Charter for Regional or Minority Languages by some of the EU member states,[40] especially since candidate states were required to ratify the same texts prior to accession.

The Charter of Fundamental Rights is not legally binding (Article 51, paragraph 2, of the charter). However, the Laeken European Council in December 2001 established a "convention" on the future of the EU and at the same time adopted a declaration setting issues that the convention is expected to consider including the possibility of the incorporation of the charter in the basic treaty.

EU external policy and minority rights

EU external policy has used fairly extensively the notion of respect for human rights, of which minority rights form an integral part. The most quoted example in that respect is the criteria for the upcoming EU enlargement. This wider category of "human rights clauses" applies to the candidates for accession but also in a slightly different form to any third country associated in commercial or other terms with the EU.

a. The general legal framework

The entry into force of the Treaty on European Union (TEU) on 1 November 1993 marked the beginning of the process of integration of human rights into the policies of the EU. The treaty considers as one of the objectives of the Common Foreign and Security Policy of the EU the development and consolidation of "democracy and the rule of law, and respect for human rights and fundamental freedoms" (Article 11 of the TEU). A second reference to human rights is included in the new title on development co-operation: "Community policy in this area shall contribute to the general objective of developing and consolidating democracy and the rule of law and to that of respecting human rights and fundamental freedoms" (Article 177, paragraph 2, of the EC Treaty).

The Treaty of Amsterdam, in force since 1 May 1999, introduced an additional element by inserting Article 6 in the Treaty on European Union that stipulated that the EU "is founded on the principles of liberty, democracy, respect for human rights and fundamental freedoms, and the rule of law, principles which are common to the member states". At the same time, Article 49 of the same treaty required that countries that wish to apply for EU membership respect the principles contained in Article 6. The Treaty of Nice, concluded in December 2000, reinforced the Article 7 mechanism sanctioning serious and persistent breaches of human rights by the EU member states. Finally, Articles 177 to 181 of the EC Treaty extended the objective of promoting human rights and fundamental freedoms to development co-operation and to all forms of co-operation with third countries.

The EU is also bound by its declarations on respect for human rights.[41] In more practical terms, the European Community since the early 1990s has included a "human rights clause" in its bilateral trade and co-operation agreements. A Council decision of May 1995 lays out the modalities of the clause in question in order to achieve consistency in its application.

To promote human rights objectives in external relations, the EU considers a variety of norms and instruments. These instruments range from traditional diplomacy and foreign policy to interventions in UN fora and bilateral dialogue.

b. EC external assistance programmes towards third countries and minority rights

The main instruments available to the European Community to promote respect for human rights are co-operation and partnership agreements with third countries. The promotion of human rights, democracy, the rule of law and good governance are an integral part of new policy. The European Community's co-operative assistance funding programmes (Phare, Tacis, Ala, Meda, Cards) amount to approximately €5 billion per annum in addition to European Development Fund (EDF) sources for the African, Caribbean and Pacific (ACP) countries (€13.5 billion under the 9th EDF between 2000-07). This assistance, however, is not exclusively devoted to human rights promotion.

More specifically, the main current dialogue arrangements of the EU with various geographical regions supporting to some extent minority rights protection are the following:

i. the Cotonou Agreement with the ACP states[42] explicitly mentions the respect for all human rights and fundamental freedoms as an integral part of sustainable development. A new procedure has been drawn up for cases of violation of this element[43] with emphasis placed on the responsibility of the state concerned. Moreover, the participatory approach within the agreement enhances the involvement of non-state actors. Modalities for this new approach are not nevertheless specified in the Cotonou Agreement. A special place within the ACP-EU assistance framework is allocated to the rights of indigenous people, which were included as a thematic priority in proposals launched by the Commission.[44]

ii. in EU-Latin America relations, the European Commission also focused on the protection of human rights among other elements and the need for measures to strengthen this protection.

iii. along similar lines, the Commission called for greater attention to be given to human rights, good governance and the rule of law in the EU's relations with Mediterranean countries. The Mediterranean partners were encouraged to accede to the relevant international instruments on human rights.

iv. in Asia, the EU has established dialogue with the members of the Association of South East Asian Nations (ASEAN) on support for human rights yet it is acknowledged by the Commission that the dialogue needs to be strengthened further.

v. more specific to minority rights is the development of relations between the EU and countries of the western Balkans. In order to support the stabilisation and association process that offers the possibility of integration into EU structures to Albania, Bosnia and Herzegovina, Croatia, Serbia and Montenegro and "the former Yugoslav Republic of Macedonia", assistance under the Community Assistance for Reconstruction, Development and Stabilisation (Cards) is provided. The main objective of the assistance programme in question is to create the adequate institutional and legislative framework and to support, *inter alia*, minority rights. The Community also collaborates with the Stability Pact for South Eastern Europe, signed in Cologne on 10 June 1999, co-ordinating efforts of major donors to the Balkans, devoted as well to the development of democracy and human rights and paying attention to the respect for minorities.

vi. the EU has concluded agreements on partnership and co-operation with Russia (1994) providing for institutionalised dialogue at all levels, further defined in the EU's Common Strategy on Russia (1999), with priority areas including human rights. A similar strategy was adopted for Ukraine, Belarus, Armenia, Azerbaijan, Georgia, Kazakhstan, Kyrgyzstan and Uzbekistan.

c. The European Initiative For Democracy and Human Rights (EIDHR)

As part of a European Parliament initiative in 1994, a new budget heading was created to promote human rights, democratisation and conflict prevention. The originality of this programme comes from the fact that support is destined mainly to NGOs and international organisations that operate in the sectors identified. It is clear that this budget line corresponds to the need to acknowledge and value the contribution of NGOs and international organisations to the implementation of human rights.

The legal basis for human rights activities of the European Union, under this specific budget heading (Chapter B7-7), is provided by Council Regulations 975/99 and 976/99 of 29 April 1999. The regulations provide for the establishment of a Human Rights and Democracy Committee which started its work in July 1999.

Combating racism, xenophobia and discrimination against minorities has been identified as a thematic and funding priority for the EIDHR during the period 2002 to 2004. This approach was recently endorsed in a European Commission communication adopted on 8 May 2001, concerning the EU's role in promoting human rights and democratisation in third countries.[45]

d. The European Union minority rights policy and enlargement

Particular attention has been paid to minorities within the context of the EU enlargement process. The Copenhagen criteria designed in 1993 for countries wishing to join the EU specifically mention that "membership requires that the candidate country has achieved stability of institutions guarantee-ing democracy, the rule of law, human rights and the respect for and protec-tion of minorities".[46]

Initially, the EU established accession partnerships with each candidate coun-try, identifying priorities for each country to fulfil the accession criteria. On the basis of the above political criterion in conjunction with the objectives set in each accession partnership, the European Commission has, since 1997, assessed the individual records of candidate states concerning the treatment of minorities on an annual basis. Each year, the Commission recommended measures for the improvement of each country's record. The issue of the Roma/Gypsies/Sinti for example has proved of a particularly problematic nature transnationally in central and eastern Europe, as these populations of around six million in central and eastern European countries, suffer from widespread prejudice and discrimination.

As part of the effort of the EU to assist candidate states in preparation for accession, three main budget possibilities have been created:

— the Phare programme aimed at assistance to the countries of central and eastern Europe (B 7-030). It was designed to facilitate and accelerate preparation for the future accession of these countries. For a long time, Phare did not dispose of a separate budget line for assistance to promote minority rights protection and as such it is difficult to calculate the total amount of assistance provided towards that aim. Each component of the national Phare allocation for every candidate state has over the years increasingly included funding for projects concerning the improvement of local protection of minorities;

— the Access programme aimed at strengthening civil society in candidate countries in central and eastern Europe (B 7-500) granted financial sup-port to NGOs targeting mostly the social integration and/or the promotion of sustainable health and social support for marginalised groups of the population. Access ceased to exist in 2002;

— the EIDHR (Chapter B 7-7), already mentioned previously, includes spe-cific references to minorities and has also been employed within the framework of enlargement.

Critique and evaluation of the practice: a mixed record

On law

From the above analysis of legal and political elements it appears quite clearly that the European Union, as an actor in the international scene, has certainly evolved towards more serious consideration for human rights and to a certain extent minority rights. The value of the Copenhagen criterion on the need for respect of the rights of minorities can be evaluated as a "soft law" provision aimed at addressing the security concerns of the EU and at showing commitment to human rights.

From a legal point of view, the primary tool that has been used to guarantee the rights of ethnic or national minorities has been non-discrimination (for instance Article 13 of the EC Treaty and the related Race Directive). It is, however, insufficient to cover the special rights required by ethnic or national minorities. At the very least and in order to have a clearer idea of the contribution of those texts to the protection of the rights of minorities, one needs to wait for the actual implementation of the "race" and "equal treatment" directives by the member states and for the subsequent case-law that will emerge from their application. Any legal action on the basis of these directives should be directed to domestic courts, due to the direct effect of EU legislation and more specifically directives, on the jurisdiction of member states. For cases that will be subjected to a preliminary ruling, interpretation by the ECJ must respect the principles contained in the directives and provide the most restrictive interpretation for any exceptions limiting the scope of rights for the victims of discrimination. Generally speaking, as outlined previously, provisions in both directives appear indeed largely in favour of victims of discrimination yet any interpretation must follow this spirit and not attempt to reduce the practical application of the rules in question.[47] Furthermore, the insertion of provisions allowing for *locus standi* for NGOs and associations to help the victim plead his/her cause constitute a path of action that needs to be exploited at its fullest by the relevant organisations. Non-governmental organisations and practitioners must also control the extent to which the domestic legislation implementing the directives is faithful to the content of the latter. Directives are in principle compulsory in their content but allow the member states to select the means to enact their content. This means that any implementing provision in an individual member state must be in full accordance with the scope and without any limitation of the corresponding provision of the directives.

From a negative perspective and on a conceptual level practitioners must bear in mind that the three components of the anti-discrimination package of the Commission do not bring any clarity to the definition of "racial or ethnic origin". The only reference to the use of this term states: "The European Union rejects theories which attempt to determine the existence of separate human races. The use of the term 'racial origin' in this Directive does not imply an acceptance of such theories". The practitioner unfortunately cannot distinguish here as to what is meant by either component of the term ("racial" and/or "ethnic" origin) and whether they should be considered jointly or separately in each case.

One of the most notable shortcomings of the Race Directive is that no systematic monitoring of member states' implementation has been devised so as to complement the other measures assisting individual litigation. After all, it is a common secret that the success of EU legislation is and always has been highly dependent on the level of implementation achieved within the individual member states. It is towards that direction both at national and European level that more pressure needs to be applied.

Turning to the European Union Charter of Fundamental Rights, the text as such is a non-legally binding document. Until a decision is taken on its possible incorporation in the basic treaty, its symbolism is accepted, though one may argue again a "soft law" value to it given the periodic references that the ECJ makes to its text in judgments.[48] Yet, it is quite difficult to consider its provisions justiciable in the narrow sense and capable of producing a shield of protection for those seeking to enforce non-discrimination on grounds of racial and ethnic origin. Article 21 certainly gives a clear mandate to act against discrimination and contains a prohibition in principle but it will be subjected to the interpretation of the ECJ as to how it must be enforced in practice. A possible course of action in this case would be to argue in favour of the "legalisation" of the charter, allowing in this way for a supplementary legal basis against discrimination.

More generally, reliance on the ECJ rather than a more straightforward solution of new and clear legislation has created an unstable record for the protection of fundamental rights and freedoms. Rendering the charter legally binding could, at least partially, solve this problem. The asymmetry of principles in the conduct of internal and external policy also provokes questions and doubts at the level of effective protection of minority rights in the EU.[49]

On policy

The Commission has been providing support to projects within the context of structural funds for actions for the period 2000-06 on combating all types of discrimination in the labour market and in the work place (Equal programme). It has also distributed support, as a result of the Community action programme 2001 to 2006 mentioned above, to projects studying discrimination and increasing awareness, under the aegis of the European Network Against Racism (ENAR) which brings together around 600 NGOs that monitor European and national anti-discrimination programmes. This type of initiative constitutes an example of action that is susceptible of highlighting the importance of respect for non-discrimination in the post-Copenhagen criteria era. Similar patterns should naturally be encouraged within member states as well.

In spite, however, of the new powers vested in the EU to take measures to combat discrimination based on ethnic origin and the inclusion of the requirement for the protection and respect for the rights of minorities in the accession criteria, enlargement and the monitoring that was performed on candidate states have shown that the Commission and indeed the whole of the EU are not in search of a new, dynamic concept of minority but rather consider the issue one of relevance only for external relations and for the Union's security agenda.

The regular Commission reports have been compiled based on information provided by the Council of Europe, the OSCE, NGOs and the candidate countries themselves. The generality of the Commission's assessment combined with lack of evidence on a number of the comments have affected the accuracy of the latter. References to "international standards" or "European standards" are not specified and suggest an internationalisation of human rights benchmarking within the EU.[49]

As already discussed above, the new norms on the question have not been numerous and have not produced noticeable effects so far. Furthermore, accession criteria on minorities have left unresolved serious breaches of minority rights despite some improvements at the legal level, particularly in the case of the Roma/Gypsies. This is a case where fundamental rights are systematically violated as well as minority rights in both the "old" and the "new" member states.[50] This mere fact leads to two very important conclusions: first, as far as the "old" member states are concerned, the political criterion has been applied to candidate states only and the respect for the rights of minorities is not a requirement for the "old" states. Second, it demonstrates a certain degree of superficiality in the treatment of the question as the "new" states are declared to satisfy all the accession criteria, yet violations of minority rights and the principle of non-discrimination subsist.

On the other hand, enlargement and the inclusion of the respect of minority rights as a condition have contributed to a certain extent towards the realisation of the need for a more consistent commitment to minority protection and the fuller integration of the requirement into existing EU standards; even more so given the signs of positive impact of minority rights conditionality on candidate states. Under EU influence, Bulgaria, the Czech Republic, Estonia, Hungary, Latvia and Slovakia have been reviewing their legislation to ensure compliance with the EU Race Directive.[51] Success stories include for example the Roma/Gypsy government strategies in Slovakia and Romania as well as integration programmes for Russian speakers and relative liberalisation of language policies in Latvia and Estonia. The EU has moreover supported financially the implementation of many of the specific priority areas identified by respective central and eastern European candidate countries in the field of minority protection.[52]

It is nevertheless currently not entirely clear what will happen in the future to the requirement for the protection of the rights of minorities in that respect, since the first ten candidate states are in the process of joining the EU and monitoring is likely to undergo a transformation in its character at least for them. Any action at this point should target the extension of application and monitoring for the protection and respect for minorities to the "older" member states as well and should apply pressure to ensure a future for the Copenhagen political criterion as a political standard with independent existence. Maintaining a high standard of monitoring and ensuring that requirements for respect for the rights of minorities are met in effective ways would avoid the deterioration or stagnation of the situation and possibly allow for improvement. Follow-up strategies to put in practice the basis that was set by the Copenhagen criteria in conjunction with the wise application of Article 7 of the TEU regarding the suspension of rights for serious and persistent violations of human rights by member states, should therefore be encouraged both horizontally and vertically within individual member states.

Conclusions

The purpose of this analysis has been mainly to examine the options under EU law for the enforcement of the principle of non-discrimination with particular regard to racial and/or ethnic origin. As the previous sections have highlighted, EU law does not appear at the moment the "natural" environment for such claims although Article 13 of the EC Treaty and its implementing directives, when implemented, could transform the current situation.

In the meantime, the EU as a body of law and policy continues to a certain extent to take into consideration human rights in its actions but this is by no means synonymous with a coherent and fully-fledged minority rights policy. At its best, given the current state of affairs, the EU has the potential to cover the non-discrimination aspect of the rights of ethnic or national minorities, which automatically leaves special rights and policies for these groups almost untouched.

* Doctoral researcher, Queen's University Belfast.

1. Christine Duparc, *The European Community and Human Rights*, Commission of the European Communities, Office for Official Publications of the European Communities, (Brussels, October 1992), pp. 11-12.

2. However, in Article A of the TEU "a new stage in the process of creating an ever closer union among the peoples of Europe ... in a manner demonstrating consistency and solidarity" [Estebanez, see note 5, p. 135.] is proclaimed, which sets an innovative approach that needs to be extended to minorities.

3. EU, *Consolidated Versions of TEU and Treaty establishing the EU*, 1997, Office for Official Publications of the European Communities, (Luxembourg, 1997), p. 13.

4. http://www.europa.eu.int/comm/external_relations /human_rights/intro/index.htm

5. Case 29/69 [1969] ECR 419.

6. Ibid, paragraph 7.

7. Lammy Betten and Nicholas Grief, *EU Law and Human Rights*, (Longman, London, 1998), p. 58.

8. Case 4/73 Nold v. Commission of the European Communities (1974), ECR 491, paragraph 13.

9. Case 36/75 Rutili v. Minister for the Interior (1975) ECR 1219.

10. Betten and Grief, op.cit. p. 62.

11. Especially in the case Defrenne v. SABENA (1978) ECR 1365.

12. Case C-262/88 Barber v. Guardian Royal Exchange Insurance Company (1990) 1 CMLR 513 at p. 547.

13. Andrew Charlesworth and Holly Cullen, *European Community Law*, (Pitman Publishing, London, 1994), p. 106.

14. A typical example of this attitude is the case National Panasonic (UK) Ltd. v. Commission, 136/79 [1980] ECR 2033.

15. Cinéthèque SA v. Fédération Nationale des Cinémas Français, joint cases 60 & 61/84 (1985) ECR 2605.

16. Case 5/88 Wachauf v. Bundesamt für Ernährung und Forstwirtschaft (1989) ECR 2609, paragraph 19.

17. Case C-260/89 [1991] ECR 2925.

18. Charlesworth and Cullen, op.cit., p. 108.

19. Horst Bickel and Ulrich Franz, Case C-274/96 (1998), ECR I-4139.

20. Roman Angonese v. Cassa di Risparmio di Bolzano, Case C-281/98 (2000), ECR I-4139.

21. It must be noted that in parallel all member states are subject to supervision on the matter by the European Court of Human Rights of the Council of Europe.

22. A3-0042/94, (O.J. 1994, C61/111).

23. The declaration reads: "all peoples have the right to respect for their language and culture and must therefore have the necessary legal means to protect and promote them".

24. European Treaty Series (ETS) No.148.

25. Its projects are funded mainly by the European Commission but also from the Irish and Luxembourgish governments as well as from the Frisian province of the Netherlands and the French and German Communities of Belgium. For more information see http://www.eblul.org

26. For a summary of the Council's main functions see http://ue.eu.int/en/info/index.htm

27. References to principles of the United Nations Charter, by inclusion of clauses referring to them in bilateral agreements, have been applied to both the Declaration of 29 June 1991 and the Council Resolution of 28 November 1991.

28. See Tampere Conclusions of the EU Presidency, http://ue.eu.int/en/info/eurocoun-cil/index.htm 16/10/99, Press Release Nr 200/1/99, at paragraph 19.

29. See Helsinki Conclusions of the EU Presidency, http://ue.eu.int/en/info/eurocoun-cil/index.htm 11/12/99, Press Release Nr 00300/1/99, at paragraph 65.

30. According to the process for acting under Article 13 within the EU, the Council must approve unanimously a proposal from the European Commission, after consulting with the EP.

31. OJ L 180, 19 July 2000, pp. 22-26.

32. OJ L 303, 2 December 2000, pp. 16-22.

33. OJ L 303, 2 December 2000, pp. 23-28.

34. OJ L 151, 10 June 1997, pp. 1-7.

35. See Article 7.3 of Council Regulation 1035/97/EC and also the agreement signed on 10 February 1999 (Council Decision of 21 December 1998, O.J. L44 of 18 February 1999).

36. Article 13 of the EC Treaty stipulates: "Without prejudice to the other provisions of this Treaty and within the limits of the powers conferred by it upon the Community, the Council, acting unanimously on a proposal from the Commission and after consulting the European Parliament, may take appropriate action to combat discrimination based on sex, racial or ethnic origin, religion or belief, disability, age or sexual orientation."

37. Mark Bell, "Article 13 EC: The European Commission's Anti-Discrimination Proposals", *Industrial Law Journal*, Vol.29, No.1, March 2000, pp. 79-84, at p. 79.

38. The budget allocated for the implementation of the programme for 2001-2006 was set at € 98.4 million according to Article 10 of the decision.

39. See for example case 283/83 Racke [1984], ECR 3791, 13 November 1984, case 15/95 EARL [1997] ECR I – 1961, 17 April 1997 and case 292/97 Karlsson, 13 April 2000, ECR I – 2737.

40. For example, France has not signed the FCNM and Belgium, Greece, Luxembourg and the Netherlands have signed but not ratified it. In the same spirit, the ECRML has not been signed by Belgium, Greece, Ireland and Portugal.

41. See for example the Declaration on Human Rights adopted at the Luxembourg European Council on 28–29 June 1991, http://www.europarl.eu.int/summits/luxem-bourg/lu1_en.pdf 11/12/98, Press Release Nr 0030/1/98 REV, part II or the Declaration on the occasion of the 50th anniversary of the Universal Declaration of Human Rights, http://www.europa.eu.int/comm/external_relations/human_rights/doc/50th-decl_98.htm

42. Agreement between the Community and its member states and 77 countries of the African, Caribbean and Pacific Group signed in 23 June 2000 for the duration of twenty years.

43. The procedure applies also for the violation of one of the other two elements, which are democracy based on the rule of law and transparent and accountable governance.

44. For more information on the funding possibilities for indigenous people under the EU budget, see for example Pamphlet No.14 of the *UN Guide for Minorities: The European Union: Human Rights and the Fight Against Discrimination*, http://www.unhchr.ch/html/racism/01-minoritiesguide.html

45. European Commission, Communication from the Commission to the Council and the European Parliament: *The European Union's Role in Promoting Human Rights and Democratisation in Third Countries*, COM (2001) 252 final, 8 May 2001.

46. For the list of the Copenhagen criteria see http://www.europa.eu.int/comm/enlarge-ment/intro/criteria.htm

47. For example, according to the principle of the reversal of proof, the alleged victim must prove facts that allow for the formulation of a presumption of discrimination. It would be detrimental to the principle if unfavourable standards and interpretation of facts were established for this presumption to apply.

48. See for example Joined cases T-377/00, T-380/00, T-260/01, T-272/01 Phillip Morris International v. Commission, 15 January 2003, not published yet, in paragraph 122 and case C-491/01, British American Tobacco Investments and Imperial Tobacco, 10 December 2002, not published yet, in paragraph 144.

49. For a critical discussion of EU minority policy on conditionality see James Hughes and Gwendolyn Sasse, "Monitoring the Monitors: EU Enlargement Conditionality and Minority Protection in the Central and Eastern European Countries", *JEMIE*, Issue 1/2003, http://www.ecmi.de/jemie/download/Focus1-2003_Hughes_Sasse.pdf

50. EU Network of Independent Experts in Fundamental Rights (CRF-CDF), Report on the situation of fundamental rights in the EU and its Member States in 2002, http://www.europa.eu.int/comm/justice_home/fsj/rights/network/rapport_2002_en.pdf in particular pp. 160-178.

51. EUMAP, *Monitoring the EU Accession Process: Minority Protection*, Open Society Institute, 2002, 24, http://www.eumap.org

52. EUMAP, 31.

CHAPTER 9

BILATERAL AGREEMENTS
AND THEIR IMPLEMENTATION

Emma Lantschner*

Introduction

Bilateral agreements typically stand at the end of a conflict or a period of suppression, during which relations between neighbouring countries were rendered difficult. This could be observed in the case of the agreement concluded between Finland and Sweden on the status of the Åland Islands[1] in the aftermath of the First World War as well as in the Gruber-De Gasperi Agreement (Austria-Italy),[2] which laid the basis for the autonomous status of the province of Bolzano-Südtirol after the Second World War. Bilateral agreements appeared again after the collapse of communism. In the first half of the last decade many countries in central and eastern Europe concluded bilateral agreements aiming to guarantee stability through respect of their borders and settlement of long-standing disputes. Such agreements also often contain commitments regarding their respective minorities. In recent years, the former Yugoslav countries, especially Serbia and Montenegro, became very active in the field of minorities, not only by adopting national (constitutional) laws on minorities, but also by concluding bilateral agreements on minorities with their neighbours.

These agreements cover issues such as the right to identity, language and education rights, media usage, and participation in decision-making processes.

The implementation mechanism of bilateral agreements is generally considered to be one of the weaknesses of this instrument. It can be examined from the political as well as the legal perspective, the political aspects of implementation having received primacy over the legal possibilities.[3]

There are four possible procedures for the implementation and monitoring of bilateral agreements.

Most of the treaties concluded at the beginning of the 1990s have been included in the Pact on Stability.[4] Article 16 of the declaration of the pact states that:

> ... the States party to the OSCE Convention establishing the International Conciliation and Arbitration Court may refer to the Court possible disputes concerning the interpretation or implementation of their good-neighbourliness agreements.

The role conferred in this context to the OSCE has been, however, the subject of lively controversy, some OSCE states considering that the guarantee mechanisms provided for, in particular the opportunity given in certain cases to third states to raise disputes, could be abused especially by the kin-states of the minorities referred to in the bilateral agreements. So far, OSCE countries have never made recourse to this provision.

Article 15 of the Pact on Stability further states that the parties "with regard to the observance of ... commitments in the implementation of the agreements and arrangements included in the Pact, [can] resort to the instruments and procedures of the OSCE, including those concerning conflict prevention, peaceful settlement of disputes and the human dimension". This also includes the opportunity to consult the High Commissioner on National Minorities (HCNM) on problems regarding the implementation of bilateral agreements. This provision has never been applied either.

Use of domestic remedies in the form of court proceedings might be another possible monitoring instrument, as long as the constitutional system allows treaty rules to operate directly in domestic law, and the rights are self-executing. Since self-executing provisions in bilateral agreements are rare, there is little likelihood of rights included in a bilateral agreement being effectively invoked before a court.

In the light of the above, the joint intergovernmental commissions (and their sub-committees on minorities),[5] which are established under many bilateral agreements, can be considered as the most effective implementation mechanism.[6] Joint commissions can contribute to confidence-building and play an important role by establishing a forum for discussion where minority issues can be addressed and where the ground for decisions, which will only be taken at a higher level, can be prepared. Furthermore, an ongoing dialogue to channel and refocus debate in a productive manner has thus been created.[7] None the less, there would still be room for further improvement of their functioning and effectiveness. The most important factor that has an impact on their effectiveness is the political good will of the contracting parties to implement the agreement and the recommendations resulting from the work of the joint commissions. This political will is conditioned by the internal development of the state in question, and its general state of democracy.

This paper will set out to give an overview of the existing joint commissions established in the field of the protection of minorities, focusing mainly on the commissions set up between Hungary and its neighbours: Croatia,[8] Slovenia,[9] Romania[10] and Slovakia.[11] Joint intergovernmental commissions also exist in the framework of some other agreements, but do not always function properly.

Description of the mechanism

Joint commissions are not comparable to a judicial body that supervises that the law of the citizens of a certain state is being abided to. It is not a mechanism which assists a person whose rights have been violated. There is no formal procedure foreseen for persons who want to bring to the commission's attention facts that run contrary to a provision laid down in a bilateral agreement. Its decisions are not directly binding on anybody.

Joint commissions are politically charged bodies, comparable to a governmental advisory organ, evaluating the overall implementation of bilateral agreements in the field of minorities and adopting recommendations which are addressed to the respective governments. The destiny of these recommendations depends on the political will of the government. No sanctions can be imposed if the recommendations are not implemented.

These are the common features of an implementation mechanism which holds a huge potential but constantly lives with the risk of inefficiency or obstruction.

In order to describe this mechanism in detail, the joint commissions based on a bilateral agreement on minorities will be examined separately from joint commissions based on a treaty on friendly relations and good neighbourliness.

Joint commissions based on a bilateral agreement on minorities

The joint commissions discussed in this part have their basis in a bilateral agreement dealing solely with the issue of minorities. This is the case of the agreements between Hungary and Slovenia and Croatia respectively.[12] The articles providing for the establishment of the joint commissions[13] are very detailed and contain information that ranges from their composition, through the frequency of the meetings and the mandate of the joint commission to the modus in which decisions are adopted.

Composition of the commission: The number of members present in the joint commissions is not defined in the agreements but agreed upon by the two parties.[14] The Hungarian-Slovenian and the Hungarian-Croatian joint commissions are both made up of two state delegations of 15 members each. Each delegation is composed of a chairman, a secretary and its members. The delegations are headed by the foreign ministers but in practice this position is normally delegated to a state secretary. The members are mainly heads of international co-operation departments or relevant ministries for the protection of minorities (ministries of education, culture and the interior).

In both conventions the presence of minority representatives in the respective delegation is foreseen by the agreement. These representatives are to be appointed by the governments upon the proposal of their minority organisations. For instance, a Hungarian member of the Croatian parliament and elected local representatives hold seats on the Hungarian-Croatian commission.

Membership in the commission, especially with regard to the governmental representatives, is not attached to specific persons, but instead to the positions that these persons hold. This has the disadvantage that the continuity of the commission is constantly endangered by political changes. On the other hand, this linkage to the position might be useful and necessary in the sense that it guarantees having members present in the joint commission who also have the political back-up to enact the recommendations adopted by the commission.

Apart from the two state delegations as described above, no external actors have been involved in the meetings of the joint commissions between Hungary, Slovenia and Croatia respectively. Such actors could be independent legal experts or representatives of international organisations. The aim of such participation would be impartial assistance to both parties when it comes to legal questions of the protection of minorities. The assistance of international organisations could, for example, be useful when it comes to the definition of terms or interpretation of standards where there is a clear understanding in public international law.[15] Moreover, external actors, like the HCNM of the OSCE, could play a conciliating role where necessary.

As relations between Hungary, and Croatia and Slovenia respectively are good and no substantial problems have appeared concerning the relatively small mutual minority groups, such involvement does not necessarily need to be sought.

The mandate of joint commissions is described in both bilateral agreements as follows:

— to discuss current issues relevant to the two minorities;
— to evaluate the implementation of obligations under the convention;
— to prepare and adopt recommendations for their respective governments concerning the implementation and, in case of necessity, the modification of the convention.

Meetings shall take place at least annually in the case of the Hungarian-Croatian commission and at least twice a year in the case of the Hungarian-Slovenian commission, which has proved not to be attainable.[16] In order to improve the reception of the work of the joint commissions within the minority group and to make it more visible to it, the meetings are increasingly often organised not in capitals but in areas where the respective minorities live.

During the meetings, the general situation of the respective minorities is assessed, and the implementation of previous recommendations is evaluated. The issues generally discussed are the preservation of culture, language and religion and developments in the field of education.

During the discussion as well as in the decision-making the minority representatives play the same role and have the same powers as any other member of the commission. Moreover, the legitimately elected leaders of the different minority organisations are being regularly consulted by the secretaries of the joint commission.

The decision on a recommendation is always taken by consensus without any possibility for anybody to veto a decision. The protocol of the meeting including the adopted recommendations is forwarded to both governments. The recommendations always propose a government action or legislative activity of the home-state.

In Hungary, like in Croatia and Slovenia, the recommendations adopted by the joint commission are reinforced by a governmental decision, determining which government departments will be responsible for the implementation of the respective recommendations. In the case of Hungary, this governmental decision is drafted by the secretary of the commission in co-operation with the Office of Hungarians Abroad and the Office for National Minorities. Once adopted by the government, it is published in the *Official Bulletin* in this way giving binding force to the recommendations.

The joint commission itself also oversees the implementation of its recommendations. As many of the members in the commission are themselves working in the governmental departments responsible for the implementation they can follow it up on a daily basis. Moreover, in the meetings of the joint commission the implementation of the recommendations adopted during the previous session is evaluated. If in the period between one meeting and the next a recommendation has not been implemented, it will be reiterated in the recommendations to be adopted until its implementation.

Joint commissions based on a treaty on friendly relations and good neigh-bourliness

Joint commissions can also be foreseen by treaties of friendly relations and good neighbourliness.[17] This is the case of the joint commissions established by the basic treaties concluded between Hungary, and Slovakia and Romania respectively.[18] As these treaties do not only deal with minority issues but are more general agreements on friendly relations and good neighbourliness, there is only one comprehensive article in each, containing a whole "law on minorities".[19]

The main difference between this group of joint commissions and the one discussed above lies in the fact that the involvement of minority representatives in the respective delegations is not explicitly foreseen by the treaties. Specifications on mandate and composition remain rather vague[20] or are lacking.

The distinction is moreover justified due to the different size of minorities which have to be protected through these treaties. The demands of these quite sizeable minority groups are more challenging for the states and are more likely to cause tensions between the states.

Procedures regarding the preparation of the meetings, voting modalities and the way of following up on the recommendations are comparable to those in the commissions that are based on a minority agreement. In this part, only the distinctive elements will be examined.

The basis for the establishment of a joint commission for co-operation on minority issues is laid down in Article 5 of both basic treaties. This article, with a view to implementing the purposes of the basic treaties, calls upon the contracting parties to establish an appropriate framework for co-operation in all fields of mutual interest. Within this framework the prime ministers and ministers for foreign affairs are supposed to meet at least annually.

Article 15 of both basic treaties is the article dealing with the issue of (mutual) minorities. One paragraph within this article,[21] making reference to

Article 5 of the basic treaties, stipulates in both cases that the contracting parties shall co-operate to assist one another in following the implementation of the content of the minority related articles. For this end they shall set up an intergovernmental joint commission.

A relatively long period of time passed between the ratification of the agreement and the first meeting of the Hungarian-Slovak joint commission.[22] During a meeting of Hungarian and Slovak prime ministers, Hungary proposed that by 30 September 1997:

— the foreign ministers, after due preparation by experts, should sign the protocol relating to the operational mechanism of the basic treaty;

— all the joint commissions intended to monitor the implementation process, which are yet to be formed, should be set up;

— the representatives of Hungary's Slovak community and Slovakia's Hungarian community should be granted a chance to participate in the joint commission charged with the monitoring of the minority rights provisions.

Only on 13 November 1998, did the Hungarian deputy state secretary at the Foreign Ministry state that an agreement was reached on the implementation mechanism. Eleven committees were designed to co-ordinate the implementation of the basic treaty. On 24 November 1998, the foreign ministers of Hungary and Slovakia signed the protocol that founded the Hungarian-Slovak Joint Commission for Minority Affairs. In this protocol the parties agreed upon the involvement of representatives of the Hungarian minority in Slovakia and the Slovak minority in Hungary in the Joint Commission for Minority Affairs.[23]

This positive development in the Hungarian-Slovak relations has to be pointed out. The basic treaty asks for a composition "as they deem necessary" (Article 15, paragraph 6), making the participation of minority members in the work of the joint commission possible but not compulsory. The agreement to involve the minorities concerned in the work of the commission is an encouraging demonstration of both parties' willingness to work effectively on the improvement of the situation of their (mutual) minorities.

The situation with regard to representation of minorities in the Hungarian-Romanian joint commission is slightly different. As explained above, the precondition for such involvement was similar to the Hungarian-Slovak commission. The treaty just says that the contracting parties shall establish an "intergovernmental expert commission" (Article 15, paragraph 10), without any further specification on mandate or who these experts could be. On 12 March 1997, a protocol was concluded between the Government of Romania and the Government of the Republic of Hungary concerning the establishment of the Romanian-Hungarian Joint Commission on Active Co-operation and Partnership.[24] In its Article 4, the protocol determines the set-up of nine expert committees, including the Special Committee for Co-operation on Minorities' Issues. The protocol includes Rules of Operation, which in their Article 4 touch on the issue of minority representation:

The co-presidents of the joint commission may invite to its sessions a representative of the organisations of the Hungarian and, respectively, Romanian national minorities from the two countries. In particular, the Romanian co-president may invite a representative of the Hungarian community in Romania, and the Hungarian co-president may invite a representative of the Romanian community in Hungary.

Firstly, this provision does not imply any obligation to invite minority representatives ("may invite"). Secondly, this invitation is only foreseen for the meetings of the full joint commission, but not for the meetings of the Special Committee for Co-operation on Minorities' Issues. In its first meeting, this special committee agreed that minority representatives will also be invited to the meetings of the special committee. They participate as permanent invited members, with a right of consultation.

After the elections in 1996, the Democratic Union of the Hungarians in Romania (DUHR) became part of the government coalition and Hungarian representatives were included in the special committee. After the elections in 2000, the DUHR, although not part of the government coalition, concluded a protocol of co-operation with the governing party, supporting the government, which further guaranteed their presence in the special committee. None the less, there is a permanent concern among minority representatives with regard to this lack of institutionalisation of the presence of minorities in the Hungarian-Romanian committee.[25]

In principle, the minority representatives do not have the same decisional power as other members of the special committee. They only have a consultative role. Even if in practice, all decisions are taken by consensus, including also the point of view of the minority representatives, this fact raises further concern among the minorities concerned.

Compared to the Hungarian commissions with Croatia and Slovenia, the commissions with Slovakia and Romania are rather small. Each state delegation consists of eight members. Initially, both commissions intended to meet twice a year. Now the parties have agreed upon annual meetings, which have not always been realised.[26] Between 1999 and 2001, the work of the Hungarian-Romanian special committee was interrupted, allegedly because of a lack of interest of the Romanian party. On 19 June 2001, the Hungarian Parliament adopted the Act on Hungarians Living in Neighbouring Countries, the so-called Status Law,[27] which caused big tensions between Hungary and Romania. The HCNM played a very important role in bringing the two disputing parties back into a discussion. As a result, the joint commission was reactivated and through its work, along with the continuing efforts undertaken by the HCNM, a rapprochement of the two positions became possible. In a Memorandum of Understanding a possible solution to various problems was found.[28]

The mandate of the joint commissions is, similar to the one of the previously examined commissions, to evaluate the situation of the Hungarian and the Romanian minorities, to phrase recommendations for the governments and to monitor their implementation. The Hungarian-Romanian commission has elaborated a working method for cases in which sensitive issues are discussed. In these cases, the commission is split into two working groups. One deals with the ordinary agenda, the other group deals with the extraordinary agenda: such a working group discussed, for example, issues of the Status Law.

With regard to the follow-up on the recommendations, the Romanian Government approves the protocol containing the recommendations as a document of a political character. In Slovakia, recommendations become binding through their inclusion in a governmental decree. As explained earlier, in Hungary the recommendations adopted by the joint commission are reinforced by a governmental decision, in this way giving binding force to the recommendations. Romanian, Slovak and Hungarian secretaries to the joint commissions or their co-chairs can ask the departments of institutions responsible for the implementation for progress reports. But the monitoring of the implementation of recommendations usually takes place, as in the case of the Hungarian-Croatian and the Hungarian-Slovenian joint commissions, during the next meeting of the joint commissions.

While political pressure can be exerted on countries reluctant to implement a recommendation, there is a lack of legal means to push the other side to implement the recommendations. However, the force of the recommendations of all joint commissions, be it the ones based on a bilateral agreement on minority issues or the ones based on a basic treaty, lies in the consensus principle, expressing the willingness of both sides to work on the situation.

Discussion of the main results in the field of minority rights

As has been described above, joint commissions can only address recommendations to their respective governments or to both governments together and have no means of forcing their implementation.

This section starts with a description of the types of issues that are discussed in the meetings, the degree of specificity of the recommendations and an assessment of their implementation. The adoption of certain measures for the protection of minorities within a state is of course not always only due to the work of the joint commission but is also related to other factors or developments within a given country. An example for this could be the recommended adoption of a piece of legislation by the Committee of Ministers of the Council of Europe with regard to the implementation of the Framework Convention for the Protection of National Minorities. In such cases, the commission can serve as a discussion forum where details of the reception of such a recommendation can be discussed.

The second part of this section discusses the role of the joint commissions, in particular the joint commission between Hungary and Romania, in finding an agreement on the implementation of the Hungarian Status Law.

Types of recommendations adopted and their implementation

The issues discussed during the meetings of the joint commissions are generally very practice-related. As a consequence, the recommendations adopted are in most cases quite detailed and specific.

The Hungarian-Croatian commission,[29] for instance, has recommended the establishment of a Hungarian educational centre in Osijek. As well as this centre, a Hungarian language department has been opened in Zagreb. Following a recommendation of the joint commission, a Croatian school and a Croatian language department have been opened in Pécs. As a result of the work of the joint commission, a library of the Hungarian minority has been opened in Beli Manastir, Croatia. Croatia has secured, as requested by Article 9 of the convention between Hungary and Croatia, the representation of the Hungarian minority at local, regional and national levels. Accordingly, the Hungarian minority is represented in the city of Osijek, the Osijek-Baranja county and in the Croatian Parliament. The same commission has recommended the opening of new border crossing points. Through the accession of Hungary to the European Union the border between Hungary and Croatia becomes an external border. Therefore, the implementation of this recommendation has been hampered by the Schengen regulations.

The Hungarian-Slovenian joint commission has also recommended the establishment of new border crossings, which in this case has been successfully implemented near to the villages where the minorities live. On the other hand, despite a recommendation of the joint commission to that effect, the use of the mother tongue in religious practice is still not fully ensured.

The Hungarian-Slovak commission dealt amongst other things with the establishment of a Hungarian university department in Slovakia and of a Slovakian university department in Hungary. The commission adopted a recommendation to that effect.[30]

At the beginning of 2001, the Slovak Government decided that a Hungarian faculty could be established with Hungarian funding within the Slovak University. However, this decision could not be implemented because Slovak universities are autonomous and they decide autonomously about the establishment of new faculties. This example shows, that in some cases, the non-implementation of a recommendation is due to the difficulty of involving the private sector or autonomous agencies.

With regard to the establishment of a Slovak faculty in Hungary, the evaluation during the following meeting showed that there is no real interest among the Slovak minority in Hungary in the establishment of a Slovak faculty in Hungary.[31] This example shows the importance of close and continuous consultations with the minority group in order to ensure that the recommendations adopted are really beneficial for the group and comply with their needs.

In another recommendation Hungary has been called upon to ensure the representation of the Slovak minority in parliament. This recommendation has not yet been implemented.

During the second meeting of the Hungarian-Slovak joint commission,[32] the parties agreed upon a yearly exchange of financial overviews of the amounts invested in the protection of minorities.

In the field of education, the committee recommended the formation of a group of Slovak and Hungarian historians who would produce a handbook on the history of Hungary and Slovakia, which would also be used as material for history classes in the schools of both countries.

The Hungarian-Romanian Special Committee for Co-operation on Minorities' Issues discussed the modification of the Romanian law on education, the use of the mother tongue in relations with public administration in Romania and the mutual recognition of diplomas. Concerning the Romanian minority in Hungary the demands raised during the meetings of the joint commission referred to the representation of the Romanian minority in the Hungarian Parliament, the publication of official documents of the municipalities in two languages, and education in the mother tongue.

The committee recommended amongst other things that Hungary should finance the kindergartens for the Romanian minorities in Hungary, whereas Romania was requested to finance the primary schools and high schools for Romanian minorities in Hungary. The Hungarian Government was requested to take initiatives to assure the representation of the Romanian minorities in the Hungarian Parliament. The Romanian Government was asked to accelerate the approval of the law for the protection of minorities, which also stipulates the establishment of a university in the Hungarian language in Romania. The committee stressed that the Romanian Government should start the construction of this university, to which Hungary shall contribute structurally and financially.[33]

The protocol of the fourth meeting of the special committee[34] gives an overview of the recommendations that have been implemented.

Education in the Romanian language is carried out in thirteen villages of Hungary. Hungary granted support of around 1.5 million euros to Romanian kindergartens and minority schools between 1999 and 2002. Some funds have been allocated by Hungary for the restoration of Romanian Orthodox churches in Hungary. However, the recommendation concerning the representation of the Romanian minority in parliament could not be implemented as there was no consensus between the parties in the Hungarian Parliament on this matter. A recommendation to that effect has since been reiterated in every protocol of the joint commission's meetings.

According to the aforementioned protocol, Romania contributed to the renovation of Romanian churches in Hungary. Moreover, the bilateral agreement for mutual recognition of diplomas has been ratified. So far, no law on the protection of national minorities has been passed, but amendments to the Law on Education and a new Law of Local Public Administration have been adopted.

In 1999, Romania amended the Law on Education,[35] which constituted a legal obstacle to the establishment of multicultural institutions, where languages other than Romanian can be used in the teaching. The modified law provides the right of persons belonging to national minorities to study and receive instruction in their mother tongue, at all levels and in all forms of education (Article 118). The law provides for the possibility of establishing, upon request and in compliance with the legal provisions, groups, classes, sections or schools with teaching in the language of national minorities (Article 119). For the teaching of Romanian language and literature in elementary schools, special curricula and textbooks are conceived for the respective minority (Article 120). Moreover, "[p]upils belonging to national minorities that attend schools with tuition in Romanian shall be granted, at request and according to the present law, the study of the language and the literature of the mother tongue as well as the history and traditions of the respective national minority, as school subjects" (Article 121). Lines of instruction in the Hungarian language for more than fifty fields of study were created in the Babes-Bolyai University, within the Medicine and Pharmacy University and within the Dramatic Art University of Târgu-Mureş.

Furthermore, Romania passed a Law of Local Public Administration[36] which provides for the use of mother tongue in public administration: "In the territorial-administrative units in which the citizens belonging to the national minorities have a share of over 20% of the number of the inhabitants, the local public administration authorities shall ensure, in the relations with them, also the use of the mother tongue ..." (Article 17). This implies amongst other things also the employment of persons speaking the minority language in positions regarding public relations (Article 90, paragraph 3). Always on the condition of holding a share of over 20%, decisions of normative character of the territorial-administrative units "shall be brought to the public knowledge also in the mother tongue of the respective minority, while those of individual character shall be communicated, at request, in the mother tongue, too" (Article 51). Moreover, in these territorial-administrative units the inscription of the name of the localities, as well as the posting of announcements of public interest also has to be ensured in the respective minority language (Article 90, paragraph 4). These are especially interesting provisions for the strong Hungarian minority in Romania, which in two counties of Transylvania make up not only 20% of the number of inhabitants but up to 84%.[37]

In a common effort of both countries, the network of border control points has been increased and is still expanding. So far no understanding has been reached regarding the preservation of monuments and military cemeteries. The text of a draft convention is still under negotiation.

In the recommendations contained in the protocol of the fourth meeting of the Hungarian-Romanian special committee,[38] the Hungarian Government was asked to agree, together with the self-governance of Romanians in Hungary, on "the most appropriate means in order to eliminate any possibility of access to the leadership of the Romanian self-governance for persons not having Romanian ethnic origin". Furthermore, the Hungarian Government was requested to "grant appropriate resources for completely financing the education in Romanian language and to take the necessary measures for continuing teachers' training as required by the process of education in Romanian language". The Romanian Government, on the other hand, "shall support the development of the professional level of Romanian educational institutions" in Hungary, "by ensuring the auxiliary means, the specialty and belletristic books [*sic*], accordingly to the peculiarities of the teaching in Romanian language". Moreover, the "Romanian Government shall ensure the effective implementation of the dispositions concerning minorities provided by the Law on Public Administration, by drafting the enforcement regulations and by enforcing them." Upon the request of the Hungarian side, the parties agreed to keep the issue of the Romanian state university in the Hungarian language on the agenda of the committee. "The Romanian Government shall examine the possibility of creating a centre of scientific research regarding the Hungarians from Romania, including the modalities of its financing".

Besides dealing with these general issues, the Hungarian-Romanian Special Committee for Co-operation on Minorities' Issues has played an important role in finding a solution to the dispute between Hungary and Romania over the Act on Hungarians living in Neighbouring Countries. A Memorandum of Understanding has been signed between the two governments laying down the conditions for the implementation of the Status Law.

The role of the joint commissions in finding an agreement on the implementation of the Hungarian Status Law

Since September 2001, it is mainly one joint commission that has been very active: the Hungarian-Romanian sub-committee on minority issues. The reason for its revitalisation after years of inactivity is the adoption and entry into force of the Hungarian Act on Hungarians Living in Neighbouring Countries,[39] granting certain benefits to persons declaring themselves of Hungarian national identity but residing in a neighbouring country.[40] The law was adopted without previously conferring with the affected neighbouring countries. The existing joint intergovernmental commissions were not consulted on the issue.

Austria has rejected the application of the law on its territory. Ukraine and Serbia and Montenegro accepted the law. There were very few reactions coming from Croatia and Slovenia, as the percentage of Hungarians living in these countries is rather low.

Slovakia and Romania, however, both countries having quite a large Hungarian minority, strongly opposed the law. Their main arguments were that the law had extraterritorial effects and that it was discriminatory towards their local populations. Hungary and Romania asked the Council of Europe's Venice Commission for an opinion on the question whether such preferential treatment of kin-minorities is in line with the principles of international law.[41]

Only three months after the adoption of the law, the sub-committee on minorities of the Hungarian-Romanian joint commission reassumed its functions and three meetings took place in September and October 2001. During these meetings the sub-commission was split into two groups: one dealing with the ordinary agenda and the second dealing only with the issue of the Status Law.

The protocol resulting from these meetings expresses the readiness of the two parties "to adopt, if necessary, within their territory, measures of positive discrimination in order to ensure the full equality of chances between the persons belonging to national minorities and the persons belonging to the majority population in their respective States." It continues by specifying that "[f]rom the Romanian point of view, the adoption of positive discrimination measures based on ethnic criteria cannot be extended to socio-economic rights."[42]

This is a more restrictive approach than the one adopted by the Venice Commission in its report, made public shortly after the signature of the protocol. The Venice Commission had found that preferential treatment may be granted to persons belonging to kin-minorities in the fields of culture and education, and only under very exceptional circumstances also in other fields, but in both cases this preferential treatment is subject to the condition that "it is shown to pursue a legitimate aim and to be proportionate to that aim."[43]

The protocol of the Hungarian-Romanian sub-committee on minorities expressed the appreciation for every support given by their governments to their co-ethnics living on the territory of the other party, but put very much emphasis on the fact that the parties have to inform each other of such activities. This was a clear message in the direction of Hungary, to avoid in the future any unilateral undertakings for the protection of its kin-minority without previously consulting or at least informing its neighbours.

These meetings and the resulting protocol together with the continuing efforts of the HCNM were the basis for the signature in December 2001 of the Memorandum of Understanding (MOU) between the Romanian and Hungarian governments.[44]

The MOU sets forth the conditions for the implementation of the Status Law "with regard to Romanian citizens". The MOU asks for amendments of the law in the field of employment, the granting and issuing of the "Hungarian certificate" as well as in the field of health care. When implementing the provisions of the memorandum, the Hungarian authorities are requested to "take also into account the recommendations of the Committee on national minorities which shall further on examine the questions concerning the Law on Hungarians Living in Neighbouring Countries."[45]

Since the signing of the MOU, the Hungarian-Romanian sub-committee on national minorities has continued to meet on a regular basis. In November 2002, Romanian and Hungarian premiers signed a new "strategic partnership" in Budapest, agreeing to continue consultations on amending the Hungarian Status Law, after Romanian Prime Minister Adrian Nastase expressed objections to some Hungarian proposed changes in the legislation.[46]

Despite this positive development, so far the necessary amendments of the law have not been adopted. A Hungarian intergovernmental working group has recommended mostly technical but also some substantial changes to the law: the number of persons eligible for educational benefits would for example be considerably expanded by granting the subsidies to institutions rather than to persons. The proposal includes also the removal of the chapter on employment from the law. In line with the recommendations of the Venice Commission, the issue of Hungarian certificates would also be modified.

Another question is whether the law will be applicable to Slovenia and Slovakia after their accession to the European Union in 2004 and to Romania after its expected accession in 2007. Hungarian Foreign Minister Laszlo Kovacs is well aware of this potential short life of the law, as the EU bans any type of differentiation on ethnic grounds. EU Enlargement Commissioner Guenther Verheugen underlined that the "Status Law must correspond with the recommendations of the Venice Commission and can only be applied on the basis of agreements with [Hungary's] neighbouring countries."[47] The latest version of the amended law stipulates that the legislation does not apply to ethnic Hungarians in EU countries. The Hungarian opposition party, which was in power in 2001 when the law was adopted, is in particular against this proposed amendment. An early sign of a development in this direction is the fact that at the beginning of March 2003, Hungary has suspended the implementation of the Status Law for Slovak citizens of ethnic Hungarian origin until the Hungarian Parliament approves amendments to the law.[48]

On 23 June 2003 the Hungarian Parliament adopted with 195 votes in favour and 173 against a series of amendments to the law. These amendments include the deletion of a reference to the unified Hungarian nation in the law's preamble and modified terms of eligibility for financial assistance.[49]

Neighbouring countries reacted in very different ways: Slovakia considered that the amended law still includes unacceptable extraterritorial provisions and criticised that Slovakia was not consulted on the draft amendments. This fact was also criticised by the Parliamentary Assembly of the Council of Europe.[50] Slovakia would therefore block the implementation on its territory of clauses that infringe its sovereignty. Some days after the adoption of the amendments, Slovakia announced the dissolving of organisations that are active in the implementation of the law in the territory. Furthermore it stated that money provided by Hungary to individuals in Slovakia who are entitled to financial subsistence under the provisions of the law would be subject to a 90% tax. Another announced counter-measure to the Status Law foresees that Slovak schools receiving such financial subsistence could see the contributions they receive from the Slovak state budget curtailed.[51]

Romania also found that the law still includes aspects that are out of line with European standards.[52] Croatian premier, Ivica Racan, said that Croatia has no objections to the implementation of the law on Croat territory and recommended that Bratislava and Budapest should seek a mutually acceptable solution.[53]

The OSCE HCNM stressed that the law has to be implemented in co-operation with Hungary's neighbours. Hungary proposed a meeting of the joint commissions to discuss ways of implementing the provisions of the law.

This case is a good example of how highly political the issue of minorities is and how carefully states have to deal with it, if they do not want to endanger friendly relations with their neighbours. It also shows that with political good will on both sides an agreement on controversial issues may be reached. A timely use of structures designed for the discussion of such issues has the potential of avoiding tensions between two states. In cases where tensions have already appeared, such structures can contribute to a relaxation of the situation and the finding of a solution. Thus, joint commissions can have a conflict-preventing and a conflict-solving effect.

Guidance for minority rights practitioners

What are the strengths and weaknesses of bilateral agreements as an instrument for the protection of minorities and the joint commissions as the most important monitoring and implementation mechanism?[54]

Every minority situation presents its own particular characteristics and there is consequently no standard means of resolving the multitude of problems that each case presents in a national context. On the whole, bilateral treaties constitute a useful and sometimes even essential addition to the international regime for the protection of persons belonging to national minorities. If effectively implemented, the substantive rights included in the existing bilateral agreements hold a considerable potential for the development of minority protection.

In this perspective, the use of bilateral agreements in comparison to general minority regulations included in international and regional instruments has the advantage that they take into account the specific historical and traditional needs of the minorities concerned.

The conclusion of these treaties often reflects a remarkable relaxation of tensions between treaty parties, and their implementation can further stimulate a climate of good-neighbourliness and co-operation. Besides having this effect, bilateral treaties constitute important instruments for the prevention of conflict between states, by providing a clear framework for contacts and contributing to transparency in the actions of the kin-state in support of the minority in question.

The relaxing effect is partly due to the fact that bilateral treaties usually contain provisions that reduce the fear of secession. They refer to the mutual recognition of borders and contain provisions on territorial integrity of states and reinforcement of the inviolability of borders.

In addition to strengthening confidence and stability among and in border regions, bilateral treaties give legal force, through confirmation and/or incorporation, to international instruments that are not legally binding documents.

Bilateral agreements must certainly not lower or compromise existing obligations or commitments.[55] To replace specific national provisions by reference
to international conventions, such as the Framework Convention for the
Protection of National Minorities, which contains more general standards,
could in a specific case be such a regression.

Further concerns may arise from the fact that vague wording and formulations potentially obstruct the effective implementation of the provisions.
Bilateral treaties may also have disintegrative effects as they normally protect only kin-minorities. Other groups of inhabitants might be placed in a
less favourable position, in particular minority groups without a kin-state.
Tensions among minority groups within a given country could thereby be
created. Bilateral treaties and their state of implementation, in particular of
their minority regulations, usually reflect the actual political orientation of
the states concerned and are subject to strong political influence. The basic
precondition for efficiency of a bilateral agreement is the political will to
apply that agreement in practice, as there is no possibility of sanctioning the
non-implementation.[56]

Notwithstanding this weakness of the monitoring and implementation
mechanism and in order to make the best of the situation, it is of utmost
importance for the minorities concerned to seek every kind of possible
involvement or participation in the process of negotiating and drafting of an
agreement and afterwards in the implementation and monitoring of the
same.

The issue of "representativity" of the person present in a joint commission for
the minority group is often difficult to resolve. First of all it has to be ensured
that the minority group makes the appointment. Sometimes there is more
than one minority organisation, as, for example, the case of the Hungarians
in Croatia. The question arises as to whether unity of a minority representation has to be sought in order to strengthen the position of a minority group.

The minority group cannot be obliged to have only one organisation. A plurality of organisations can be based upon territorial division of the minority
group or different political directions. It is important to make sure that
minority representatives present in the joint commissions are able to represent a plurality of minority views. In order to exert pressure on decisions to
be taken in the joint commission, a concerted direction of impact of the
minority groups is an asset, whether this position is the expression of a single
minority organisation or a common position agreed upon between different
minority organisations. Communication between the various organisations
and the support by its minority of the person representing a minority in a
joint commission is therefore of utmost importance.

In some of the commissions the appropriate representation of minorities is
questionable. In the Hungarian-Romanian commission, for instance, while
the minority representatives are members of the minority group in question,
in most cases they are at the same time members of a governmental department, like the Office of National Minorities or the like. This might have the
advantage that these members also have the possibility to follow up on the

implementation of the recommendation on a daily basis, as this is linked to their activities within the governmental departments. On the other hand, their impartiality is not guaranteed. In any case, the government has to abstain from any attempt to influence the position of the minority representative. Moreover, participation of a minority party in the governmental coalition should not condition the participation of a minority representative in the joint commission.

Minority representatives should be seen in their linking role: they can depoliticise issues, because they have a more practical approach. Ideally, they are in constant consultation with their group and should therefore be able to inform the joint commission about the real practical needs of their minority. But the flow of information has to be two-way. It is a fact that most of the joint commissions consider it to be the responsibility of the minority representatives to report back to their minority group and inform them about the results and the conclusions of the meeting of the joint commission. In order to render the work of the joint commissions more transparent, not only for the minority groups concerned but also for other minorities or the majority population, the results of the meetings should be published.

In order to bring the work of the joint commissions in the field of minorities into a broader context of mechanisms for the protection of minorities and in an effort to improve the efficiency of existing mechanisms, contacts and exchange of information with other monitoring bodies could be sought. One such monitoring body could be the Advisory Committee for the Framework Convention for the Protection of National Minorities (ACFC).[57] During its country visits, the ACFC could be informed about the activities of the joint commissions, the success or the failure of its work. If considered to be necessary or useful, written information could be sent for the ACFC's attention. The ACFC in its opinions could look into the level of participation of minority representatives in the work of the commission (based on Article 15 of the FCNM) or the potential discriminatory effects bilateral agreements might have on other groups (based on Article 4 of the FCNM).

Another body that could be involved on an ad hoc basis in the activities of the joint commission is the High Commissioner on National Minorities of the OSCE. His involvement could be taken into consideration, or requested by members of the joint commission and therefore also by the minority group through its representative in the joint commission, if an agreement on a particular issue cannot be reached between the parties.

Considering all this, the concrete role of minority rights practitioners could consist firstly of organising and channelling the consultation with members of the minority group in order to ensure that the commission member is aware of the most urgent needs of the group and is able to represent the plurality of views of the group. This is especially important when there is more than one minority organisation in a country.

Secondly, the minority representative has to be fully informed about the legal obligations of the state under public international law in order to guarantee that these standards cannot be lowered or circumvented in any way by a recommendation of the joint commission.

Thirdly, the joint commission has to ensure that the results of its meetings are disseminated, especially among the minority group, but also among the majority population. Minority rights practitioners can support this dissemination. Publicity of the work of the joint commission contributes on the one hand to transparency and a better acceptance of the work of the commission, on the other hand to a better control that can be exerted through public opinion and minority rights activists on the implementation of recommendations. Moreover the results can be brought in the broader context of monitoring mechanisms at the international level.

Fourthly, minority rights practitioners should make sure that other minorities, in particular minorities without a kin-state, benefit from the work of the joint commission.

Fifthly, minority rights practitioners could also seek the involvement of external actors, such as the ACFC, through providing it with information during its country visits or through written information sent to the committee. And finally, minority rights practitioners could call for an involvement of the HCNM of the OSCE, if an agreement cannot be reached between the parties.

Concluding remarks

Dealing with minority issues is per se a political issue. It is therefore hardly conceivable, that the work of the joint commissions in the field of minorities could be made less dependent on political developments. In cases where the representation of minorities within the commission is not guaranteed by the bilateral agreement or a subsequent protocol this could even mean the absence of minority members in the commission.

That being said, joint commissions should be perceived as a forum for discussion and a possibility to deal with misunderstandings and problematic issues between neighbouring states. They can assume this role properly only under certain conditions. First of all there has to exist a political will to use this mechanism not only as a conflict-solving but more importantly as a conflict-preventing mechanism. Unilateral steps for the protection of the kin-minority should be avoided in order not to endanger friendly relations between the states. If differences appear with regard to the implementation or interpretation of a bilateral treaty, they should be resolved through bilateral negotiations and discussions in the bodies provided for by the treaties.

Secondly, when meetings are convoked, the representatives of the relevant minority groups must be granted the same decisional powers as all the other members of the commission in order to ensure that the recommendations adopted are beneficial for the minorities concerned. However, participation of minority representatives should be ensured not only in the implementation process but already during the drafting and conclusion of the bilateral agreement itself. In most cases the agreements are negotiated in the absence of the minority community they were designed to protect. States with a larger minority community tend to be reluctant to involve the minorities, while the kin-states expressly enforce their involvement.[58]

Thirdly, the solution of a controversial issue during a meeting depends mainly on the type of mandate the negotiating partners have received from their respective governments concerning a concrete question. It is therefore important that the heads of the two state delegations are high ranking officials or political representatives with a strong political back-up and a comprehensive mandate and that the overall composition of both state delegations is balanced.

When it comes to the implementation of the recommendations it has to be ensured that this is not curtailed through governmental decrees or circumvented through too large a margin of discretion for the state authorities or the administration. Implementation is often also hampered because of a lack of (or untimely) funding. Another obstacle for the implementation of certain recommendations arises from the difficulty of efficient involvement of the private sector.

Even if there is the permanent danger of politicisation of the work of the commissions and of inefficiency it has to be considered a positive fact that the minority issue is extensively discussed in government when transforming the recommendations into a governmental decree and the consequent awareness of minority issues in the work of the government. By making the documentation of the work of the joint commissions available to a broader public, public awareness can also be raised.

The role of minority rights practitioners consists basically in assisting and supporting the activities of the minority representative in the joint commission, co-ordinating and enhancing the information flow from the minority group to the commission through the minority representative and the dissemination of the results of the work of the commission among the minority group, but also among the majority population and other international actors in the field of minorities.

* Researcher at the European Academy Bolzano, Minorities and Regional Autonomies, currently doctoral candidate in Law (University of Graz).

1. For the text of the agreement see, for instance, Hurst Hannum (ed.), *Documents on Autonomy and Minority Rights* (Dordrecht 1993), pp. 141-3. As stated by Myntti, this agreement is often quoted as an example of a long-standing bilateral treaty. However, the Åland Agreement was not a legally binding treaty and only later it developed into international customary rule seen to oblige Finland to safeguard the Ålanders' autonomy: Kristian Myntti, "The Åland Model – its Background and Special Characteristics", in Harry Jansson and Johannes Salminen (eds.), *The Second Åland Islands Question – Autonomy or Independence?* (Mariehamn 2002), p. 110.

2. The text of the treaty can be found in German at the following website: http://zis.uibk.ac.at/stirol_doku/dokumente/19460905.html

3. Kinga Gál, "Bilateral Agreements in Central and Eastern Europe: A new Inter-State Framework for Minority Protection?" ECMI Working Paper No. 4, 1999, at http://www.ecmi.de/doc/download/working_paper_4.pdf 2-3.

4. Florence Benoît-Rhomer, *La question minoritaire en Europe*, Council of Europe Publishing (Strasbourg, 1996), pp. 31-37. The Pact on Stability (not to be confused with the Stability Pact for South Eastern Europe) is also known as the "Balladur Plan" because it was proposed by the French Prime Minister Edouard Balladur. The pact was adopted by the representatives of 52 member states of the OSCE at a conference held in Paris on 20-21 March 1995. It consists of a declaration and a list of bilateral agreements which the participating states decided to include.

5. Hereinafter "joint commissions".

6. Emma Lantschner and Roberta Medda, "Bilateral Approach to the Protection of Kin-Minorities", in European Commission for Democracy through Law (ed.), *The Protection of National Minorities by their Kin-State*, (Strasbourg, 2002), pp. 107-133, at pp. 119-120; Kinga Gál, op.cit., p. 13.

7. Patrick Thornberry, "Hungarian Bilateral Treaties and Declarations", in Arie Bloed and Pieter van Dijk (eds.), *Protection of Minority Rights Through Bilateral Treaties. The Case of Central and Eastern Europe* (The Hague, 1999), pp. 127-161, at p. 159.

8. The Intergovernmental Commission for Implementation of the Agreement between the Republic of Croatia and the Republic of Hungary on the Protection of the Hungarian Minority in the Republic of Croatia and the Croatian Minority in the Republic of Hungary, established in Osijek, 5 April 1995, hereinafter "Hungarian-Croatian commission".

9. Hungarian-Slovenian Intergovernmental Minority Commission, established in Ljubljana, 6 November 1992, hereinafter "Hungarian-Slovenian commission".

10. Special Committee for Co-operation on Minorities' Issues of the Hungarian-Romanian Inter-Governmental Joint Commission on Active Co-operation and Partnership, established in Budapest, 12 March 1997, meeting for the first time on 9 October 1997, hereinafter "Hungarian-Romanian commission".

11. Hungarian-Slovak Joint Commission for Minority Affairs, established in Budapest, 8 February 1999, hereinafter "Hungarian-Slovak commission".

12. Convention on Providing Special Rights for the Slovenian National Minority Living in Hungary and the Hungarian National Community Living in Slovenia (6 November 1992); Convention between the Republic of Croatia and the Republic of Hungary on the Protection of the Hungarian Minority in the Republic of Croatia and the Croatian Minority in the Republic of Hungary (5 April 1995).

13. Article 15 for the Hungarian-Slovenian commission, Article 16 for the Hungarian-Croatian commission.

14. The agreements only speak about the delegation of "an appropriate number of members".

15. This proposal was made at the Meeting of Representatives of Joint Commissions on "Joint Commissions and the Implementation of Bilateral Agreements in the Field of Minorities", Stability Pact Project of the Council of Europe concerning Minorities,

Poiana Brasov, 18-19 November 2002.

16. So far six meetings of the Hungarian-Slovenian commission have taken place (4 April 1995 in Ljubljana, 20-21 May 1996 in Budapest, 4-5 November 1997 in Lendava/north-east Slovenia, 1-2 February 1999 in Szentgotthárd/western Transdanubia/Hungary, 3-4 February 2000 in Ljubljana, 8-9 May 2001 in Szentgotthárd/western Transdanubia/ Hungary) and six meetings of the Hungarian-Croatian commission (30 June 1995 in Zagreb, 23-24 September 1996 in Budapest, 13-14 November 1997 in Zagreb, 28-29 September 1999 in Pécs, 25-26 January 2001 in Osijek, 19 December 2002 in Pécs).

17. Hereinafter "basic treaties".

18. Treaty on Good Neighbourliness and Friendly Co-operation between Slovakia and Hungary, (19 March 1995); Treaty on Understanding, Co-operation and Good-Neighbourliness between the Republic of Hungary and Romania (16 September 1996).

19. Kinga Gál, op.cit., p. 7.

20. "… whose composition will be determined as they [the contracting parties] deem necessary" (Article 15.6 of the Hungarian-Slovak commission).

21. Article 15.6 for the Hungarian-Slovak commission, Article 15.10 for the Hungarian-Romanian commission.

22. The basic treaty was signed in 1995, ratified in 1996 and the first meeting of the Hungarian-Slovak commission took place on 8 February 1999 in Budapest.

23. Linda Schweiger, "Bilateral Agreements: A Political Tool Complementary to International Minority Protection", E.MA thesis European Master's Degree in Human Rights and Democratisation, (2001), p. 44.

24. Hungarian Official Journal, 1997/59, p. 4487.

25. This concern was expressed by Mr Arpad Marton, representative of the Hungarian minority in Romania in the Hungarian-Romanian joint commission, at the Meeting of Representatives of Joint Commissions on "Joint Commissions and the Implementation of Bilateral Agreements in the Field of Minorities", Stability Pact Project concerning Minorities, Poiana Brasov (18-19 November 2002).

26. So far there have been three meetings of the Hungarian-Slovak commission (8 February 1999 in Budapest, 29 September 1999 in Bratislava, 30 March 2001 in Budapest), and five meetings of the Hungarian-Romanian commission (1997 in Bucharest, 1998 in Budapest, 1999 in Bucharest, 2001 in Budapest, 2002 in Gyula).

27. Act LXII of 2001 on Hungarians Living in Neighbouring Countries, entered into force on 1 January 2002. See later in this chapter.

28. See later in this chapter.

29. Information gathered at the Meeting of Representatives of Joint Commissions on "Joint Commissions and the Implementation of Bilateral Agreements in the Field of Minorities", Stability Pact Project of the Council of Europe concerning Minorities, Poiana Brasov, 18-19 November 2002.

30. Official report of the first meeting of the Hungarian-Slovak Joint Commission for Minorities (Budapest, 8 February 1999), see website of the Governmental Office for Hungarians Abroad, at http://www.htmh.hu

31. Linda Schweiger, op.cit., pp. 47-48.

32. Official report of the second meeting of the Hungarian-Slovak Joint Commission for Minorities, (Bratislava, 29 September 1999), see website of the Governmental Office for Hungarians Abroad, at http://www.htmh.hu

33. Linda Schweiger, op.cit., pp. 50-52.

34. Protocol of the IV Meeting of the Joint Committee on National Minorities of the Joint Intergovernmental Commission on Co-operation and Active Partnership between Romania and Hungary, signed on 19 October 2001 in Budapest.

35. Law on Education No. 84/1995 amended by Law No. 151/1999. See also the Opinion on Romania, adopted on 6 April 2001 by the Advisory Committee on the

Framework Convention for the Protection of National Minorities, paragraphs 52-55.

36. Law of Local Public Administration no. 215/2001, published in the Official Gazette, Part I, No. 204 of 23 April 2001. See also Governmental Decision No. 1206/2001 on the adoption of application guidelines for the provisions concerning the right of citizens belonging to a national minority to use the mother tongue in local public administration, as stipulated in the Law of Local Public Administration No. 215/2001.

37. In Covasna and Harghita counties (south-eastern Transylvania) 76.17% and 84.41% of the population respectively, speak Hungarian. For more details about Hungarians in Romania, see Cathy O'Grady, Zoltán Kántor and Daniela Tarnovschi, "Hungarians of Romania", Center for Documentation and Information on Minorities in Europe – Southeast Europe, June 2001, at http://www.greekhelsinki.gr/–bhr/english/countries/romania/hun_rom.doc

38. Protocol of the IV Meeting of the Joint Committee on National Minorities of the Joint Intergovernmental Commission on Co-operation and Active Partnership between Romania and Hungary, signed on 19 October 2001 in Budapest.

39. For a comment on that law, see Sergiu Constantin, "The Hungarian 'Status Law' on Hungarians Living in Neighbouring Countries", in *European Yearbook of Minority Issues* (The Hague 2001/02), pp. 593-622; Kinga Gál, "The Hungarian Legislation on Hungarians Living in Neighbouring Countries", in European Commission for Democracy through Law, *The Protection of National Minorities by their Kin-State* (Strasbourg, 2002), pp. 157-174.

40. Originally the law was supposed to be implemented with respect to Hungarians living in Austria, Croatia, Romania, Serbia and Montenegro, Slovakia, Slovenia and Ukraine.

41. Report of the Venice Commission on the preferential treatment of national minorities by their kin-state, adopted by the Venice Commission at its 48th Plenary Meeting, (Venice, 19-20 October 2001), CDL-INF (2001) 19.

42. Protocol of the IV Meeting of the Joint Committee, op.cit.

43. Report of the Venice Commission, op.cit.

44. Memorandum of Understanding between the Government of the Republic of Hungary and the Government of Romania concerning the Law on Hungarians Living in Neighbouring Countries and issues of bilateral co-operation, signed in Budapest on 22 December 2001.

45. Ibid., part II, paragraph 11.

46. *RFE/RL Newsline* Vol. 6, No. 224, Part II, 2 December 2002.

47. *RFE/RL Newsline* Vol. 6, No. 224, Part II, 2 December 2002.

48. *RFE/RL Newsline* Vol. 7, No. 44, Part II, 7 March 2003.

49. *RFE/RL Newsline* Vol. 7, No. 118, Part II, 24 June 2003.

50. PACE resolution No. 1335(2003) of 25 June 2003.

51. *RFE/RL Newsline* Vol. 7, No. 122, Part II, 30 June 2003.

52. *RFE/RL Newsline* Vol. 7, No. 118, Part II, 24 June 2003.

53. *RFE/RL Newsline* Vol. 7, No. 122, Part II, 30 June 2003.

54. Emma Lantschner and Roberta Medda-Windischer, op.cit., pp. 126-129.

55. Max van der Stoel, "Minority Rights, Participation and Bilateral Agreements", Address of the High Commissioner on National Minorities of the OSCE to an international seminar on Legal Aspects of Minority Rights: Participation in Decision-Making Processes and Bilateral Agreements on Minority Rights (Zagreb, 4 December 2000), 4, at http://www.osce.org/hcnm/documents/speeches/2000/hcnm_speech2000_8.pdf

56. Kinga Gál, op.cit., p. 18.

57. Based on Article 18 of the Framework Convention for the Protection of National Minorities, which says: "The Parties shall endeavour to conclude, where necessary, bilateral and multilateral agreements with other States, in particular neighbouring States, in order to ensure the protection of persons belonging to the national minorities concerned."

58. Emma Lantschner and Roberta Medda-Windischer, op.cit., p. 126.

Useful websites

Chapter 4

http://www.coe.int/T/E/Human_rights (Council of Europe human rights website)

http://www.echr.coe.int/Convention/webConvenENG.pdf (European Convention on Human Rights – ECHR)

http://www.echr.coe.int/Eng/EDocs/RulesofCourt2002.htm (Rules of the European Court of Human Rights)

http://www.echr.coe.int/Eng/Judgments.htm (Decisions and judgments of the European Court of Human Rights)

Chapter 5

http://www.humanrights.coe.int/minorities/eng/sitemap.htm (Council of Europe minorities homepage for state reports, ACFC opinions, state comments and resolutions on monitoring by the Committee of Ministers)

http://www.coe.int/T/E/human_rights/minorities (this website contains updated information and documents on the various activities of the secretariat of the Framework Convention for the Protection of National Minorities (FCNM). These include:

- updated news briefs about monitoring of the FCNM;
- basic legal texts; public reports and opinions produced during the monitoring process, such as Committee of Ministers resolutions, Advisory Committee opinions and state reports; descriptions of ongoing co-operation activities;
- Stability Pact projects and intergovernmental developments;
- links to websites dealing with the protection of persons belonging to national minorities)

http://www.humanrights.coe.int/minorities/eng/sitemap.htm (3rd Activity Report of the Advisory Committee for the Protection of National Minorities, covering the period November 2000 until May 2002)

http://www.greekhelsinki.gr/english/reports/index.html (Greek Helsinki Monitor website for comprehensive information on the FCNM, including alternative state reports written by civil society organisations) http://www.minelres.lv (Minelres also provides a valuable resource on minority issues)

http://www.minorityrights.org (the website of Minority Rights Group International contains valuable information on minorities and treaty monitoring internationally)

http://www.ecmi.org (is the site for timely information and scholarly analysis of minority issues in Europe)

Chapter 6

http://www.coe.int/T/E/Legal_Affairs/Local_and_regional_Democracy/Regio nal_or_Minority_languages (most of the legal documents concerning the ECRML and the operation of its monitoring mechanism may be found on this site)

Chapter 7

http://www.osce.org/docs/english/1990-1999/summits/helfa75e.htm (CSCE, "Helsinki Final Act", 1975)

http://www.osce.org/docs/english/1973-1990/follow_ups/vienn89e.htm (CSCE, "Concluding Document of the Vienna Meeting (1986) of representatives of the participating states of the Conference on Security and Co-operation in Europe, held on the basis of the provisions of the Final Act relating to the follow-up to the Conference", 1986–89)

http://www.osce.org/docs/english/1990-1999/summits/paris90e.htm (CSCE, "Charter of Paris for a New Europe", 1990)

http://www.osce.org/docs/english/1990-1999/hd/cope90e.htm (CSCE, "Document of the Copenhagen Meeting of the Conference on the Human Dimension of the CSCE", 1990).

http://www.osce.org/docs/english/1973-1990/other_experts/gene91e.htm (CSCE, "Report of the CSCE Meeting of Experts on National Minorities", Geneva, 1991)

http://www.osce.org/docs/english/1990-1999/hd/mosc91e.htm (CSCE, "Document of the Moscow Meeting of the Conference on the Human Dimension of the CSCE", 1991).

http://www.osce.org/docs/english/1990-1999/summits/hels92e.htm (CSCE "Helsinki Document, The Challenges of Change", 1992)

http://www.osce.org/docs/english/1990-1999/summits/buda94e.htm (CSCE, "Budapest Document, Towards a Genuine Partnership in a New Era", 1994)

http://www.osce.org/docs/english/1990-1999/summits/lisbo96e.htm (OSCE, "Lisbon Declaration on a Common and Comprehensive Security Model for Europe for the Twenty-First Century", 1996)

http://www.osce.org/publications/handbook/files/handbook.pdf (OSCE, "OSCE Handbook", 2000) http://www.osce.org/docs/english/1990-1999/summits/istadecl99e.htm (OSCE, "Istanbul Summit Declaration", 1999)

http://www.osce.org/publications/survey (OSCE, "OSCE Mission Survey")

http://www.osce.org/publications/annual_report/files/annual_report_2002.p df (OSCE, "Annual Report on OSCE Activities", 2002)

http://www.osce.org/hcnm/documents/recommendations/hague/index.php3 (Foundation on Inter-Ethnic Relations, "Hague Recommendations Regarding the Education Rights of National Minorities", 1996)

http://www.osce.org/hcnm/documents/recommendations/oslo/index.php3 (Foundation on Inter-Ethnic Relations, "Oslo Recommendations Regarding the Linguistic Rights of National Minorities", 1998)

http://www.osce.org/hcnm/documents/recommendations/lund/index.php3 (Foundation on Inter-Ethnic Relations, "Lund Recommendations on the Effective Participation of National Minorities in Public Life", 1999)

Chapter 8

http://www.eumap.org (EUMAP, "Monitoring the EU Accession Process: Minority Protection", Open Society Institute, 2002)

http://www.europa.eu.int/comm/enlargement/intro/criteria.htm (European Commission, "EU Enlargement – a Historic Opportunity")

http://www.europa.eu.int/comm/external_relations/human_rights/rm/index. htm (European Commission, "The EU's Human Rights and Democratisation Policy: Protecting and Promoting the Rights of Minorities")

http://www.europa.eu.int/comm/europeaid/projects (European Commission, "Europeaid: Programmes and Projects")

http://ue.eu.int/pesc/human_rights/en/99/main3.htm (European Council, "Human Rights in the European Union", in particular part 3.1)

http://www.eumc.eu.int (European Monitoring Centre on Racism and Xenophobia – EUMC)

http://www.europarl.eu.int/comparl/libe/elsj/charter/art21/default_en.htm (European Parliament – Committee on Citizens' Freedoms and Rights, Justice and Home Affairs, "Freedom, security and justice: An Agenda for Europe")

http://www.europa.eu.int/abc/treaties_en.htm (List of EU treaties including the Treaty on European Union and the Treaty establishing the European Community, as amended by the Treaty of Amsterdam)

http://www.unhchr.ch/html/racism/01-minoritiesguide.html (United Nations, "The European Union: Human Rights and the Fights Against Discrimination", Pamphlet No.14)

Chapter 9

http://www.eurac.edu/miris (Minority Rights Information System for all bilateral agreements discussed in this contribution):

- the Memorandum of Understanding between the Government of Romania and the Government of the Republic of Hungary
- Protocol concluded between the Government of Romania and the Government of the Republic of Hungary concerning the establishment of the Romanian-Hungarian Joint Commission on Active Co-operation and Partnership
- Protocol of the 4th meeting of the Joint Committee on National Minorities of the Joint Intergovernmental Commission on Active Co-operation and Partnership between Romania and Hungary)

http://www.htmh.hu (Government Office of Hungarians Abroad for bilateral agreements concluded by Hungary with its neighbours (also in English) and protocols of the meetings of the joint commissions (only in Hungarian))

http://www.venice.coe.int/ (Report of the Venice Commission on preferential treatment)

SELECTED BIBLIOGRAPHY

While this bibliography is chapter specific many of the titles will cover a wider range of minority rights issues too.[1]

Chapter 1

Ghandhi, P. R., *The Human Rights Committee and the Right of Individual Communication* (Aldershot, 1998).

Kastanas, Elias, "The Preventive Dimension of the Activities of United Nations Treaty Bodies", in Sicilianos, L.-A. (ed.), *The Prevention of Human Rights Violations* (The Hague, Boston, London, 2001), pp. 57-66.

McGlue, Hannah, "The Jurisprudence of the United Nations Human Rights Committee and Other Treaty Monitoring Bodies", 2 *European Yearbook of Minority Issues* (2002/3), forthcoming.

Morawa, Alexander H. E, "The Individual as a Party to International Human Rights Litigation, With Particular Reference to the Issue of 'Abuse of the Right to Petition'", 4 *Journal of International Relations* (1997), pp. 11-28.

Morawa, Alexander H. E, "The Jurisprudence of the United Nations Human Rights Committee and Other Treaty Monitoring Bodies", 1 *European Yearbook of Minority Issues* (2001/2), pp. 461-85.

Nowak, Manfred, "The International Covenant on Civil and Political Rights", in: Raija Hanski and Markku Suksi (eds), *An Introduction to the International Protection of Human Rights* (Turku/Åbo, 2nd ed. 1999), pp. 79-100.

Nowak, Manfred, *U.N. Covenant of Civil and Political Rights. ICCPR Commentary* (Kehl am Rhein, 1993).

Opsahl, Torkel, "The General Comments of the Human Rights Committee", in Opsahl, Torkel (ed.), *Law and Equality, Selected Articles on Human Rights* (Oslo, 1996), pp. 403-17.

Pentassuglia, Gaetano, *Minorities in International Law* (Strasbourg, 2002).

Pocar, Fausto, "Current Developments and Approaches in the Practice of the Human Rights Committee in Consideration of State Reports", in Eide, Asbjørn and Helgesen, Jan (eds.), *The Future of Human Rights Protection in a Changing World* (Oslo, 1991), pp. 51-58.

Tomuschat, Christian, "Making Individual Communications an Effective Tool for the Protection of Human Rights", in Beyerlin, Ulrich, Bothe, Michael,

Hofmann, Rainer and Petersmann, Ernst-Ulrich (eds), *Recht zwischen Umbruch und Bewahrung. Völkerrecht – Europarecht – Staatsrecht. Festschrift für Rudolf Bernhardt* (Berlin, 1995), pp. 615-34.

Weiss, Norman, "Einführung in den Individualrechtsschutz nach dem Internationalen Pakt über bürgerliche und politische Rechte", 1 (1) *MenschenRechtsMagazin* (1996), pp. 7-11.

Chapter 3

Akhavan, Payam, "Enforcement of the Genocide Convention: A Challenge to Civilization", 8 *Harvard Human Rights Law Journal* (1995), pp. 229-58.

Bils, Iris, "Internationale Schutzmechanismen zur Durchsetzung von Minderheiten- und Volksgruppenrechten", Ph.D. thesis, Bayerische Julius-Maximilians-Universität (1995) Würzburg on file at the Law Faculty of the University of Leipzig.

Blumenwitz, Dieter, *Internationale Schutzmechanismen zur Durchsetzung von Minderheiten- und Volksgruppenrechten* (Köln, 1997).

Gray, Christine, "Legality of Use of Force (Yugoslavia v. Belgium) (Yugoslavia v. Canada) (Yugoslavia v. France) (Yugoslavia v. Germany) (Yugoslavia v. Italy) (Yugoslavia v. Netherlands) (Yugoslavia v. Portugal) (Yugoslavia v. Spain) (Yugoslavia v. United Kingdom) (Yugoslavia v. United States of America): Provisional Measures", 49 *International and Comparative Law Quarterly* (2000), pp. 730-36.

Lippman, Matthew, "The Convention on the Prevention and Punishment of the Crime of Genocide: Fifty Years Later", 15 *Arizona Journal of International and Comparative Law* (1998), pp. 415-514.

Selbmann, Frank, *Der Tatbestand des Genozids im Völkerstrafrecht* (Leipzig, 2002).

Thornberry, Patrick, *International Law and the Rights of Minorities* (Oxford, 1991).

Zeller, Karl, *Das Problem der völkerrechtlichen Verankerung des Südtirol-Pakets und die Zuständigkeit des Internationalen Gerichtshofs* (Vienna, 1989).

Chapter 4

Berg, Leif, "Bringing Cases before the European Commission and Court of Human Rights", Institute for Human Rights, Åbo Akademi University (Åbo, 1997).

Dijk, P. van, and Hoof, G.J.H. van, Heringa, A.W., Schokkenbroek, J.G.C., Vermeulen, B.P., Viering M.L.W.M., and Zwaak, L.F., *Theory and Practice of the European Convention on Human Rights* (The Hague, 1998).

Gomien, Donna, *Short Guide to the European Convention on Human Rights*, 2nd edition (Strasbourg, 1998).

Varennes, Fernand de, "To Speak or not to Speak: The Rights of Persons Belonging to Linguistic Minorities", working paper prepared for the UN Sub-Committee on the Rights of Minorities (Geneva, 18 April 1997, UN Doc. E/CN.4/ Sub.2/AC.5/1997/WP.6).

Varennes, Fernand de, "A Guide to the Rights of Minorities and Language", Constitutional and Legal Policy Initiative (COLPI) (Budapest, 2001).

Varennes, Fernand de, *Language, Minorities and Human Rights,* Martinus Nijhoff Publishers (The Hague, 1996).

Chapter 5

Alfredsson, G., "A frame with an incomplete painting. Comparison of FCNM with international standards and monitoring procedures", 7(4) *International Journal on Minority and Group Rights* (2000).

Framework Convention for the Protection of National Minorities, adopted on 1 February 1995, entered into force on 1 February 1998, ETS No. 157, *Collected texts,* Council of Europe Publishing (2nd edition), August 2001.

Hofmann, R., "Protecting the Rights of National Minorities in Europe. First Experiences of the Council of Europe FCNM", *German Yearbook of International Law* (2001), p. 237 et seq.

Phillips, A., "The Framework Convention for the Protection of National Minorities: a Policy Analysis", MRG policy paper (London, 2002).

Phillips, A., "FCNM: from Analysis to Action", MRG Briefing, September 2002.

Steketee, F., "The Framework Convention: a Piece of Art or a Tool for Action?", 8(1) *International Journal on Minority and Group Rights* (2001).

Thornberry, P., "The FCNM: a Provisional Appraisal and Memory of the Baltic States", *The Baltic Yearbook of International Law* (2002).

Troebst, Stefan, "The Council of Europe's Framework Convention for the Protection of National Minorities revisited", European Centre for Minority Issues (ECMI) Working Paper No. 2, December 1998.

Chapter 7

Alfredsson, Gudmundur and Türk, Danilo, "International Mechanisms for the Monitoring and Protection of Minority Rights: Their Advantages, Disadvantages and Interrelationships", in Bloed, Arie, Leicht, Liselotte, Nowak, Manfred and Rosas, Allan (eds), *Monitoring Human Rights in Europe. Comparing International Procedures and Mechanisms* (Dordrecht, 1993), pp. 169-86.

Arifi, Teuta, "Substantial Progress, though not Enough: Implementation of the Recommendations of the OSCE High Commissioner on National Minorities to Macedonia, 1993-2001", in Zellner, Wolfgang, Oberschmidt, Randolf and Neukirch, Claus (eds), *Comparative Case Studies on the*

Effectiveness of the OSCE High Commissioner on National Minorities (CORE Working Paper No. 9, forthcoming) (Hamburg, 2003).

Birmingham, Katherine, *The OSCE and Minority Issues* (The Hague, 1995).

Bloed, Arie, "Die OSZE und nationale Minderheiten: Eine neue Herangehensweise", in Mohr, Manfred (ed.), *Friedenssichernde Aspekte des Minderheitenschutzes in der Ära des Völkerbundes und der Vereinten Nationen in Europa* (Frankfurt/Oder, 1996), pp. 153-65.

Brett, Rachel, "The Human Dimension Mechanism of the CSCE and the CSCE Response to Minorities", in Lucas, Michael R. (ed.), *The CSCE in the 1990s: Constructing European Security and Cooperation* (Baden-Baden, 1993), pp. 143-60.

Brown, James F., "Aktuelle und potentielle Konfliktmöglichkeiten in Südosteuropa", in Heydrich, Wolfgang, Krause, Joachim, Nerlich, Uwe, Nötzold Jürgen and Rummel, Reinhardt (eds), *Sicherheitspolitik Deutschlands. Neue Konstellationen, Risiken, Instrumente* (Baden-Baden, 1992), pp. 395-413.

Cohen, Jonathan, *Conflict Prevention Instruments in the Organization for Security and Co-operation in Europe. An Assessment of Capacities* (London 1998).

CSCE, "Report of the CSCE Human Dimension Mission to the Republic of Moldova, January 30 – February 4, 1993".

Dorodnova, Jekatarina, "Beneath the Smooth Surface: Implementation of the Recommendations of the OSCE High Commissioner on National Minorities to Latvia, 1993-2001", in Zellner, Wolfgang, Oberschmidt, Randolf and Neukirch, Claus (eds), *Comparative Case Studies on the Effectiveness of the OSCE High Commissioner on National Minorities* (CORE Working Paper No. 10, forthcoming) (Hamburg2003).

Horváth, István, "Facilitating Conflict Transformation: Implementation of the Recommendations of the OSCE High Commissioner on National Minorities to Romania, 1993-2001", in Zellner, Wolfgang, Oberschmidt, Randolf and Neukirch, Claus (eds), *Comparative Case Studies on the Effectiveness of the OSCE High Commissioner on National Minorities* (CORE Working Paper No. 8) (Hamburg, 2002).

Kemp, Walter A. (ed.), *Quiet Diplomacy in Action: The OSCE High Commissioner on National Minorities* (The Hague/London/Boston, 2001).

Kulyk, Volodymyr, "Revisiting a Success Story: Implementation of the Recommendations of the OSCE High Commissioner on National Minorities to Ukraine, 1994-2001", in Zellner, Wolfgang, Oberschmidt, Randolf and Neukirch, Claus (eds), *Comparative Case Studies on the Effectiveness of the OSCE High Commissioner on National Minorities* (CORE Working Paper No. 6) (Hamburg, 2002).

Neukirch, Claus, *Konfliktmanagement und Konfliktprävention im Rahmen von OSZE-Langzeitmissionen* (Baden-Baden, 2003).

Oberschmidt, Randolf 2002, "Ten Years of the Office for Democratic Institutions and Human Rights – An Interim Assessment", in Institute for Peace Research and Security Policy at the University of Hamburg (ed.), *OSCE Yearbook 2001* (Baden-Baden, 2002), pp. 387-400.

Oberschmidt, Randolf and Zellner, Wolfgang, OSCE *at the Crossroads* (CORE Working Paper No. 2) (Hamburg, 2001).

OSCE Office for Democratic Institutions and Human Rights, *OSCE Human Dimension Commitments: A Reference Guide* (Warsaw, 2001).

Sarv, Margit, "Integration by Reframing Legislation: Implementation of the Recommendations of the OSCE High Commissioner on National Minorities to Estonia, 1993-2001", in Zellner, Wolfgang, Oberschmidt, Randolf and Neukirch, Claus (eds), *Comparative Case Studies on the Effectiveness of the OSCE High Commissioner on National Minorities* (CORE Working Paper No. 7) (Hamburg, 2002).

Schöpflin, George, "Hungary and its neighbours", 7 Chaillot Paper (Paris, 1993).

Simhandl, Katrin, *Der Hohe Kommissar für nationale Minderheiten der Organisation für Sicherheit und Zusammenarbeit in Europa. Das Amtsverständnis Max van der Stoels im Lichte der Theorien über das Nationale* (Baden-Baden, 2002).

Tomuschat, Christian, Törnudd, Klaus et al. (on behalf of the CSCE Office for Democratic Institutions and Human Rights), "Report of the CSCE ODIHR Mission on the Study of Estonian Legislation", December 1992.

Troebst, Stefan, "Ethnopolitical Conflict in Eastern Europe and the OSCE: An Interim Appraisal", ECMI Brief No. 1 (Flensburg, 1998)http://www.ecmi.de/doc/download/brief_1.pdf

Van der Stoel, Max, "Peace and Stability through Human and Minority Rights" in Zellner, Wolfgang and Lange, Falk (eds), *Speeches by the OSCE High Commissioner on National Minorities* (Baden-Baden, 1999, 2nd enlarged ed. 2001).

Wright, Jane, "The OSCE and the Protection of Minorities", 18(1) *Human Rights Quarterly* (1996), pp. 190-205.

Zaagman, Rob, "Conflict Prevention in the Baltic States: The OSCE High Commissioner on National Minorities in Estonia, Latvia and Lithuania", ECMI Monographs No. 1 (Flensburg, 1999) http://www.ecmi.de/doc/download/monograph_1.pdf

Zaagman, Rob , "The CSCE High Commissioner on National Minorities: An Analysis of the Mandate and the Institutional Context", in Bloed, Arie (ed.), *The Challenges of Change: the Helsinki Summit of the CSCE and its Aftermath* (Dordrecht, 1994) pp. 113-75.

Zaagman, Rob, Zaal, Hannie, "The High Commissioner on National Minorities: Prehistory and Negotiations", in Bloed, Arie (ed.), *The Challenges of Change: the Helsinki Summit of the CSCE and its Aftermath* (Dordrecht, 1994), pp. 95-111.

Zellner, Wolfgang, "On the Effectiveness of the OSCE Minority Regime. Comparative Case Studies on Implementation of the Recommendations of the High Commissioner on National Minorities of the OSCE", 111 *Hamburger Beiträge zur Friedensforschung und Sicherheitspolitik* (Hamburg, 1999).

Chapter 8

Alston, P. and Weiler, J.H.H., "An 'Ever Closer Union' in Need of a Human Rights Policy: The European Union and Human Rights" in Alston P. (ed.), *The EU and Human Rights* (Oxford University Press, 1999). Also at http://www.jeanmonnetprogram.org/papers/99/990101.html#fn1

Bell, Mark, "Article 13: The European Commission's Anti-discrimination Proposals", *Industrial Law Journal*, Vol. 29, No.1 (March 2000), pp. 79-84.

European Commission, Communication from the Commission to the Council and the European Parliament, "The European Union's Role in Promoting Human rights and Democratisation in Third Countries", Brussels, 8 May 2001, COM (2001) 252 final.

European Community, "Declaration against Racism and Xenophobia", *Official Journal*, C 158, 25 June 1986, pp. 1-3.

European Council, "Resolution of the Council and the Representatives of the Governments of the Member States, meeting within the Council of 23 July 1996 concerning the European Year against Racism (1997)" *Official Journal*, C 237, 15 August 1996, pp. 1-4.

European Council, "Resolution of the Council and the Representatives of the Governments of the Member States, meeting within the Council of 5 October 1995 on the fight against racism and xenophobia in the fields of employment and social affairs" *Official Journal*, C 296, 10 November 1995 pp. 13-14.

Guild Elspeth, "The EC Directive on Race Discrimination: Surprises, Possibilities and Limitation", *Industrial Law Journal*, Vol. 29, No. 4 (December 2000), pp. 416-23.

Hofmann Rainer, "National Minorities and European Community Law", in Ziemele, I. (ed.), *Baltic Yearbook of International Law*, Volume 2, 2002, pp. 159-74.

Niessen, Jan, "Assistance aux organizations actives dans les domaines de la lutte contre la discrimination et pour l'égalité du traitement", 4 *Associations Transnationales/Transnational Associations* (July-August 1998), pp. 201-13.

Pentassuglia, Gaetano, *Minorities in International Law: An Introductory Study* (Strasbourg, 2002), in particular pp. 144-57.

Toggenburg, N. Gabriel, "The Race Directive: A New Dimension in the Fight Against Ethnic Discrimination in Europe", *European Yearbook of Minority Issues*, Volume 1, 2001/2, pp. 231-244.

Toggenburg, N. Gabriel, "Minorities (...) the European Union: Is the Missing Link an 'or' or a 'within'?", *European Integration*, Vol. 25(3), September 2003, pp. 273-84.

Witte, Bruno de, "Politics versus Law in the EU's Approach to Ethnic Minorities", EUI Working Paper, RSC No.2000/4.

Chapter 9

Bloed, Arie and Dijk, Pieter van (eds), *Protection of Minority Rights through Bilateral Treaties, the Case of Central and Eastern Europe* (The Hague, 1999).

1. See also: http://book.coe.int

Appendices

EXTRACTS FROM THE EUROPEAN CHARTER
FOR REGIONAL OR MINORITY LANGUAGES

Article 15 – Periodical reports

1. The Parties shall present periodically to the Secretary General of the Council of Europe, in a form to be prescribed by the Committee of Ministers, a report on their policy pursued in accordance with Part II of this Charter and on the measures taken in application of those provisions of Part III which they have accepted. The first report shall be presented within the year following the entry into force of the Charter with respect to the Party concerned, the other reports at three-yearly intervals after the first report.

2. The Parties shall make their reports public.

Article 16 – Examination of the reports

1. The reports presented to the Secretary General of the Council of Europe under Article 15 shall be examined by a committee of experts constituted in accordance with Article 17.

2. Bodies or associations legally established in a Party may draw the attention of the committee of experts to matters relating to the undertakings entered into by that Party under Part III of this Charter. After consulting the Party concerned, the committee of experts may take account of this information in the preparation of the report specified in paragraph 3 below. These bodies or associations can furthermore submit statements concerning the policy pursued by a Party in accordance with Part II.

3. On the basis of the reports specified in paragraph 1 and the information mentioned in paragraph 2, the committee of experts shall prepare a report for the Committee of Ministers. This report shall be accompanied by the comments which the Parties have been requested to make and may be made public by the Committee of Ministers.

4. The report specified in paragraph 3 shall contain in particular the proposals of the committee of experts to the Committee of Ministers for the preparation of such recommendations of the latter body to one or more of the Parties as may be required.

5. The Secretary General of the Council of Europe shall make a two-yearly detailed report to the Parliamentary Assembly on the application of the Charter.

Article 17 – Committee of experts

1. The committee of experts shall be composed of one member per Party, appointed by the Committee of Ministers from a list of individuals of the highest integrity and recognised competence in the matters dealt with in the Charter, who shall be nominated by the Party concerned.

2. Members of the committee shall be appointed for a period of six years and shall be eligible for reappointment. A member who is unable to complete a term of office shall be replaced in accordance with the procedure laid down in paragraph 1, and the replacing member shall complete his predecessor's term of office.

3. The committee of experts shall adopt rules of procedure. Its secretarial services shall be provided by the Secretary General of the Council of Europe.

EXTRACTS FROM THE STATUTE OF THE INTERNATIONAL COURT OF JUSTICE

Article 34

1. Only states may be parties in cases before the Court.

2. The Court, subject to and in conformity with its Rules, may request of public international organisations information relevant to cases before it, and shall receive such information presented by such organisations on their own initiative.

3. Whenever the construction of the constituent instrument of a public international organisation or of an international convention adopted there-under is in question in a case before the Court, the Registrar shall so notify the public international organisation concerned and shall communicate to it copies of all the written proceedings.

Article 35

1. The Court shall be open to the states parties to the present Statute.

2. The conditions under which the Court shall be open to other states shall, subject to the special provisions contained in treaties in force, be laid down by the Security Council, but in no case shall such conditions place the parties in a position of inequality before the Court.

3. When a state which is not a Member of the United Nations is a party to a case, the Court shall fix the amount which that party is to contribute towards the expenses of the Court. This provision shall not apply if such state is bearing a share of the expenses of the Court.

Article 36

1. The jurisdiction of the Court comprises all cases which the parties refer to and all matters specially provided for in the Charter of the United Nations or in treaties and conventions in force.

2. The states parties to the present Statute may at any time declare that they recognise as compulsory *ipso facto* and without special agreement, in relation to any other state accepting the same obligation, the jurisdiction of the Court in all legal disputes concerning:

    a. the interpretation of a treaty;

    b. any question of international law;

   c. the existence of any fact which, if established, would constitute a breach of an international obligation;

   d. the nature or extent of the reparation to be made for the breach of an international obligation.

3. The declarations referred to above may be made unconditionally or on condition of reciprocity on the part of several or certain states, or for a certain time.

4. Such declarations shall be deposited with the Secretary-General of the United Nations, who shall transmit copies thereof to the parties to the Statute and to the Registrar of the Court.

5. Declarations made under Article 36 of the Statute of the Permanent Court of International Justice and which are still in force shall be deemed, as between the parties to the present Statute, to be acceptances of the compulsory jurisdiction of the International Court of Justice for the period which they still have to run and in accordance with their terms.

6. In the event of a dispute as to whether the Court has jurisdiction, the matter shall be settled by the decision of the Court.

EXTRACTS FROM THE CONVENTION ON THE PREVENTION AND PUNISHMENT OF THE CRIME OF GENOCIDE

Article 1

The Contracting Parties confirm that genocide, whether committed in time of peace or in time of war, is a crime under international law which they undertake to prevent and to punish.

Article 2

In the present Convention, genocide means any of the following acts committed with intent to destroy, in whole or in part, a national, ethnical, racial or religious group, as such:

- a. killing members of the group;
- b. causing serious bodily or mental harm to members of the group;
- c. deliberately inflicting on the group conditions of life calculated to bring about its physical destruction in whole or in part;
- d. imposing measures intended to prevent births within the group;
- e. forcibly transferring children of the group to another group.

Article 3

The following acts shall be punishable:

- a. genocide;
- b. conspiracy to commit genocide;
- c. direct and public incitement to commit genocide;
- d. attempt to commit genocide;
- e. complicity in genocide.

Article 4

Persons committing genocide or any of the other acts enumerated in Article 3 shall be punished, whether they are constitutionally responsible rulers, public officials or private individuals.

Article 5

The Contracting Parties undertake to enact, in accordance with their respective Constitutions, the necessary legislation to give effect to the provisions of the present Convention, and, in particular, to provide effective penalties for persons guilty of genocide or any of the other acts enumerated in Article 3.

Article 6

Persons charged with genocide or any of the other acts enumerated in Article 3 shall be tried by a competent tribunal of the State in the territory of which the act was committed, or by such international penal tribunal as may have jurisdiction with respect to those Contracting Parties which shall have accepted its jurisdiction.

Article 7

Genocide and the other acts enumerated in Article 3 shall not be considered as political crimes for the purpose of extradition.

The Contracting Parties pledge themselves in such cases to grant extradition in accordance with their laws and treaties in force.

Article 8

Any Contracting Party may call upon the competent organs of the United Nations to take such action under the Charter of the United Nations as they consider appropriate for the prevention and suppression of acts of genocide or any of the other acts enumerated in Article 3.

Article 9

Disputes between the Contracting Parties relating to the interpretation, application or fulfilment of the present Convention, including those relating to the responsibility of a State for genocide or for any of the other acts enumerated in Article 3, shall be submitted to the International Court of Justice at the request of any of the parties to the dispute.

EXTRACTS FROM THE EUROPEAN CONVENTION FOR THE PEACEFUL SETTLEMENT OF DISPUTES

Preamble

The governments signatory hereto, being members of the Council of Europe, Considering that the aim of the Council of Europe is to achieve a greater unity between its members;

Convinced that the pursuit of peace based upon justice is vital for the preservation of human society and civilisation;

Resolved to settle by peaceful means any disputes which may arise between them,

Have agreed as follows:

Chapter I – Judicial settlement

Article 1

The High Contracting Parties shall submit to the judgment of the International Court of Justice all international legal disputes which may arise between them including, in particular, those concerning:

    a. the interpretation of a treaty;

    b. any question of international law;

    c. the existence of any fact which, if established, would constitute a breach of an international obligation;

    d. the nature or extent of the reparation to be made for the breach of an international obligation.

Article 2

1. The provisions of Article 1 shall not affect undertakings by which the High Contracting Parties have accepted or may accept the jurisdiction of the International Court of Justice for the settlement of disputes other than those mentioned in Article 1.

2. The parties to a dispute may agree to resort to the procedure of conciliation before that of judicial settlement.

Article 3

The High Contracting Parties which are not parties to the Statute of the International Court of Justice shall carry out the measures necessary to enable them to have access thereto.

[...]

Chapter IV – General provisions

Article 27

The provisions of this Convention shall not apply to:

a. disputes relating to facts or situations prior to the entry into force of this Convention as between the parties to the dispute;

b. disputes concerning questions which by international law are solely within the domestic jurisdiction of States.

Article 28

1. The provisions of this Convention shall not apply to disputes which the parties have agreed or may agree to submit to another procedure of peaceful settlement. Nevertheless, in respect of disputes falling within the scope of Article 1, the High Contracting Parties shall refrain from invoking as between themselves agreements which do not provide for a procedure entailing binding decisions.

2. This Convention shall in no way affect the application of the provisions of the Convention for the Protection of Human Rights and Fundamental Freedoms signed on 4th November 1950, or of the protocol thereto signed on 20th March 1952.

Sales agents for publications of the Council of Europe
Agents de vente des publications du Conseil de l'Europe

AUSTRALIA/AUSTRALIE
Hunter Publications, 58A, Gipps Street
AUS-3066 COLLINGWOOD, Victoria
Tel.: (61) 3 9417 5361
Fax: (61) 3 9419 7154
E-mail: Sales@hunter-pubs.com.au
http://www.hunter-pubs.com.au

BELGIUM/BELGIQUE
La Librairie européenne SA
50, avenue A. Jonnart
B-1200 BRUXELLES 20
Tel.: (32) 2 734 0281
Fax: (32) 2 735 0860
E-mail: info@libeurop.be
http://www.libeurop.be

Jean de Lannoy
202, avenue du Roi
B-1190 BRUXELLES
Tel.: (32) 2 538 4308
Fax: (32) 2 538 0841
E-mail: jean.de.lannoy@euronet.be
http://www.jean-de-lannoy.be

CANADA
Renouf Publishing Company Limited
5369 Chemin Canotek Road
CDN-OTTAWA, Ontario, K1J 9J3
Tel.: (1) 613 745 2665
Fax: (1) 613 745 7660
E-mail: order.dept@renoufbooks.com
http://www.renoufbooks.com

CZECH REPUBLIC/
RÉPUBLIQUE TCHÈQUE
Suweco Cz Dovoz Tisku Praha
Ceskomoravska 21
CZ-18021 PRAHA 9
Tel.: (420) 2 660 35 364
Fax: (420) 2 683 30 42
E-mail: import@suweco.cz

DENMARK/DANEMARK
GAD Direct
Fiolstaede 31-33
DK-1171 COPENHAGEN K
Tel.: (45) 33 13 72 33
Fax: (45) 33 12 54 94
E-mail: info@gaddirect.dk

FINLAND/FINLANDE
Akateeminen Kirjakauppa
Keskuskatu 1, PO Box 218
FIN-00381 HELSINKI
Tel.: (358) 9 121 41
Fax: (358) 9 121 4450
E-mail: akatilaus@stockmann.fi
http://www.akatilaus.akateeminen.com

FRANCE
La Documentation française
(Diffusion/Vente France entière)
124, rue H. Barbusse
F-93308 AUBERVILLIERS Cedex
Tel.: (33) 01 40 15 70 00
Fax: (33) 01 40 15 68 00
E-mail: commandes.vel@ladocfrancaise.gouv.fr
http://www.ladocfrancaise.gouv.fr

Librairie Kléber (Vente Strasbourg)
Palais de l'Europe
F-67075 STRASBOURG Cedex
Fax: (33) 03 88 52 91 21
E-mail: librairie.kleber@coe.int

GERMANY/ALLEMAGNE
AUSTRIA/AUTRICHE
UNO Verlag
Am Hofgarten 10
D-53113 BONN
Tel.: (49) 2 28 94 90 20
Fax: (49) 2 28 94 90 222
E-mail: bestellung@uno-verlag.de
http://www.uno-verlag.de

GREECE/GRÈCE
Librairie Kauffmann
28, rue Stadiou
GR-ATHINAI 10564
Tel.: (30) 1 32 22 160
Fax: (30) 1 32 30 320
E-mail: ord@otenet.gr

HUNGARY/HONGRIE
Euro Info Service
Hungexpo Europa Kozpont ter 1
H-1101 BUDAPEST
Tel.: (361) 264 8270
Fax: (361) 264 8271
E-mail: euroinfo@euroinfo.hu
http://www.euroinfo.hu

ITALY/ITALIE
Libreria Commissionaria Sansoni
Via Duca di Calabria 1/1, CP 552
I-50125 FIRENZE
Tel.: (39) 556 4831
Fax: (39) 556 41257
E-mail: licosa@licosa.com
http://www.licosa.com

NETHERLANDS/PAYS-BAS
De Lindeboom Internationale Publikaties
PO Box 202, MA de Ruyterstraat 20 A
NL-7480 AE HAAKSBERGEN
Tel.: (31) 53 574 0004
Fax: (31) 53 572 9296
E-mail: books@delindeboom.com
http://home-1-worldonline.nl/~lindeboo/

NORWAY/NORVÈGE
Akademika, A/S Universitetsbokhandel
PO Box 84, Blindern
N-0314 OSLO
Tel.: (47) 22 85 30 30
Fax: (47) 23 12 24 20

POLAND/POLOGNE
Głowna Księgarnia Naukowa
im. B. Prusa
Krakowskie Przedmiescie 7
PL-00-068 WARSZAWA
Tel.: (48) 29 22 66
Fax: (48) 22 26 64 49
E-mail: inter@internews.com.pl
http://www.internews.com.pl

PORTUGAL
Livraria Portugal
Rua do Carmo, 70
P-1200 LISBOA
Tel.: (351) 13 47 49 82
Fax: (351) 13 47 02 64
E-mail: liv.portugal@mail.telepac.pt

SPAIN/ESPAGNE
Mundi-Prensa Libros SA
Castelló 37
E-28001 MADRID
Tel.: (34) 914 36 37 00
Fax: (34) 915 75 39 98
E-mail: libreria@mundiprensa.es
http://www.mundiprensa.com

SWITZERLAND/SUISSE
Adeco – Van Diermen
Chemin du Lacuez 41
CH-1807 BLONAY
Tel.: (41) 21 943 26 73
Fax: (41) 21 943 36 05
E-mail: info@adeco.org

UNITED KINGDOM/ROYAUME-UNI
TSO (formerly HMSO)
51 Nine Elms Lane
GB-LONDON SW8 5DR
Tel.: (44) 207 873 8372
Fax: (44) 207 873 8200
E-mail: customer.services@theso.co.uk
http://www.the-stationery-office.co.uk
http://www.itsofficial.net

UNITED STATES and CANADA/
ÉTATS-UNIS et CANADA
Manhattan Publishing Company
2036 Albany Post Road
CROTON-ON-HUDSON,
NY 10520, USA
Tel.: (1) 914 271 5194
Fax: (1) 914 271 5856
E-mail: Info@manhattanpublishing.com
http://www.manhattanpublishing.com

Council of Europe Publishing/Editions du Conseil de l'Europe
F-67075 Strasbourg Cedex
Tel.: (33) 03 88 41 25 81 – Fax: (33) 03 88 41 39 10 – E-mail: publishing@coe.int – Website: http://book.coe.int

Ollscoil na hÉireann, Gaillimh

3 1111 40155 2896